If These WALLS Could TALK:
NEW YORK GIANTS

Stories from the
New York Giants' Sidelines,
Locker Room, and Press Box

Ernie Palladino

TRIUMPH
BOOKS

Library of Congress Cataloging-in-Publication Data

Palladino, Ernie.
  If these walls could talk : stories from the New York Giants' sidelines, locker room, and press box / Ernie Palladino.
    pages cm
  ISBN 978-1-60078-877-2 (pbk.)
  1. New York Giants (Football team)—History. 2. New York Giants (Football team)—Anecdotes. I. Title.
  GV956.N4P34 2013
  796.332'64097471—dc23
                                                                    2013018371

This book is available in quantity at special discounts for your group or organization. For further information, contact:

  Triumph Books LLC
  814 North Franklin Street
  Chicago, Illinois 60610
  (312) 337–0747
  www.triumphbooks.com

Printed in U.S.A.

ISBN: 978-1-60078-877-2

Design by Amy Carter

Photos courtesy of Getty Images unless otherwise indicated

For Andrew, as tough a guy
as you'll find in any locker room.

CONTENTS

FOREWORD

To call the past 20 years of Giants history "interesting" would be a gross understatement. For a team that had risen from the turbulence of the 1970s to regain its status as an NFL power, the era from 1993 to 2013 has included the kind of success our organization expects from itself and what our fans expect of us.

We've certainly had our ups and downs. Not every team is a winner, and some seasons brought back the cold sweats that accompanied the lean years of my youth. As a high school and college student still years away from joining the family business, I watched my late father, Wellington Mara, brave those losing seasons with grace and dignity.

All that had changed when I left my life as an attorney and joined our organization in an official capacity in 1991. The turnaround started a decade earlier with coach Ray Perkins claiming our first postseason berth since 1963. Bill Parcells continued the job with Super Bowl championship seasons in 1986 and 1990.

We dipped again my first two years here, but things picked up in 1993 when we hired Dan Reeves and once again reached the postseason. In the last 20 years under Reeves, Jim Fassel, and Tom Coughlin, we have earned nine playoff berths compared to six appearances in the previous 29 years. We played in three Super Bowls and won two of them—in 2007 and 2011. In addition to our success on the field, we built a new, state-of-the-art stadium in partnership with the Jets that was paid for entirely with private funds. In 2014 MetLife Stadium will host Super Bowl XLVIII, the league's first open-air Super Bowl in a cold-weather city.

Our franchise is proud of our accomplishments in the past two decades. As Parcells always said, "You are what your record says you are." The record over the past 20 years says we are winners—sometimes on a grand scale. It didn't occur by accident. It happened because we have had good people who do a good job: decision makers, excellent players, and outstanding coaches.

It was not always smooth. Seasons rose and fell. Coaches were replaced. Players came and went. General managers retired. We endured the loss of loved ones, including my father, Wellington Mara; his good friend and co-owner Bob Tisch; and the thousands who died one sunny Tuesday morning in September 2001, many of them Giants fans.

Between these covers you will read about the most productive stretch in our franchise's 88-year existence. *If These Walls Could Talk* is not a history lesson. Far from a rundown of box scores and a litany of down-and-distance situations, this is a book about the individuals who engineered that success told by many of our people.

Ernie Palladino, who has covered the New York Giants for more than 20 years, explains why this period was so successful through his observations and the voices of many others. Some of the tales—like our quarterback's foray into hosting a television comedy show—might make you laugh. Others—such as the account of my father's funeral and its on-field aftermath—will lift your spirits. Still others—like Jason Whittle's vigil at the bedside of his dying friend in the wake of 9/11—may break your heart. Some might even exasperate you.

The stories all share a common denominator. Whether describing on-field exploits or off-field hijinks, Ernie's characterizations demonstrate how the competitiveness and will to win of every one of these contributors made them so valuable to our organization.

This is the story of our last 20 years as told by many of the people who are responsible for our success. As Parcells said, you are what the record says you are. Our record says our people are winners. After reading this book, I think you'll agree.

—John Mara

CHAPTER 1
SUPER MEMORIES

Trains, Horse Races, and Poker Games

Jim Fassel remembers it as "the day I lost my mind." His team had just taken a bad 31–21 loss in Detroit to send the 2000 season into a tenuous 7–4 situation. Sensing a sag in his team's confidence and the need to take some media heat off his players, Fassel decided to take the psychological offensive that Tuesday night. He talked over his plan with the team's savvy publicity director, Pat Hanlon, but even Hanlon's suggestion that he could make himself the target of ridicule couldn't change his mind. So with Hanlon's blessing— "Let the good times roll," he told Fassel—the coach went to bed.

What happened the next day amounted to Fassel's Douglas MacArthur's "I Shall Return!" moment. With all the fury and passion of a modern day patriot, Fassel riffed and ranted his way through a 25-minute playoff guarantee—the greatest ever issued in the bowels of Giants Stadium. "If you have the crosshairs or the lasers, you can put them directly on my chest!" Fassel said as his widened eyes panned over the cameras and notebooks in the Wednesday media room. "I'll take full responsibility! This is a poker game! I'm shoving my chips to the middle of the table! I'm raising the stakes here, and anybody who wants in, get in! Anybody who wants out, get out! I'm loving every bit of this! *This team is going to the playoffs!"*

Far from a polished declaration, the monologue amounted to a fullblown assault on the English language as Fassel mixed and matched metaphors while adding the real news that he would closely oversee his assistant coaches' responsibilities. He announced lineup changes, too, putting veteran defensive starters such as Jessie Armstead, Jason Sehorn, Sean Williams, and Mike Barrow on special teams to shore up the flagging kick coverage units. "We're in a horse race and we're coming around the last corner. My whole life right now is getting this team across the finish line," Fassel said. "I'm taking total control over everything. I'm gonna be everywhere. I'm going to question everything that's going on around here. And we're only going to do what I say we're going to do. You got any questions about it, then bring it to me!"

Just moments before he had previously addressed his players in similar terms. "I told them I'm driving the train," he said. "All they need to do is listen and follow along. I plan on having a short fuse with anything else. I'm redefining things around here. I like to be in control. I'm gonna grab that right now and set the course. I'll set the course, and I'll set the expectations."

When he finished he went upstairs to visit with general manager Ernie Accorsi and then-vice president John Mara. "Well, I did it," he told Accorsi.

"I said, 'Oh, geez, what did he do?'" Accorsi said.

"I just guaranteed the playoffs," Fassel said.

Whether it was the words or the lineup changes or a renewed commitment from his players, the rant worked. The Giants won their last five regular season games and then beat the Philadelphia Eagles and Minnesota Vikings in the playoffs to advance to Super Bowl XXXV in Tampa, Florida, against the Baltimore Ravens.

Fassel showed he had his players' back that day. And in those final weeks, his players showed they had his back.

41–0

The issues surrounding the 2000 NFC championship game encounter with the Vikings revolved around four visiting players: Daunte Culpepper, Cris Carter, Randy Moss, and Robert Smith. How would the Giants prevent that potent group from running and passing them straight out of Giants Stadium? This was an offense that put up 397 points. The offense didn't set a record, but that unit was just two years removed from its NFL all-time high, 556-point season of 1998. The explosive potential was still there—even if the Vikings had fallen to fifth in the league in points scored.

General manager Ernie Accorsi was well aware of that and spent the practice week battling some terribly dark thoughts. "I'm thinking we're going to have to score 40 points to have a chance," Accorsi said. "All week long in my dreams, the Vikings scored 8,000 points. All I dreamt of was Randy Moss, Cris Carter, and Robert Smith running up and down the field."

He couldn't even look defensive coordinator John Fox in the eye, even though they were office neighbors. It wasn't just the natural paranoia that afflicts all members of a football team's hierarchy. Accorsi's teams had been to these games before, and he has known championship nightmares all too well. In his stint as the Browns' general manager from 1985 to 1992, he saw Cleveland lose three AFC Championship Games, two in horrific fashion. John Elway's legendary 98-yard drive in 1986 led to an overtime loss, and the next year, running back Earnest Byner fumbled on the Denver 3 to wreck a late fourth-quarter comeback. To think about the potency of Minnesota's offense causing the loss of a fourth conference championship was almost too much to bear and certainly too much to talk about with Fox.

He avoided him all week until the day before the game when Fox asked him directly about his aloofness. "I don't even want to think about our defense," Accorsi told the coordinator. To which Fox prophetically answered, "We'll be fine. We might even shut them out."

While Accorsi worried a hole in his stomach, Fassel gave the media what they were looking for. Of course, he said, the Giants would run, run, run to control the clock and keep Cunningham and his points machine off the field. Low-risk, conservative play would win this game. A Republican couldn't have said it better. But in reality Fassel and offensive coordinator Sean Payton had far more liberal plans in mind. "Everybody's asking how we're gonna keep Cunningham, Moss, and Carter off the field, and meanwhile we're planning on throwing the shit out of the ball," Fassel said.

And so they did. Kerry Collins had the best game of his career, going 28-of-39 for 381 yards and five touchdowns. Four of those came as he built a 34–0 first-half lead. Defensively, Jason Sehorn covered Moss so well that the moody, ultra-deep threat just plain quit.

Walking off the field at halftime, Fassel chatted with Fox. "Before the game I'd asked him how many points we'd need from the offense to win this thing, and he said probably 28, maybe 30," Fassel said. "Well, we're up 34–0. He says, 'Look, just run the ball. Chew the clock. This team is explosive, and they can come back on us very quickly.'

"I looked at him. Remember, we're up 34–0. So I said, 'Listen, if they score 34 points in a half against this defense, *you're fired*.'"

Collins didn't stop throwing the ball until the fourth quarter when running back Joe Montgomery took over and helped the offense run off the final

12:53. Accorsi, whose championship game track record wouldn't allow him to relax, finally made his way to the field with 7:31 remaining. There he watched Montgomery pick up one first down after another to run out the clock.

He finally exhaled.

"Winning the Super Bowl is what you work for," said Accorsi, who would hand over the GM reins to Jerry Reese one year too early to enjoy that thrill. "Getting there is also an incredible experience. That would be my greatest thrill."

Losing Super Bowl XXXV

The Giants went to five Super Bowls between 1986 and 2012. Their only loss came in 2000 under Fassel. Despite the four Lombardi Trophies that gleam in the showcase of the Timex Performance Center's reception area, that single 34–7 blowout in Super Bowl XXXV to the Baltimore Ravens stings as profoundly years later as it did the night of January 28, 2001.

Accorsi had said before the game that losing a Super Bowl is the worst thing in sports because only the winner is remembered. He is living proof. "That game still irritates me," Accorsi said. "I never felt we had the intensity for that Super Bowl game. I always thought we were too happy after the 41–0 Vikings win. I know the players played hard, but I never felt good about our preparation. It was too light-hearted for me."

Accorsi also let it be known the following training camp that he was none too happy with Fassel's decision to rent out a movie theater and conduct a ring ceremony for winning the conference title. The object, Accorsi maintained, is to win the Super Bowl. Anything short of that is failure. "When you're involved in this game, there's one thing that becomes clear: you play for the ultimate goal," he said. "And the ultimate goal is not the NFC Championship Game."

Accorsi had worried about that game for two weeks since the day after the Giants vanquished the Vikings. So great on that day, Collins seemed nervous and tentative in the following practices. Those same deficiencies carried over to gameday in Tampa.

And the Ravens sensed it. "The Super Bowl was over in a series," recounted the Ravens' massive defensive tackle Tony Siragusa, whose hole-clogging allowed Ray Lewis and the rest of a ferocious front seven to sack Collins four times. "I watched Collins standing at the line, getting ready to call out the signals. He wasn't looking up the field or at his receivers or the defensive backs covering those receivers. He was looking at us, the guys who were coming to get him. I thought, *man, this game is over.*"

Collins threw four interceptions that day and only completed 15-of-39 passes for 112 yards. "I stunk today. This is the most disappointing loss I've ever been involved with not only because we lost, but the way we lost," Collins said. "Anything I put up ended up in the wrong spot."

As bitter as that loss was for Accorsi, Collins, and even Fassel, it was even tougher to swallow for two players. Lomas Brown, the old left tackle, had waited 16 years to reach a Super Bowl. Brown would eventually get his ring—as a reserve with the 2002 Tampa Bay Buccaneers—but at that point, he had no way of knowing if he'd ever return to the NFL's greatest show. "It hurts," Brown said. "It really, really hurts."

Just as pained but more philosophical was Brown's left-side mate, Glenn Parker. The old guard knew from Super Bowls, having played in four straight with Marv Levy's Buffalo Bills from 1990 to 1993. But he never experienced the thrill of winning one. "Let's face it," Parker said. "From when you're a kid growing up, second place is not good enough. But losing the Super Bowl will not define my career. Although you want to win, that's what it's all about. But that's what made those Buffalo teams what they were. We lost, but we kept on going." Unfortunately for Parker, his fifth Super Bowl was his last. He finished his career as a Giant after 2001.

As for Fassel he admitted to pain but was proud his team had exceeded all preseason expectations. They had after all been predicted to finish last in the NFC East. "This loss will take a while to go away," he said after the game. "But my feeling of pride and the way they've worked this year will not go away. We're going to be back in this game."

He was wrong about that. The Giants wouldn't reach another Super Bowl until 2007. Another coach and another quarterback would lead them there. "You don't get over some losses," Fassel said at a fan gathering in 2008.

When Losing Is Winning

Tom Coughlin's Giants had already gone through a lot in 2007 when they reached the regular-season finale against the 15–0 New England Patriots. Michael Strahan's bitter contract dispute with new GM Reese had turned what should have been a quiet training camp into a turbulent one. To make matters worse, just-retired running back Tiki Barber had taken his new job as an NBC football analyst to a vitriolic level, criticizing quarterback Eli Manning's leadership abilities during an on-air panel discussion. "Sometimes it was almost comical the way he would say things [during locker room speeches]," Barber told his national viewing audience. That didn't quite sit well with Manning. At the urging of his roommate and backup Tim Hasselbeck, Manning stunned his teammates when he stepped out of his laid-back public persona for the first time in his career and fired back. "I guess I could have questioned Tiki's leadership skills last year with calling out the coach and having articles about him retiring in the middle of the season and how he's lost his heart," he said. "As a quarterback you're reading that your running back has lost his heart to play the game, and it's about the 10th week. I can see that a little bit at times."

Once the regular season started, the defense gave up 80 points in the first two weeks but rebounded with a goal-line stand in Washington. However, there was even controversy surrounding that. During the week leading up to the game, linebacker Antonio Pierce, a team leader, had infamously interrupted reporters' questions with repeated blasts from an air horn.

Still riding on that defensive stand, the Giants had done well enough in an uneven season to clinch a playoff spot at 10–6. A circus catch in the end zone by Amani Toomer in Chicago and Ahmad Bradshaw's 151-yard rushing effort in Buffalo, which included his 88-yard touchdown run through the snowflakes, locked the Giants into the No. 5 seed. That made the outcome irrelevant against Tom Brady, his turbo-charged offense, and his Patriots team looking to make history as the NFL's first 16–0 squad in the regular season. And that was just as well because the Giants' injury situation was anything but advantageous. Bradshaw was hurt and unavailable.

The smart money said the usually conservative Coughlin would play this one safe. Get Manning out of there early. Let Brandon Jacobs play a quarter or a half, then sheath him in bubble wrap, tuck him on the sidelines, and keep him healthy for the next week's wild-card trip to Tampa Bay. Empty the bench to preserve key defensive starters such as Justin Tuck and Osi Umenyiora for the big stuff down the road. As it happened the smart money wasn't so smart. Coughlin told his team Wednesday that, "We're playing to win the game." He meant it.

Damned if they almost did. The Giants lost 38–35 but put a mighty scare into a Bill Belichick-coached squad that didn't just beat opponents—they pulverized them with an NFL-record 589 points.

Manning went 22-of-32 for 251 yards and four touchdowns, beginning a magical turnaround for the quarterback Reese called "skittish" after a horrendous performance against the Vikings just five games before. Jacobs played the whole game, running 15 times for 67 yards and catching five passes for 44 yards and a touchdown. Kickoff returner Domenik Hixon ran one back 74 yards for a touchdown.

Manning's touchdown throws to Kevin Boss and Plaxico Burress built a 28–16 lead with 9:12 left in the third quarter, and even though Brady (32-of-42, 356 yards, two touchdowns) would bring his team charging back, the Giants still held a 28–23 lead three minutes into the fourth quarter.

Brady, however, was Brady. He spotted Randy Moss alone deep on a busted coverage and hit the receiver for a 65-yard touchdown to pull ahead. Just under seven minutes later, Manning threw his only interception of the game, and Laurence Maroney scored from five yards out to put the Patriots up by 10.

Manning's touchdown pass to Burress with 1:04 remaining left the Giants just short. The Patriots had their slice of history. But the Giants gained something more valuable than a line in the record book. On a week where playoff-bound coaches habitually rested their stars and produced half-hearted efforts, Coughlin's group had hung with the most formidable team in history and nearly survived. The Eli who stumbled to a four-interception game against Minnesota and fumbled five times against the Bills entered the playoffs sky-high with confidence.

The overall effort also earned the praise of at least one Hall of Fame coach, John Madden. "It's one of the best things to happen in the NFL in the past 10 years," Madden said in a message he left on Coughlin's answering machine that night. "I believe there is only one way to go out and play the game, and that's to win the damned thing…I'm a little emotional right now, but the NFL needed that, and you guys should be proud."

They kept the lessons gleaned from that game in their memory banks just in case. "You just learn that you have to be able to answer their call," Manning said. "You have to figure out a way when they're kind of at their best, and they're moving and getting into the rhythm of the game. You have to find a way to back off and answer their response."

Other factors certainly helped. The offensive line had come together to provide outstanding pass protection. Jeremy Shockey, a thorn in Manning's psyche, sat out with a broken leg. The defense had hit its zenith. And the running game had gotten into gear. The near-win against the Patriots brought it all together at just the right time. The game in Tampa—a rather desultory 24–14 victory against the Bucs—featured Manning going 20-of-27 for 185 yards and two touchdowns for his first playoff success.

That allowed his team to play the No. 1-seeded Cowboys, the team that handed the road warriors their only defeat away from home. The Giants trailed 14–7 until 46 seconds remained in the first half. Then Manning took over. He led his squad on a 71-yard drive, ending it with a 4-yard scoring pass to Amani Toomer to enter intermission tied at 14. Rookies Steve Smith and Kevin Boss had caught big passes in the drive, but it really came down to Manning's poise. "He put us in the Super Bowl with 46 seconds left before halftime of the Dallas game," Reese said later. "In my mind that was the biggest drive of our season."

Manning then led a drive that culminated in the fourth quarter Jacobs touchdown run that counteracted the Cowboys' go-ahead field goal in the third. He finished a modest 12-of-18 for 163 yards and two touchdowns, but his management of the 21–17 win, and an end zone interception in the final seconds by R.W. McQuarters enabled the Giants to become the first team in history to beat a No. 1 seed in the divisional round.

That loss to New England gave Coughlin's team all the confidence it needed. As for Manning he'd freeze the next week against second-seeded Green Bay but in a literal—not figurative—sense.

Ice Bowl II

Manning called the 2007 NFC Championship Game victory in Green Bay "my all-time favorite game." Packers fans called it just plain cold.

With a base temperature of minus-1 degree and a windchill factor of minus-23, the 23–20 overtime victory represented the third-coldest game in NFL history and the coldest in Giants history. It also came in a close second to the most frigid game ever played at Lambeau Field—the immortal, original Ice Bowl in which the Packers beat the Cowboys 21–17 for the 1967 NFL title.

Manning's only real concession to the conditions was the glove on his left (non-throwing) hand; other players and coaches went to more extreme measures to stave off frostbite. Comfort in that kind of weather was not even an option.

Longtime equipment managers Eddie Wagner and brothers Ed and Joe Skiba had used much forethought in furnishing the players with a skin-warming gel mountain climbers used on the frigid heights, foot warmers, and oversized stuffed gloves. But even that didn't help Burress. After about three or four routes—10 minutes time—during pregame warm-ups, Burress bailed out and scurried inside just as he lost all feeling in his hands.

He covered himself in Vaseline and then went one step further. Taking the foot warmers, which were supposed to be worn over socks, he taped them directly to the bare bottoms of his feet.

Straight onto the skin.

Head trainer Ronnie Barnes warned him that his feet would soon feel like he'd set them afire. As if Burress cared. "That's what I need," Burress said. "Do you know how cold it is out there? Let 'em burn. I'm not going to freeze."

The insides of the helmets were outfitted with sheep fleece. The iconic orange buckets by the bench were filled with chicken broth instead of Gatorade. The heaters were turned up full blast, and Burress and his fellow receivers made ample use of them during the TV timeouts. "I can't describe how bad it was," wide receiver Amani Toomer said. "Breathing in the air would burn your lungs. It was just ridiculous."

They got through it, though. Manning, going 21-of-40 for 251 yards with no touchdowns and no interceptions, outplayed the great Brett Favre,

With his face beet red, Giants head coach Tom Coughlin barks at his team during the 2008 NFC Championship Game in Green Bay, Wisconsin, which represented the third coldest game in NFL history. *(AP Images)*

who went in with a 43–5 record when the Lambeau mercury sank below 34 degrees. Burress caught 11 passes for 151 yards mostly against Pro Bowl cornerback Al Harris.

Kicking a football the cold turned rock hard, Lawrence Tynes put through a 47-yarder in overtime—after missing from 43 and 36 in regulation—to become the unlikeliest of heroes in the unlikeliest of playoff runs. Tynes took his sock off after the game to reveal a blackened foot that would not normalize for eight days. Tom Coughlin—redeemed after nearly getting fired the previous season—was heard on the sideline responding to an official's comment about his beet-red face: "This year they're talking about my face. Last year they were talking about my ass."

11

Manning never forgot that game. "Not just because it was the NFC Championship game," Manning said, "it was being in Green Bay, playing a game in negative-20 degrees. All those factors make a game special."

Men In Black

The photo of Strahan getting off the plane in Phoenix told all one needed to know about the Giants' attitude heading into Super Bowl XLII against the undefeated Patriots.

Black jacket. Black tie. Black pants.

Black shirt optional.

They filed out one by one: Manning, Burress, Strahan, and the rest of them all dressed in the same fashion as team captain Pierce.

Men In Black.

Will Smith and Tommy Lee Jones were absent, but the Giants' aim remained similar to their cinematic models: Dispatch this otherworldly team on the NFL's greatest stage.

For the Giants the most unlikely of appearances in this Super Bowl was simply straight business. Coughlin had given Pierce the responsibility of picking out the uniform to wear for the plane ride down. Pierce decided that black—the color of mourning he hoped would shroud the Patriots' locker room that Sunday—was the only appropriate hue. It would represent the death of the New England dynasty.

"All black was perfect with all the hype that was going around with the Patriots that year," Pierce said. "We were dressed to go to a funeral to end all that stuff. There was so much talk about that perfect season and Tom Brady. It was supposed to be a dream season for them, but we dressed in all black to give them a nightmare ending. It was fitting."

But it seemed for much of the week the Giants would be the mourners. Burress, the star wide receiver who caught the winning 13-yard touchdown pass from Manning with just 35 seconds remaining, slipped in the shower and severely sprained his ankle. The Giants didn't reveal the injury until midweek, and then the media and countless Giants fans spent the rest of Burress' limited practice time wondering about his availability. "If anyone could ever know how close he came to not playing," receivers coach Mike Sullivan said after the game. "He shouldn't have been out there."

It, of course, all worked out. David Tyree, Burress' practice field replacement, received the lion's share of snaps that week and responded with "The Helmet Catch" during the winning drive. And Burress was healthy enough to get open in the end zone for the final points in the stunning, 17–14 victory. But it all started with a fashion statement courtesy of Pierce. "When we got off the plane and all the cameras were there and people saw us coming off in all black, it let you know right there that we were ready to play," Pierce said.

Two Improbable Catches

The fact that Manning connected on two legendary passes in Super Bowls XLII and XLVI might almost have been expected—given the expectations that surrounded him. He was a first-round draft pick after all. He was the once-in-a-lifetime talent Accorsi risked everything for him on Draft Day 2004.

Who caught those passes was another story. Tyree and Mario Manningham became two of the unlikeliest targets—for different reasons—to find a place in the highlight reels. Tyree had caught all of four passes for 35 yards in 12 games during 2007. His true value remained in kick coverage, and there was no doubt about his standing there among the league's best. Fast and fearless he'd fly down the field and either force the opposing punt returner to fair catch or he'd be David-On-The-Spot to down Jeff Feagles' pitching wedges inside the 5.

But receiving? No. When the Giants lined up in a four-wide receiver formation on third-and-5 of their decisive drive against the Patriots in Super Bowl XLII, Tyree was nothing more than a fourth option and little more than a decoy. It was quite unlikely a pass would come his way, one that would keep a drive alive while down 14–10 with 1:15 remaining as the Patriots aimed to become the league's first undefeated champion since the 1972 Dolphins.

On top of that, Tyree had one of the poorest leaps on the team at just 30 inches. If not for the Patriots' pass rush, Manning would have waited for Steve Smith or Burress to come open. Instead a pack of linebackers, defensive backs, and defensive linemen defeated blocks and converged on the quarter-back. Tyree saw the jailbreak and cut off the post route he was assigned in the original play call of Phantom.

Defensive end Jarvis Green got a hand on Manning, and defensive end Richard Seymour followed. Linebacker Mike Vrabel was in the quarterback's face. Manning almost went down. Referee Mike Carey had his whistle raised to blow the play dead but held that fateful breath for another split second—just long enough to let Manning spin out of it, find space behind the gag-gle of defenders, and spot Tyree matched up against physical safety Rodney Harrison 32 yards down the middle of the field. *No*, thought Burress, watching from his clear-out route on the left side.

Off it went. Having cut across from his split wide-right spot, Tyree jumped—all 30 inches, it seemed. The ball hit his fully-extended hands just as the NFL's hardest-hitting safety got there. Harrison bent him backward as Tyree miracu-lously pinned the ball against his helmet and kept his head up just enough to create a two-inch space that kept the ball from hitting the ground. Burress ran over and grabbed Tyree by the head. "Man, you just saved the Fucking Super Bowl," he told Tyree, who answered, "I don't know what's going on."

Tyree's receiving talents had been underrated his whole career. Still strug-gling over the mid-season death of his grandmother, he was behaviorally reformed and spiritually reborn after a 2004 marijuana arrest. Then he made the catch of his life. "Some things don't make sense," Tyree said. "I guess that catch was one of them."

The catch didn't win the game. Smith still had to make a great third-down grab on the sideline, and Burress had to shake loose of Ellis Hobbs to get wide open in the end zone for the 13-yard, game-winning touchdown. But without Tyree's heroics, the Giants most surely would have lost.

Four years later Manning-to-Manningham also became a legendary and just as unlikely connection. Not that Manningham was underrated. When healthy he was one of the main pass-catchers on that 2011 team. He caught 39 passes for 523 yards and four touchdowns that year slightly down from his production of the two previous seasons because of injuries that limited him to 12 games.

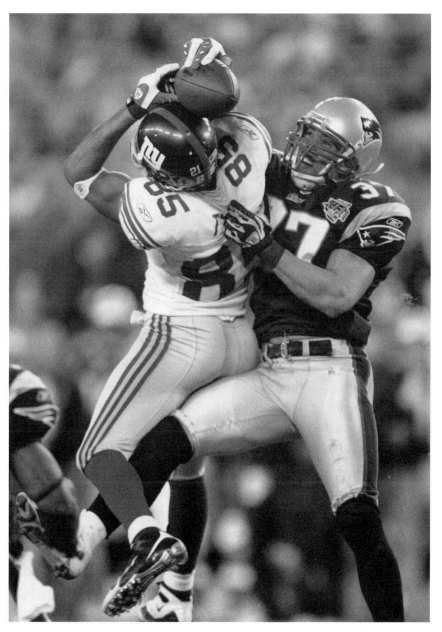

Wide receiver David Tyree, the fourth option on the third-and-5 play, snares the "Helmet Catch," the signature play of Super Bowl XLII, while being defended by New England Patriots safety Rodney Harrison. *(AP Images)*

Besides a penchant for dropping easy throws, Manningham's biggest problem involved an only recently cured issue with the sideline. His errant footwork more than once cost his team valuable third-down conversions because he misjudged the paint. In negotiating pro football's tightrope, he had been a drive's fatal accident waiting to happen. Even in his new, fairly reliable state, he was still an iffy proposition near the boundary. Moreover, he'd been overshadowed by two flashier receivers, humongous-handed Hakeem Nicks and the Salsa-tional Victor Cruz.

None of that kept Manning from finding Manningham for a big 38-yard catch as the Giants worked their way out of a familiar position against the Patriots. Backed up on their 12-yard line and down 17–15 with 3:46 to go, Manning again came under pressure. This time he didn't need a great escape like four years earlier. But this pass was still challenged. Manning threw a perfect strike between defensive backs Sterling Moore and Patrick Chung— as long as Manningham stayed inbounds. *Freeze your feet*, Manningham told himself. The receiver reeled it in as Moore grabbed him from behind, and Chung slammed him from the side. Manningham's left foot came down on its side about three inches short of the left boundary as he began his violent journey over the line. His right foot had come down close but inbounds. Replay review confirmed the on-field completion call.

Manningham was still at Michigan when Tyree made his catch. Now he had one of his own. "There's nothing harder than a sideline catch," he told *The New York Times* a year later. "There's nothing prettier either."

Like Tyree's catch, it didn't win Super Bowl XLVI, but it sure helped. It put the ball at the 50. From there Nicks caught a 14-yard pass to the 36, Bradshaw ran for 7, Nicks caught another pass for 4, and Bradshaw ran for one before the featured back raced in from the 6 behind a "Jumbo" alignment using Tony Ugoh as an eligible tackle.

Tyree and Manningham had something else in common, too. They both became ex-Giants in short order. Tyree missed the 2008 season because of offseason knee surgery and a lingering hamstring injury and was released on the final cutdown of his injury-marred 2009 training camp. He was one of Coughlin's hardest cuts. "David Tyree is such a class act," Coughlin said.

"When he came in to see me, I had a lot of emotions running through my head. He put everything at ease. He had a big smile on his face. I told David he is forever etched in the annals of New York Giants history. That will never change. That moment in history will stand forever in time."

"This is part of the journey," Tyree said. "It's not like it's a great day. But at the same time, I'm filled with expectations about what's next on this track." He picked up with the Ravens where he spent an uneventful season on special teams. "The Helmet Catch" would count as his final NFL reception and a signature way to wrap up a career.

Tyree later became an outspoken opponent of the New York legislature's proposal on gay marriage, saying he'd gladly trade his famous catch for defeat of the measure. Citing religious beliefs as his reason for going against ex-teammate Strahan's and team vice president Steve Tisch's support of the proposal, Tyree called same-sex marriage "the first steps toward anarchy."

With the Giants unwilling to sign Manningham to a long-term mega-contract, they let him test the 2012 free-agent market. He wound up with San Francisco but missed the 49ers' Super Bowl XLVII appearance after he tore his ACL in a Week 16 loss to Seattle.

Super Prep

Four months after the Giants won Super Bowl XLVI, the New York Yankees asked Coughlin to throw out the ceremonial first pitch in a late June game. Coughlin came through with a fastball high and inside. "Close enough," he told the media. "I might have gotten the call."

Reporters didn't know Coughlin prepared for his moment in the Yankee Stadium spotlight for two weeks. Determined not to bounce it and incur what certainly would have been a round of light-hearted razzing from the stands, Coughlin measured off a 60-foot, 6-inch patch of the team's Timex Performance Center training ground and rigged up a temporary mound and plate. He practiced throwing off it three or four times each week during 30-minute sessions.

That stood as a prime physical example of the coach's manic—some might call it maniacal—philosophy on preparation. On a weekly basis, he bombarded his team with stats, situations, and information about everything from opponents' tendencies to weather conditions to the playoff picture. In the end the players had an overwhelming amount of information at their disposal, some of which actually came in handy in key moments.

Middle linebacker Kawika Mitchell benefitted from one such piece of minutia in 2007. During the staff's film study for Super Bowl XLII against the Patriots, the coaches noticed New England center Dan Koppen would hunch over the ball and look up to identify where each of the linebackers were stationed. He would then look down at the ball and keep his head down until the snap. He never glanced upward again to notice any shifts.

Defensive coordinator Steve Spagnuolo told Mitchell that when Koppen looked at him, he should step back as if he was dropping into coverage. Then when Koppen looked down, he should begin his charge forward toward the unsuspecting center; Mitchell might get himself an easy sack. Mitchell did exactly that early in the second quarter and produced the first of five sacks on Tom Brady.

Special Party

Winning a Super Bowl is a memorable experience for any player. But for Rich Seubert, the starting left guard in Super Bowl XLII, that night in Arizona went beyond special. Seubert had come all the way back from a mangled leg that kept him out of football in 2004. The chase for a Super Bowl ring was the only thing that motivated him through the painful rehab, the uncertainty of a roster spot every year thereafter, and the constant punishment of the seasons that eventually led him to San Luis Obispo, California, where year-round warmth makes his battered body hurt just a little less.

For Seubert the aftermath of Super Bowl XLII was touching, joyous, and uproarious. "There were a lot of dark days and dark nights," said Seubert, who was released in training camp of 2011. "But I made it back, and winning a Super Bowl was what every little kid thinks about. I wasn't done, so I wouldn't call it closure, but if that was the last game I ever played, I would have been happy."

Seubert's wife, Jodi, a constant source of encouragement during his rehab, viewed the game with his parents and was the first one Seubert sought after time expired. "I gave her a kiss and said, 'We did it.' We did it together," Seubert said. "She gets the most credit for keeping me into it and keeping me rehabbing. We just hugged each other and gave each other a big old kiss."

Then came the postgame party back at the Giants' hotel, the Wild Horse Pass Resort, about 45 minutes away from Glendale and the University of Phoenix Stadium. The mood on the bus was as wild as one might expect. There was plenty of screaming and yelling, but even that didn't compare to the reception the players received back at the hotel. "Everybody's in the lobby, screaming and high-fiving us," Seubert said. "Then we go into the party. There were three rooms, and I didn't even know it. I never made it out of the first room with the band and the people and the food. I don't even remember the party. I heard there was karaoke in the other room. It was very cool."

The parade through lower Manhattan's Canyon of Heroes, the interviews, the adulation that followed were imprinted indelibly in Seubert's memory. He would play three more years, but nothing compared to winning the Super Bowl. "It was a special moment in time for me," Seubert said.

Rooney Mara Wins Out

It takes an earthshaking event for a Mara to miss a playoff game. So when the Giants' senior vice president in charge of player personnel, Chris Mara, skipped the Giants' 37–20 NFC semifinal win in Green Bay on January 15, 2012, everyone knew he had a pretty darned good reason.

His daughter, Rooney Mara, was up for Best Actress in a drama at the Golden Globes in Hollywood that night. Somehow, Rooney and her older sister, Kate, had acquired some considerable acting chops while growing up as football royalty. Rooney had gotten the nod for her graphic star turn as Lisbeth Salander, the antisocial, bisexual computer hacker in *The Girl with the Dragon Tattoo*. It was a role that made her straight-laced, 54-year-old father wince as Rooney depicted rape and other sexual outrages on the big screen. But he was no less proud of his second daughter to hit it big in films five years after Kate broke out in *The Shooter*.

So Mara was faced with a choice. Accompany the 26-year-old granddaughter of Wellington Mara and great-granddaughter of fabled Pittsburgh Steelers owner Art Rooney to the Golden Globes or witness what would become the next step toward a second Super Bowl title in four years. No-brainer there. Put on the Brooks Brothers and hit the red carpet. Televisions and cell phones would have to suffice for game viewing. And for anyone questioning his decision to spend that night in Los Angeles instead of Green Bay, he had an answer all loaded up. "Yeah, this isn't exactly a piano recital," he told one inquisitor.

The dad didn't exactly put the game on the back burner while hobnobbing with the Hollywood glitterati. He caught the first quarter in his hotel room and watched most of the second quarter in Rooney's room before they headed to the ceremonies. The old man got a bit antsy on the red carpet, however. Rooney had to stop for interviews every few feet, and the bumper-to-bumper nature of it all kept Chris from his appointed date with any available TV screen. His patience exhausted, Mara bolted from the carpet and headed into a suite at the Beverly Hilton to join several Sony executives who had planned to watch the game, too. He made it through most of the fourth quarter before he absolutely had to head into the ceremony. Out came the cell phone. In came text messages from friends, and his frequent arm pumps alerted the rest of the table to each snippet of good news.

It was over in a few minutes. The game, that is. The Giants moved on to the NFC Championship matchup against the 49ers. But Chris had to settle for going 1–1 that evening. Rooney lost out on the hardware as Meryl Streep took her eighth win for her portayal of Margaret Thatcher in *The Iron Lady*.

Interception, Blackburn!

Until the fourth quarter of Super Bowl XLVI, Chase Blackburn had made three interceptions and four pass breakups in a seven-year career. Obviously the Giants never regarded the affable middle linebacker as a huge weapon in their pass defense. As a matter of fact, Blackburn wasn't even part of any alignment until after Thanksgiving of 2011. The Giants had cut him after the 2010 season, and only a spate of injuries to the linebackers prompted them to re-sign him on November 30.

To think after more than half a season of unemployment that he'd pull off the pivotal defensive play in the 21–17 win against the Patriots was unfathomable. Yet with his team down 17–15 on the second play of the fourth quarter and with Brady scrambling away first from Linval Joseph and then Rocky Bernard at the Patriots 43, there was Blackburn fronting tight end Rob Gronkowski 50 yards downfield at the Giants 8. He was never supposed to have coverage responsibilities on the downfield drifter. "I had to carry Gronkowski," Blackburn said. "I heard the crowd go wild a little bit and I thought we had a sack. But I continued to see Gronk go up the field and I just tried to stay with him."

A completion there might have produced a touchdown for the 6'6", 265-pound tight end. He needed only to catch it, turn, and run untouched behind Blackburn's last line of defense. At worst Gronkowski might have fallen, succumbing to the ankle sprain that only slightly cut down on his outstanding speed and agility. The masterful Brady likely would have brought the Patriots to pay dirt in one or two more plays against a shaken defense.

Instead the 6'3", 247-pound run-stopper was right there. Speedy rookie Jacquian Williams, who normally would have covered Gronkowski, was given the Patriots' other fast tight end, Aaron Hernandez, because of Gronkowski's ankle limitations. And it wasn't Michael Boley, the weak-side linebacker who also made Blackburn look like he should be timed with a calendar not a stopwatch. It was just Blackburn. And the unheralded linebacker was in perfect position to leap, grab, and cradle Brady's throw as Gronkowski turned instantly into a safety. He got above Blackburn all right but couldn't break up the textbook catch. "He just threw it up for grabs," Blackburn said. "When I saw him look back, I looked back for the ball. And when I spotted it, I tried to just block out and go up for a rebound like in basketball."

Super Bowl XLVI's only turnover swung momentum back in the Giants' favor. It was a game changer. It got a street named after him, too. Blackburn Avenue sits in the middle of a housing development in Jersey City, New Jersey, where Bergen Avenue and Montgomery Street intersect.

None of it would have happened if Blackburn had just gone on with his life after the Giants let him go after 2010. He had moved back to Dublin, Ohio, with his wife and two sons, prepared to take a job as a substitute middle school math teacher. It wasn't because he had given up on football. He hadn't. Instead of sitting on the couch getting fat and depressed, Blackburn continued to work out like a demon to remain in football shape. But he also realized that he needed to get on with his life in case football had given up on him.

When Boley and Mark Herzlich went down November 28 against the New Orleans Saints, Blackburn's phone finally rang. "You in shape?" Reese asked. When the answer came back an unequivocal yes, Blackburn was re-signed, and countless scores of eighth graders were deprived of the privilege of being taught algebra by a real, live linebacker. Out came the suitcase he kept packed with bare necessities for such occasions—jeans, shorts, some dress shirts, T-shirts, underwear, and a business suit. Soon came other numbers— sums more applicable to his current life—like the number three. That represented his third career interception—made just five days after he arrived back in East Rutherford—and it came against Green Bay and eventual MVP Aaron Rodgers. "From the moment he arrived, it was like he never left," Coughlin said. "He absorbed where we were really fast, jumped right back into special teams, jumped into the linebacker role, and progressed."

And then came the biggest pick of any of the Giants' 22 that season. "I knew it was a long way," Blackburn said. "[Gronkowski] stopped for a second, and I stopped with him. I was thinking it was a sack, but then as soon as I saw him go vertical, I knew I had to run to catch up with him."

That wasn't the only big play he made that game, just the most important. In the second quarter, he laid such a vicious hit on BenJarvis Green-Ellis that he not only sent the running back to the sideline but also shook up defensive end Jason Pierre-Paul.

Clearly the work during his forced vacation paid off big time. "It happened because Chase had spent the time preparing when nobody was watching, when he wasn't on any team's payroll," Coughlin said. "He intended to be ready if he got the opportunity. If he hadn't done that, it's quite possible the outcome of the Super Bowl might have been different."

Linebacker Chase Blackburn, who didn't join the Giants team until after Thanksgiving, makes a pivotal fourth-quarter interception in front of New England Patriots tight end Rob Gronkowski during Super Bowl XLVI. *(AP Images)*

Super Slogans

Motivational slogans don't win games, but they don't hurt the cause either. They can turn into mission statements for entire seasons, carrying with them team identity and purpose. Those are exactly what "Talk is Cheap; Play the Game" and "Finish!" brought as defining themes for the Giants' two Super Bowl-winning seasons under Coughlin.

"Talk is Cheap; Play the Game" sprang forth from the turbulence of 2006. Along with the mighty on-field struggles to 8–8 that preceded a first-round playoff exit in Philadelphia, there was much chatter going on in and out of the locker room. Having already announced he would make that season his last, Barber blasted Coughlin for abandoning the run in a loss to Jacksonville. Shockey had described the team as being "out-coached" in a bad loss to Seattle. The media was beating down Coughlin's door, crying for the ouster of what they perceived as an intractable, rude, and inaccessible head coach.

Like many coaches Coughlin had always believed in slogans and quotes to get his team fired up. Players could always count on hearing the words of such luminaries as George Patton, Winston Churchill, and even romantic poets in Coughlin's Saturday night speeches. Other minor slogans were plastered around any area players congregated.

But the upheaval of 2006 made "Talk is Cheap; Play the Game" a perfect motto for the upcoming season since there had been so much of the former and not nearly enough of the latter. It went on T-shirts, placards, printed materials, and stayed on the players' lips throughout a season that saw the Giants become road warriors with an 11–1 record away from the Meadowlands, including four postseason victories through Super Bowl XLII. "We focused on how good we were on the playing field—not talking about it," Coughlin said.

"I remember after we lost that playoff game at Philly, talking to coach Coughlin on the bus," Pierce said. "And I was like, 'Man, we just waited too long to stop talking. All of us.' It was a whole group of us from the front office to the coaches to the players. We waited too long and did too much."

The players found their T-shirts hanging in their lockers during the off-season conditioning program. Predictably some of the more outspoken members of that group saw them simply as free apparel. "He wants us to talk with our play," Burress said. "That's fine, too, but that's not the character of our football team. Our team is very outspoken. We have guys who wear their emotions on their sleeve. You can't just change them by making a T-shirt."

But the locker room culture did change. The season was relatively devoid of player controversy. The 10–6 Giants finished second in the NFC East to Dallas. The slogan simply solidified the changed nature of Coughlin and his hierarchy. At the insistence of management, he softened his personality to become more player and media friendly. Conservative offensive coordinator John Hufnagel was gone, replaced by quarterback coach and huge Manning supporter Kevin Gilbride. Chris Palmer replaced Gilbride as the quarterback coach. The defensive side was also changed with Spagnuolo taking over for Tim Lewis.

In the end that team overcame the preseason predictions of a last-place finish to make the playoffs and go on an incredible Super Bowl run. "Whatever the phrase it has to be appropriate to the moment or the season," Hanlon said. "In '07, our locker room was in a state of transition. It had been a chatty locker room. What that phrase did was tell them, 'Let's stop talking and let's start doing.' It was Tom's way of reinforcing that thought. In the New York marketplace, it's easy to confuse rhetoric with productivity. But talking about it isn't going to get it done. Tom just streamlined the expectations. The point was not—don't say anything. It was think about what you say because at the end of the day it's about what you produce not what you say."

"Finish!" came about in 2011 because the previous season's 10–6 team failed to do enough to get into the playoffs. Instead the Giants finished in a first-place tie with the Philadelphia Eagles only to get bumped from a postseason berth because Philly swept the season series. They would have made it had they "finished" during a 38–31 loss to the Eagles on December 19. Instead leading 31–10 with just over eight minutes remaining, the Giants fell apart. Starting at the 7:28 mark, Michael Vick produced three touchdown drives. DeSean Jackson put the finishing touches on the 28-point deluge with a devastating 65-yard punt return for a touchdown as time expired. It was the NFL's first game-winning punt return for a touchdown in history.

Coughlin unveiled the slogan for that season on the first day of the 2011 minicamp. "Finish" what you start, no matter what it takes. "The necessity to come up with that was obvious," Hanlon said. "We hadn't finished. We hadn't finished games, hadn't finished practices, hadn't finished the season."

Coughlin hit that theme in every team meeting throughout the season. A piece of tape assistant video director Ed Triggs saw on ESPN's *SportsCenter* backed up the words. It showed a San Francisco University High School girls cross country runner collapsing and crawling across the finish line to help her team win a state championship for her ALS-stricken coach. His pre-race message had been "It's purely determination that allows you to finish. You need to finish. That's the point."

Coughlin showed that video to his team before the first Philadelphia game, and the Giants came away with a 29–16 victory at Lincoln Financial Field. They "finished" enough games to go 9–7 and make yet another magical playoff run, winning a first-round game at home against the Atlanta Falcons and then road games against Green Bay and San Francisco before beating the Patriots again in Super Bowl XLVI.

That year, however, wouldn't end before an allusion to the 2007 battle cry. As the New York Jets and Giants prepared for their Christmas Eve encounter, Jets coach Rex Ryan said he had no doubt his team was the better team. Still piqued over a sloppy, losing effort against the Washington Redskins the week before, Coughlin responded that Wednesday. "I just say, regardless of the talk, it will be decided at 1:00 Saturday afternoon," Coughlin said. "Regardless of what is said: Talk is cheap; play the game."

The Giants won 29–14.

They all went as examples of Coughlin's meticulous and all-encompassing attention to details. "I've never been around anybody who puts as much thought or consideration into his message to his players and how he frames that message," Hanlon said. "He's forever compiling thoughts and phrases and quotes and he has his brain trust in Triggs and [coaching assistant] Chris Pridy to share ideas and bounce things off. I've never been around anybody who takes that kind of time."

Meeting Obama

The Giants have gone to the White House twice to be honored for Super Bowl wins under Coughlin. The coach obviously had become comfortable with Rose Garden ceremonies. Otherwise he might not have gone off the reservation with president Barack Obama on his second visit on June 8, 2012 just as the election campaigns kicked into high gear.

Enough with the grip, grin, present-jersey-to-the-chief script. Coughlin was thinking politics. "We both have the goal to get back here next year," Coughlin said, turning to Obama.

The president threw in his own thoughts, warning the sportswriters who had questioned Manning's growing status as a quarterback that, "the next time Eli says he thinks he's an elite quarterback, you might just want to be quiet."

But it was the normally staid and stoic Coughlin who really brought down the house when talking about his team's character. "Offense, defense, and special teams doing their job, though having different objectives, but playing in harmony for each other for the good of everyone. Wouldn't it be nice if Congress operated the same way?"

CHAPTER 2

RIVALS

Gragg vs. Strahan

Dan Reeves called it the worst fight he'd ever seen. But Michael Strahan's ultimate off-season workout tiff with Scott Gragg marked only the zenith in the great defensive end's campaign to become a daily tormentor to the affable giant of a man. Gragg had come to the Giants as a second rounder out of Montana in 1995, and Strahan almost immediately made it his mission to get under the right tackle's skin. Bull rushing, speed rushing, beating Gragg at seemingly every turn, Strahan would issue a steady stream of verbal abuse at him during training camp drills. "Don't be sad, Gragg," he was overheard saying during one particular pass-rush drill as the 6'8", 315-pound Gragg slinked back to the huddle.

One day during the 1996 offseason program, however, Gragg got the better of Strahan as he worked over the defender's ribs, abdomen, and face. Strahan, shorter at 6'5" and lighter at 255, basically snapped. He ripped the helmet off Gragg's head and brought it down on his crown tomahawk style. Blood gushed as Gragg fell to the ground. And then Strahan jumped on top of him and commenced beating him with his fists. Reeves called a halt to it, and several teammates pulled the irate Strahan off the now defenseless tackle. Everything would have settled quietly had the incident been contained to the two. Instead the animosity spread. Jessie Armstead went after Howard Cross. Other players made threatening gestures toward each other.

It took several minutes for the roiling pot of emotions to reduce to a simmer. Once things did calm down, Strahan and Gragg made up quickly. Strahan apologized in the locker room, to which Gragg chuckled and said, "You really got me with a good shot." All the aggravation Strahan gave him paid off as Gragg had a productive career as a four-year starter for the Giants and another five for the 49ers.

As for training camp donnybrooks in general, Jim Fassel attempted to end all that after a brawl-filled opening three days of the 1997 training camp. He instituted punishment sprints for offenders—five extra 40-yard dashes after practice for the whole team. As a result the outright fighting tailed off.

But tempers still flared, including Strahan's. Fassel had to pull him aside after guard Jerry Reynolds, working double-teams with Gragg, poked

Strahan twice in the eye during one drill. Strahan ripped Reynolds' helmet off, slammed it against the ground—not on his head, much to Fassel's relief—and dressed down Reynolds. That got Strahan a warning to back off.

All Tied Up

One of the strangest games in Giants history involved a total of two touchdowns—one each for the Giants and Washington Redskins—in a 7–7 Sunday night tie at then-named Jack Kent Cooke Stadium in 1997. Not only did it mark the team's first and only tie since 1983, but it marked the second-half return of an old Super Bowl hero, Jeff Hostetler, in a Redskins uniform.

The man who replaced the injured Phil Simms to lead the 1990 Super Bowl championship run, Hostetler was only playing on November 23 because Redskins starter Gus Frerotte had knocked himself out of the game at half-time. The operative phrase being "knocked out." In his zeal to celebrate his 1-yard touchdown scramble just before the half ended, Frerotte had head-butted the padded stadium wall and was on his way to the hospital with a sprained neck and a rather distorted view of his surroundings.

As happy as the 7–4 Giants may have been to see "Hoss," they still had some business to tend to. Frerotte's touchdown had put them in a 7–0 halftime hole and threatened to neutralize the one-game division lead they held over Washington. Chris Calloway's 6-yard touchdown catch moments after he drew a third-quarter pass interference penalty temporarily relieved the situation while at the same time creating the setting for one of the wildest overtimes ever.

Far from typical sudden-death scenarios where cautiousness and conservatism from the sidelines would lead offenses to struggle for just enough yardage to try that winning field goal, this one featured daring shots, incredible breakups, and turnovers. Hostetler threw two of his three total interceptions during the extra period, with Jason Sehorn's pick stopping the Redskins at the Giants 41.

The Giants also recovered a fumble. But they never got closer than the 36, where Brad Daluiso missed a 54-yard field goal attempt wide left. Daluiso basically could have been blamed for two misses when linebacker Marvcus Patton charged in with 2:12 remaining in overtime and blocked his second 54-yard try. But a keen-eyed official had seen Patton signaling for a time-out moments before and awarded it just before the snap. Not wanting to risk another block, Jim Fassel pulled Daluiso off and had Brad Maynard punt it into the end zone. "It did enter my mind to play for the tie on the road," Fassel admitted. "I wanted to play for the win, but at the same time I didn't want to go out of here with a loss either, so I changed my mind."

The Giants also benefited from another of the Redskins' self-inflicted wounds when receiver Michael Westbrook was hit with an unsportsmanlike conduct penalty for tearing his helmet off while arguing an out of bounds call. The flag moved them back from the Giants 38 to well out of field goal range. Hostetler did get the Redskins back to the 36 on a throw to Henry Ellard, but Scott Blanton's field goal try into a light wind fell well short.

A defense that would later disintegrate in the closing minutes of that season's wild-card playoff game against the Minnesota Vikings intercepted four passes, recovered a fumble, and sacked Frerotte and Hostetler four times. Football people like ties about as much as children like brussels sprouts. But the ever-optimistic Fassel said he saw his team grow closer from it. "A lot of people expected us to go down there and get beat and beat soundly," he said. "We didn't approach it that way. The team handled it very well. It shows me this is a team that'll fight together."

At the time the tie did no harm to the Giants' NFC East title hopes. "We didn't lose ground," fullback Charles Way said. "We didn't gain ground. It's not a disaster. It's a tie."

Strahan's Hands

Great players experience moments when the game moves in slow motion, in perfect concert with the player's movements, in a symphony of action and reaction that winds up in glorious achievement. It happened for Strahan in overtime at Philadelphia's Veterans Stadium on October 31, 1999 when the Giants record was still solid enough at 4–3 to hope for a postseason berth. The

Giants defensive end Michael Strahan struts after returning a fumble for a touchdown in 2001, which catapulted the Giants to victory much like his interception return in overtime against the Philadelphia Eagles in 1999.

season would eventually get away from them and wind up at 7–9, but on this day, Strahan pulled his team's posteriors out of a tough spot with an overtime interception and return for a touchdown.

The prelude: the Eagles went into that game at 2–5, only twice having scored as many as 20 points. But the Giants had fallen behind 17–3 by halftime. Fassel didn't greet those circumstances with his usual good nature. The air in the halftime locker room bore a distinct blue tint as the coach spewed profanity and kicked over a chair. "Oh, man, I was scared," safety Sam Garnes said. "He got on us pretty tough with a couple of choice words."

It worked, and the Giants eventually came back and tied it on Kent Graham's throw to tight end Pete Mitchell in the back of the end zone with two minutes left in regulation. Eagles quarterback Doug Pederson drove to the Giants 45 with nearly five minutes gone in the extra period. Christian Peter charged in, hands high, and tipped the ball. Up it went in a straight line. The whole world seemed slowed to a crawl for Strahan as he settled under it. "I saw the ball get tipped," Strahan said. "It went straight up in the air, and I said, 'This is too good to be true.' It's moving in slow motion end over end. I stuck my hands out."

The ball fell into his mitts perfectly as if some heavenly entity had placed it there. He cradled it, and with only slow offensive linemen in pursuit, he covered his 44-yard journey to the end zone uncontested for the second and last interception return for a touchdown of his career. "He got the ball in his hands and laid his head back and ran," Armstead said. "He was in his big old Rolls Royce and nobody was gonna catch him."

A fumble return in 2001 against the Seattle Seahawks would mark his third touchdown. On this day, however, his achievement stood as a career moment. "It's a good thing I've got good hands," Strahan said. "If I didn't, I think everybody in New York would probably hate me right now."

Fassel was able to go into a bye week relieved and happy, blissfully ignorant of a future that would hold three straight losses and six setbacks in the final eight games. For just a little while, though, the coach could enjoy what his great defensive end had wrought. "When he took off with that ball, it was euphoric," Fassel said. "That was the longest it took him to run that ball in. It was unbelievable."

Loving the City of Brotherly Love

In the eight seasons from 1993 to 2000, Reeves' and Fassel's teams dominated the Philadephia Eagles. Despite stars like Randall Cunningham, Donovan McNabb, William Fuller, and Jeremiah Trotter dotting the Eagles' roster, the Giants rolled to a 12–4 record against them in the regular season. As part of that dominance, they were 6–2 at that dumpy house of horrors the great city of Philadelphia called Veterans Stadium.

With its seams spaced so wide on the pieces covering the baseball sliding pits that one could put his thumb through them, the artificial turf was so bad that a player could get hurt just looking at it. Chicago Bears receiver Wendell Davis actually blew out *both* his knees when launching himself off that surface for a pass.

The visitors' locker room was hot and cramped. The only redeeming features were the numerous holes and cracks in the wall that offered a direct view —if one was so inclined—into the Eagles cheerleaders' shower room. More than one player peeped until a 2002 lawsuit against the NFL caused stadium authorities to break out the spackle. Forty-four former cheerleaders alleged that players from 29 teams had spied on them.

And the fans, well, they were no less crazy than they are now. Veterans Stadium was the only building in the NFL equipped with its own holding cell and municipal court. A judge was kept on-duty to mete out immediate justice to brawling drunkards—as common down there as cheesesteaks.

But the Giants of that time never thought twice about heading into that nest of lunacy. "We loved going down there," Graham said. "They were down at the time, and we seemed to have their number. We usually always beat them."

Beating the Eagles wasn't exactly a quiet or painless experience. The vocabulary emanating from the stands above the players' tunnel could be brutal, but that was just part of playing in Philly. "You'd come out. They'd boo the snot out of us," Graham said. "Howard Cross would come out of the tunnel and raise his arms and say, 'Give us more!' It was kind of an honor. But I couldn't even repeat what they said. They hated us. The words were not kind to be diplomatic about it."

Nor were the Eagles' own on-field actions—whether they were getting beat at the Vet or at Giants Stadium. Graham got some firsthand experience in that department as a starter during his second go-around with the Giants. His 16–15 win at Giants Stadium on October 3, 1999 came at the price of three interceptions—and a couple of teeth. And he knew just who to thank…uh…to blame: safety Brian Dawkins. "He knocked my teeth out on a blitz in the Red Zone," Graham said. "We had a slant that went to the left. I knew Dawkins was coming free and I let it go, and he hit me right underneath the chin. I lost two teeth and got a pretty bad concussion out of that one. I didn't come out, though. I tried to play the game anyway, but things were so confused. I made this one decision where I threw a pick right at a guy. I couldn't figure out what happened until I saw it on film later, and that's when I realized, *Oh, I had a concussion*."

That guy was Trotter. After that third-quarter interception, Graham was pulled from the game, and Kerry Collins was inserted. Graham failed a number of cognitive tests that week, one of which included the question, "How many nickels are in $1.35?" Collins started the following week, but Fassel went back to Graham for four more starts. Collins started the final six games, and Graham became a Pittsburgh Steeler after the season.

But he never forgot the Eagles. "We just enjoyed beating Philly," he said.

Pressure Games

The most pressurized game Fassel ever coached was not Super Bowl XXXV. It wasn't the 41–0 NFC championship victory against the Vikings two weeks prior to that either.

It was the NFC semifinal that postseason against the Eagles. Fassel felt the full historical weight of the NFL's most storied franchise that day at Giants Stadium for good reason. After taking his team from 7–9 in 1999 to 12–4 division champ with home-field advantage throughout the playoffs in 2000, the ever media-conscious Fassel knew losing to the second-place Eagles would have created a firestorm. "We'd beaten Philly for four years, eight straight times, and now we had home-field advantage," Fassel said. "If we'd lost that game, I'd have had some heavy artillery coming after me."

Foremost in his mind were the old nightmares from a horrible, fourth-quarter implosion against the Vikings in the 1997 wild-card game. Created by a failure to recover an onside kick and problems in pass coverage, Minnesota's 10-point comeback in the final two minutes left that season's Coach of the Year numb.

He was determined not to have a repeat. "That was the most high-pressure game I ever coached," he said. "The media talked all week long about how we'd defense them. I wouldn't let [the players] believe it, though. I was harder on them that week than I'd ever been."

Things didn't exactly go according to plan. The Giants won 20–10, but they did it without benefit of an offensive touchdown. Ron Dixon's 97-yard return of the opening kickoff got them on the board immediately, and Sehorn's acrobatic 32-yard interception return for a touchdown in the second quarter, coming after Daluiso's first of two field goals, put them up 17–0. The defense allowed just 186 yards in total offense and 46 rushing yards. "I took a deep breath after that one," Fassel said. "I just enjoyed it but just for a while. I went into the practice bubble [where postgame gatherings were held for the VIPs] and then on the drive home I said, 'Enough of that.' I was on to Minnesota. I enjoyed it for an hour, hour and a half."

Stoicism never did suit Fassel. He was an emotional coach and wasn't afraid to show it to the people around him. On the day the '97 team climaxed their last-to-first climb from the previous year with a division-clinching 30–10 win December 13 against Washington at Giants Stadium, Fassel barely knew where he was. "That was the one time in my life I was like a robot," Fassel said. "People asked me how I was doing; I didn't know. Somebody asked me what I had for breakfast; I didn't know. I couldn't remember. All I'm thinking is *First-and-10, what am I gonna do? Second-and-15?* I was like a computer. You have to remember what we did that year. We were the only team the magazines picked *unanimously* to finish last. Then we go last-to-first and become the first team to ever go undefeated in the NFC East. We accomplished a lot. What we did that year was incredible."

The Giants sealed their perfect division record (7–0–1) in Dallas during the final week. But the Washington game clinched the title and allowed general manager George Young to go out on a high note. Fassel wanted the win as much for the GM as for his team. It was Young who recommended him to

Wellington Mara for both an assistant's job in 1991 and the head coaching job in '97. And Fassel wasn't about to let that debt go unpaid. "Pat Hanlon came into the locker room after all the cameras and reporters had gone and said George was outside on the bench crying," Fassel said. "Everybody had been hammering George that year: cap problems, he hadn't built a team, all that stuff. I went out, but he had gone already. But later he came in and gave me a big hug and said, 'Thanks. You'll never know as long as you live how much that meant to me. I didn't want to go out on the bottom.' I just said, 'Thank me? Thank you!' He got Executive of the Year, and I got Coach of the Year."

It made all the anxiety over the Washington game worth it. Fassel's sanity returned moments after time expired. "I woke up after the game," Fassel said.

0–2½

Giants chairman and executive vice president Steve Tisch stood in the team's practice bubble the week before Super Bowl XLII, reminiscing about the moment 2007 turned around. Spun on its axis was more like it. The final 51 seconds at FedEx Field against the Redskins did it. A Week 3 goal-line stand for the ages sealed a 24–17 life-or-go-down-the-toilet victory. "That was amazing," Tisch said. "We were 0–2½ and we came up with that stand. It saved our season."

The three plays that stopped quarterback Jason Campbell, fullback Mike Sellers, and running back Ladell Betts from getting into the end zone halted a horrible defensive slide that, had it continued, most certainly would have cost first-year defensive coordinator Steve Spagnuolo his job at season's end if not sooner. Losses in the first two games to the Cowboys and Packers with Spags' new, supposedly more aggressive defense allowing a whopping 80 points and 846 yards of total offense had the media barking.

The players were none too happy either, even as Spagnuolo beckoned them to continue to "believe in the system." Clearly Coughlin's team was in trouble. So was he. Another loss and the playoffs would turn into a long shot, a pipe dream. Coughlin most certainly would not get another chance especially after management defied rabid calls for his head and extended him a year after the controversy-filled 8–8 mess of 2006.

Then came those last 51 seconds at FedEx.

Safety James Butler and cornerback Aaron Ross had combined to take down Antwaan Randle El on Campbell's 20-yard throw to the 1, and with no timeouts and star running back Clinton Portis on the bench injured, Campbell spiked the ball to stop the clock and set up the momentous stand.

Second down: Linebacker Kawika Mitchell defended a throw to Sellers in the flat with a well-timed hit.

Then things got interesting. "If I put you in that huddle, your ears would bleed," defensive tackle Barry Cofield said. "At that point it's not about technique. It's not about the call. It's all about getting fired up and realizing what's at stake. We just came off the ball and did what we had to do."

That was quite simply to stop Betts from getting a measly 36 inches. The Giants had done well in that area all day, holding the Redskins to 82 rushing yards. Having given up a short touchdown run to the now-injured Portis, they had to come back from a 17–3 halftime deficit to finally pull ahead on Eli Manning's 33-yard, fourth-quarter touchdown pass to Plaxico Burress. The whole season lay right there with the final two plays.

Third down: Coming out of the I-formation, Betts took it to the inside of the left tackle. Mitchell met him there and threw him for no gain.

Fourth down: Betts ran almost the same play. Defensive end Justin Tuck slid behind the line and caught his ankles, starting Betts downward. Ross, the rookie cornerback, submarined him from the side. Osi Umenyiora was in the frame. Mitchell was there. So was Antonio Pierce and Butler. Betts was dropped for a two-yard loss. Ross threw his hands up in celebration while running from the pile. The league's 29th-ranked defense had finally done something to hang its hat on. "It's not good to be 0–2 in this league," defensive end Michael Strahan said. "And to come here and have a game that tight, for us to stop them like that, it was a lot of emotion, a lot of relief just for this team."

Things improved tremendously from that point. Five more victories followed. The Giants finished 10–6 thanks in large part to Spagnuolo's system. And just at the right time, Manning got hot and led them to a Super Bowl victory. None of it happens without the goal line stand. "Just the jubilation you feel when you're running off the field after making a big stop like that in the division, on the road, I'll never forget it," Cofield said.

Neighborhood Watch

Given the track record against their Giants Stadium and MetLife Stadium co-tenant New York Jets since 1996, it's no wonder some in the Giants front office call Gang Green "the JV." Five straight victories in the quadrennial, inter-conference meetings would tend to make any Giant stick out his chest a bit more especially when recalling that only their 13–6 win in 1996 and their 31–28 overtime victory in 2003 were close.

Few of those, however, brought more satisfaction than the 2011 affair, a 29–14 win at one-year-old MetLife. It wasn't the matchup itself as much as what preceded the Christmas Eve game. Sure the win moved the Giants a step closer to an NFC East title that Coughlin's team parlayed into a Super Bowl championship. But it also put mouthy coach Rex Ryan and his brash team in their place.

Ryan had stirred the pot at his Wednesday press conference. The Jets had been to the AFC Championship game the two previous seasons, so Ryan was full of confidence even as the Jets were struggling to an 8–8, non-playoff record. Undoubtedly the sting of an awkwardly handled opening of MetLife the year before also lingered. The Giants won a supposedly secret coin flip in the commissioner's office and got to play the first game there, with the Jets following on Monday night. The Jets, though, thought they got screwed royally, placed once again in the shadow of the Giants by commissioner Roger Goodell.

Though no Giant ever called their neighbors the junior varsity to their face, the Jets clearly bristled under an inferiority complex. Ryan sought to break that and secure a third-straight playoff appearance at the same time. "I never came here to be little brother to anybody," Ryan ranted. "So it's on. There's no way I'm going to be second fiddle. If we were playing the New York Yankees, I don't want to be second fiddle to them. I recognize they're an excellent team. But I think we're better." Coughlin simply dusted off his team's battle cry from 2007 in response: "Talk is cheap; play the game."

It didn't stop there. The Jets followed their coach's word by wrapping up an early Christmas present. The walls outside the Giants' locker room bore a mural depicting their Super Bowl logos. When Coughlin's players arrived, they found the painting covered up with a black curtain. Two players tore the curtain down, but a few minutes later, some of the Jets put it back up.

Big mistake. Nothing like a little in-your-face disrespect to get a team's engine going.

The defense smothered Ryan's group. Victor Cruz took a short pass 99 yards for a touchdown. As the teams left the field, Brandon Jacobs answered a Ryan barb by threatening to punch him in the mouth. As the Giants approached their locker room door, down came the curtain once and for all. "This is Giants Stadium!" Pro Bowl offensive lineman David Diehl shouted. "This game was about respect. Walking in here today, we knew we were the away team. But to have all our logos blocked, all the Super Bowl trophies this organization's won, and everything we stand for...we all saw it as a sign of disrespect."

Linebacker Mathias Kiwanuka brought it all down to its most basic level. "Talk all you want, all day long," he said. "But after school when that bell sounds, you got to be ready to fight."

Across the Line

For all the personal rivalries in the NFL, it would be hard to top the bitterness that existed between Pro Bowl defensive ends Strahan and Tuck and their offensive line counterparts. Strahan and Eagles right tackle Jon Runyan battled yearly from 2000 to 2007, looking at each other eye to eye and hating every minute of it. For Tuck, Cowboys left tackle Flozell Adams was only a peripatetic acquaintance since Tuck usually lined up on the other side. But on the few occasions they did meet, Adams left his mark in violent, underhanded fashion.

In the second quarter of the second game of 2009, a 33–31 Giants win to christen the new Cowboys Stadium, Tuck was lined up over Adams in an adjusted alignment. He beat the massive, 6'7", 340-pound Adams off the snap. Adams, reputed as one of the league's preeminent cheap-shot artists, leg whipped Tuck as he went by and sent the defensive captain sprawling onto his left shoulder, tearing his labrum.

Tuck, who suffered such intense pain that he was unable to resume a three-point stance, could no longer continue. The man, who had not missed a game since a foot injury cost him six games in 2006, headed for the doctors the next day right after he let Adams have it in the press. "Bush league," was the term Tuck used, adding he only wished he could have returned to "punish" Adams.

That triggered a cross-country verbal battle. "Bush? What does that mean?" responded the Pro Bowl tackle, who was flagged on the play for tripping and later fined $12,500. "I've never, ever heard that term. He said he hurt his shoulder. I'm like, 'Well, stay up.' That's all I know. He fell down. Stay up."

As if the rivalry between the Cowboys and Giants wasn't intense enough, Tuck said Adams "makes me hate the Cowboys a little bit more. I did say hate. I stand by what I said right after. It was a bush-league play. Normally people go to the Pro Bowl for blocking and tackling not tripping people."

Though Tuck didn't miss a game, he was limited to a situational role the following week against the Tampa Bay Buccaneers. Tuck never did return to his old self even after he resumed his starting job. He played in pain throughout the season, saw his effectiveness decrease, and eventually submitted to off-season surgery.

That took care of the steady ache, but Tuck never lost his distaste for Adams. And vice versa. As the teams headed for the halftime locker room in their December 5 rematch, Adams pushed Tuck from behind and started a melee. "I felt somebody shove me to the ground," Tuck said. "It takes a coward and some words I can't say to push a guy in the back."

Adams called Tuck "a nobody." The Giants, though, had the last laugh that year. They swept the Cowboys, winning the second game 31–24.

The Strahan-Runyan matches were slightly more civilized—and lopsided. Strahan dominated Runyan year in, year out with his zenith coming in the 2000 playoff game when Strahan ran over the 330-pound right tackle to nail

McNabb for his second strip-sack of the game. After a Week 2 domination that same season, Strahan was asked by a television reporter about his match with Runyan. "Who?" Strahan said. "Jon Runyan who?"

The two continued to throw barbs at each other throughout their careers, but it rarely degenerated into dirty play. In fact Strahan at one point referred to their rivalry as "a dance, and you want to be the lead." Only a few months after Strahan retired, the future congressman representing New Jersey's Third District paid his foe a tremendous compliment. "He was the type of guy who threw everything at you," Runyan said. "Even if he was hurt, he'd do everything he could. The biggest thing was he wasn't going to beat you with one move. He'd wait for you to get out of position and then he'd take advantage of it. He wouldn't set you up, but he would wait and react off something you might do stupidly."

Runyan's job was to protect McNabb. Strahan didn't let him do it very well. He registered 21½ career sacks on Philadelphia quarterbacks, and his 12½ of McNabb made the Syracuse product the most sacked of any of Strahan's victims. The majority of those came against Runyan. Asked if Runyan would miss him, the tackle offered a decidedly non-political answer. "No," he said.

Shady Dealings

The war of words between Umenyiora and Philadelphia's LeSean "Shady" McCoy started during the lockout of 2011 and intensified from there. It probably never should have happened at all since Umenyiora's contract squabbles were none of the running back's business in the first place. But when McCoy decided to weigh in on the matter, it understandably triggered an alternately mean-spirited and comical exchange that carried all the way over into the 2012 season.

Having filed an affidavit that general manager Jerry Reese went back on a promise in April 2008 to either renegotiate his contract or trade him to another team, Umenyiora was in the midst of his usual contract squabbles. The controversy escalated as efforts to reach a new collective bargaining agreement remained stalemated between the players union and league management.

That's when McCoy jumped in via Twitter on June 16. Unprovoked, McCoy called him, "Overrated n soft 3rd best d-line on his team, honestly." Umenyiora fired a tweet back, calling McCoy "Lady GaGa."

In an interview the following day, Umenyiora said, "That little Chihuahua or poodle in the backfield, he doesn't have to block me. If you have something to say, say it man-to-man. You can't be a Twitter gangster. That's easy to do, trying to be a tough guy. Say it to my face, and we'll see what happens." In another interview he said, "I mean, he's a girl, man. Who does stuff like that? If he has more things to say, he can say 'em to my face. Don't be no Twitter gangster, man." Umenyiora left no doubt where his emotions were. "Yeah, me and him, we had words on the field both times we played," he said. "I hate him; he hates me, period. He chose to take it off the field and make it public when it's something between me and him. He let the whole world know about it, so I'm going to respond."

McCoy had rushed for 175 yards on 24 carries in two games against the Giants in 2010, and had apparently called Umenyiora an "African motherfucker." Umenyiora fired back but noted it was the harshest language he'd ever heard. "There's a real hatred toward Philly, and there's a real hatred toward us," Umenyiora said. "But I feel things like that stay on the football field because at the end of the day we're all brothers. But he decided to take it so far that there's no going back from it now."

From there, it was game on—sometimes in good fun. In May of 2012, Umenyiora tweeted, "Happy Mother's Day LeSean McCoy! Enjoy your special day!!" to which McCoy answered, "lol let the beef begin!"

An ESPN interview followed in which McCoy referred to Umenyiora as a "ballerina." "Osi, to be honest, is a good player," McCoy said. "He thinks he is better than he really is. I think he's a ballerina in a Giants uniform." Umenyiora couldn't let that pass. "He's probably right," he said, voice dripping with sarcasm. "I might be a ballerina in a Giants uniform. I'm lucky that I got the contract. I'm lucky to be playing 10 years in the league, won Super Bowls. All that is pure luck."

Whether or not the animosity raised the two adversaries to another level is debatable. They called a truce a week after the ballerina comment when the two met on the field following McCoy's 123-yard performance in the Eagles' 19–17 win at Lincoln Financial Field. Umenyiora had four tackles and a sack. "Osi said, 'You're a heck of a player, we're in this business, let's get over this,'" McCoy told a Philadelphia radio station. Umenyiora called the feud "irrelevant" and added, "It was about time that ended, and I'm glad all that stuff is over with." McCoy gained only 45 yards in the Giants' season-ending, 42–7 win at the Meadowlands with Umenyiora making three tackles.

Husband vs. Wife

Before hamstring problems undermined 2007 first-round cornerback Aaron Ross, he worked out harder than any of his teammates. He couldn't help it. His fiancée was Olympic sprinter Sanya Richards, and the workouts Ross did with her were tougher than anything Coughlin could concoct. "My training is pretty easy compared to hers," Ross said in August 2008, only days before Richards began her quest for an individual Olympic gold medal in Beijing, China. She only struck gold with the relay team in that one but would win the 400 in the 2012 Olympics in London after their marriage and the cornerback's subsequent move to the Jacksonville Jaguars.

At the time, though, Ross would regularly join Richards for workouts. They weren't jogs through the park either. They may have started off easy enough, but by the time they climaxed with eight 200-meter sprints with only two minutes of rest between them, Ross was begging for mercy. He usually couldn't complete the sprints at all. While Richards sweated right through them, Ross would do the first four and then have to stop for water. He'd return from his little break just in time for the last one, maybe two.

The workouts weren't the first time the future gold medalist took Ross' breath away. That would have been in Ross' freshman year at the University of Texas when fellow Longhorn Richards called him over for a chat in the student union. It was love at first sight, though the marriage proposal would have to wait until December 16, 2007. At least Ross got it on videotape—just the way Richards wanted it.

NBC was in Ross' apartment, filming a piece on Richards in prelude to the Olympics. "He asked me, 'What do you want for Christmas?'" Richards said. "I said, 'You know what I want. I want to get married.' And he said, 'Well, you can just continue to wear your promise ring,' and I said, 'No.' At that point, Ross dropped to one knee and with camera rolling said, "How about this one instead?"

The ring was worth waiting for. A five-karat stone adorned the center, and five one-karat stones decorated the band. Ross never made it over to Beijing. He was a bit busy winning the job at starting left cornerback in his second season. He did, though, ask Coughlin for permission. "Yeah, it just wasn't going to happen," he said without bitterness.

The Jaguars were more accommodating. They let him go to London, and Richards responded with her 400-meter win. This time, the world's cameras caught Ross planting a big congratulatory kiss on his wife. During the 2013 offseason, Ross would continue his union with the Giants, signing as a free agent with New York following his release after one year in Jacksonville.

CHAPTER 3

THE HIGHS, LOWS, AND PRANKS OF THE REGULAR SEASON

Surf and Turf

Rodney Hampton had the day of his life in the 17–10 wild-card playoff victory against the Minnesota Vikings in 1993, going for 161 yards and two touchdowns. Most important were the blocks he received from an offensive line that had struggled mightily in the previous week's 16–13 loss to the Dallas Cowboys.

But the line came together that windswept January 9, 1994 day at Giants Stadium just in time to provide Phil Simms some much-needed security and to lay some huge blocks during Hampton's rushing clinic. And none of it would have happened without a team-building get-together the previous Monday at Manhattan's famed Smith & Wollensky steakhouse.

The offensive line along with backup quarterbacks Dave Brown and Kent Graham and the training staff rang up a $3,000 bill on steak and lobster there. "It turned into a forget-about-yesterday thing," said massive guard William Roberts. "We wanted to forget about it and have a good time."

Oh, they did. Especially Roberts. In a career that lasted 14 seasons between the Giants and New England Patriots, Roberts weighed around 300 pounds. So one might say he got his money's worth at the dinner when he washed down a huge rib eye with an eight-pound lobster. "It was in the tank for a long time," Roberts said.

The return that Sunday on their $3,000 investment was considerable. The run blocking allowed Hampton to race all over the Vikings. On a day where the famous gusts of the Meadowlands held Simms to 94 yards passing—the quarterback called it one of the three worst weather days he'd ever encountered—Hampton rushed 33 times.

Never was Hampton more effective than on his 51-yard touchdown run in the third quarter to bring the Giants back from a 10–3 deficit. Hampton took Simms' pitch and swept right and then cut back behind blocks by Doug Riesenberg and pulling guard Bob Kratch on Roy Barker. Linebacker Fred Strickland almost had him at the Vikings 47, but tight end Howard Cross threw his body in there to spring him.

Defensive end Chris Doleman and linebacker Carlos Jenkins pursued, and Jenkins might have caught Hampton if not for the running back's stiff-arm at the 30. Safety Vencie Glenn had the last shot, slipping off a Chris Calloway block at the 5. Hampton stiff-armed him, too and reached the end zone with 12:06 left in the third quarter.

Second on the all-time Giants rushing list—Tiki Barber eventually would eclipse Hampton's 6,897 yards—Hampton scored the game-winner on a 2-yard run on the next possession. The generally quiet Hampton said he was glad to get the work. "When you get pumped up and you keep making plays, you want the ball in your hands at all times," he said. "I'm just happy they continued to call my number."

The Vikings came into the game with 45 sacks, but they never laid a hand on Simms in 26 dropbacks. And guard Eric Moore, facing Doleman on a sprained ankle, found enough inner strength to lay other key blocks to aid Hampton's ground clinic. Perhaps the steak and lobster had fueled him with extra energy.

Glickman Remembers 1936

Marty Glickman sat no more than 20 feet away from the burning torch at Berlin's Olympic Stadium, staring up at the white marble wall before him. The list of track and field winners of the 1936 Olympics, which Hitler attended, were emblazoned in gold along with their times. His name was not among them.

By the time Glickman paid his second visit to Olympic Stadium, he had long been retired as the voice of the Giants. He had made his name as a broadcasting great with his dulcet tones ringing over the radio airwaves during the home game blackout days of the 1960s and early '70s. Now he was in Berlin as a guest of the Giants, who had come reluctantly to a once-divided city as part of the preseason American Bowl series to train with and play against the San Diego Chargers.

On this day, though, Glickman was transported back to his freshman year at Syracuse and to the Olympics where the football/track star and his friend, Sam Stoller, were scheduled to run the 400-meter relay. He had dreamed of the baton pass and of standing on the gold medal platform. The 18-year-old

Glickman never thought about returning to that ground in the future, having never run in those or any Olympics games. Glickman and Stoller were Jewish, and having two Jews on a winning relay would never fit in with the world's appeasement of Germany's blossoming madman. So U.S. Olympic Committee president Avery Brundage pulled the two. (Turns out that two African Americans, Ralph Metcalfe and Jesse Owens, provided the insult to the prejudiced leader.) More than half a century later, Glickman's voice still bore the hurt from his exclusion. "I sit here and I look up there and I think about me and Sam Stoller," he said. "I was lucky. I was only 18. I had my whole career ahead of me. Sam was devastated by it. He was a senior, and in those days, when you finished college competition, that was it. I had three more years of college to look forward to. I had 1940 to look forward to. I was gonna get even."

Because of World War II, 1940 and 1944 never happened. By the time the games resumed in London in 1948, Glickman was married with children and well into his legendary broadcast career. On this day in 1994, he was no longer angry or frustrated as he was that week when he gazed at the box holding Germany's mustachioed dictator. Glickman had come back to watch two football teams play an American game in the same venue Hitler used to promote his Aryan Race. "I didn't experience that run. I didn't experience that stick pass. I didn't stand on the winning podium," said Glickman, who died on January 3, 2001. "I didn't do all those things. But I'm here, and they're not. Hitler certainly is not." Glickman had gotten even in his own way.

Snowball Game

When little kids have a snowball fight, it's harmless fun. When a pack of liquored up, frustrated adults do it, child's play turns into anything but. It became downright dangerous on December 23, 1995 as a 5–11 season wrapped up against the Chargers in a Giants Stadium still filled with snow from the previous night's storm. Only 50,243 fans showed up in the 76,000-seat building with many having bought their spots from season-ticket holders who did not want to brave the cold weather for a meaningless game.

What transpired in the stands was just plain scary. "I had season tickets for 22 years, and that was the worst experience I ever had," said Tommy Bamundo, at the time a 43-year-old Brooklynite sitting in Section 123A, an end zone area just to the right of the goalpost. "I was there for Joe Pisarcik, the scab games, and that one, and those three were the worst ever."

For pure danger what became known as "the Snowball Game" took the cake. Aside from nearly causing the first forfeit in NFL history as fans pelted the field with snowballs and iceballs in the fourth quarter, three officials were hit, and a San Diego equipment manager was knocked cold. "We were just watching and shaking our heads. We couldn't believe what was going on. It wasn't funny at all," Bamundo said.

Fights broke out all over the stands, resulting in 175 ejections from the stadium and 15 arrests. Even more surprising than the unrest—on a level more appropriately found in Philadelphia's rowdy Veterans Stadium—was the cross section of offenders. A local police chief, several lawyers and doctors, and a number of teachers were caught in the act, which made the end zones appear as if there had just been dusted in a passing snowstorm.

The mayhem even drifted over to Bamundo's section. "This guy from the lower deck came up and said we threw a snowball and hit him," Bamundo said. "We didn't throw anything. But he went to the littlest guy of our group and said, 'Yeah, I'll bet you did it,' and he hit him in the head. And then one of our guys got into it. Most of our group were cops. They started beating the hell out of each other. That was the only brawl we ever had."

The occasional snowball had come down earlier, but the flurry turned into a storm with 14:57 remaining in the game. The Giants had blown a 14-point halftime lead, and Dave Brown had just missed fullback Charles Way on a second-and-5 pass. Hit in the face by a well-aimed ice ball, Chargers equipment man Sid Brooks went down shortly after that. He lay unconscious for five minutes as action came to a halt.

Fifteen fans suffered snowball-related injuries and were treated at the stadium's first-aid station, though none were hospitalized. Ten security guards were injured by either flying snowballs or flying fists. The players weren't immune to the barrage either. San Diego's great linebacker Junior Seau was

Linebacker Lewis Bush and another Chargers player cover their heads to avoid getting pelted with snowballs as disgruntled fans made their displeasure known, resulting in 175 ejections, during the December 23, 1995 game at Giants Stadium. *(AP Images)*

hit in the helmet, and the Giants had to huddle on the sideline with their helmets on as they met with the coaches.

San Diego's Shaun Gayle returned an interception 99 yards for a touchdown with 5:44, which intensified the deluge. "It's hard enough to lose, but when it gets to the point where you can't meet on the sideline with the coaches, that's awful," Giants linebacker Corey Miller said. "We had to huddle on the sidelines with our helmets on. Who'd want to be part of that, of fans who act that way? It's pathetic."

Chargers coach Bobby Ross was livid. "We were like sitting targets, and it wasn't snowballs," he said. "It was ice."

Things got so bad that referee Ron Blum cleared the field and ordered stadium announcer Bob Sheppard to inform the crowd of a possible forfeit. "The whole thing—the endangerment of the players and officials on the field, the coaches on the sideline—was a concern," Blum said. "To be honest I was very close to forfeiting the game. One more incident like the one we had after the [99-yard] touchdown by San Diego, and we would have forfeited the game. They just totally barraged the end zone."

The Giants took immediate action. Then vice-president John Mara set about identifying the offenders. If they were one-time-only attendees, the original holders of the tickets were punished. Seventy-five original holders were held responsible for the alternate buyers' behavior and had their seats revoked. They were replaced by the top names on the waiting list. Those few seats represented the deepest cut into a list that reached more than 100,000 names before the new MetLife Stadium opened in 2010.

The incident proved a huge embarrassment for what had been regarded as a staid, buttoned-up organization and fan base. Unlike the Jets fans who set fire to some upper deck seats in 1988, Giants fans simply did not behave that way. The Giants let the people of San Diego know that, too as they bought ad space in *The San Diego Union-Tribune* to issue a letter of apology. "You don't pay your money to come and try to hurt somebody," an irate Dan Reeves said. "We're not out there in an arena looking like gladiators where you're sitting targets for someone who had too much to drink or doesn't have enough guts to come down and face you face-to-face. They have to throw it from the stands."

Said VP of communications Pat Hanlon: "That was a miserable end to a miserable season. It was a bad scene, and what happened to Sid was awful. It was an absolute nightmare."

Calloway's Nightmare

Before Amani Toomer broke out in 1999, there was Chris Calloway. Picked up as a Class B free agent in 1992 from the Pittsburgh Steelers, the steady possession receiver led the Giants in catches for four straight years from 1995 to 1998. But his highlight season was 1997 when he caught 58 passes for 849 yards and eight touchdowns while helping New York rebound from 6–10 to a 10–5–1 division championship.

For all of Calloway's efficiency, he unfortunately is remembered for a nightmarish play in the Giants' first-round playoff game that season. To say he fumbled the game away would be too harsh because a lot of other things had to happen in the final 90 seconds of that 23–22 loss to Minnesota that left coach Jim Fassel ashen afterward. But Calloway's mishandling of Eddie Murray's onside kick certainly started the ball rolling.

It was shocking, to say the least. Calloway was not a spectacular receiver, but he was reliable. And when he was called out to the field as part of the hands team—the gaggle of wide receivers, defensive backs, and running backs coaches called upon to handle obvious onside kick attempts—it was assumed Murray would have to execute something exceptional for Minnesota to get the ball again.

Things had not gone particularly well for the Vikings up until then. The smothering Giants defense had forced two Randall Cunningham fumbles in the first quarter, which the Giants converted into two field goals. A Jason Sehorn interception had led to another field goal after a 56-yard scoring drive capped by a Danny Kanell touchdown pass to Aaron Pierce. The Giants had led 19–3 at halftime.

But the game began to sour for the Giants in the third quarter. Barber fumbled at the Giants 4, and the Vikings converted that into a touchdown. Then the defense started squabbling among themselves. Cornerback Phillippi

Sparks got into it on the field with Conrad Hamilton in the fourth quarter. The argument later spilled over to the sidelines and escalated into a physical confrontation between Sparks, Hamilton, and linebacker Jessie Armstead. Defensive linemen Keith Hamilton and Michael Strahan also jawed at each other on-field and off.

Cunningham connected on a 30-yard touchdown pass to Jake Reed right in front of safety Tito Wooten to pull the Vikings to within two points with 1:30 remaining. The play proved controversial because Reed's toe appeared to land on the end line. It probably would have been overturned in the current era of replay review, but without such a provision back then, the play stood despite safety Percy Ellsworth's protests.

Then came the onside kick. Recover the ball and the Giants run out the clock and head to Green Bay. Calloway had good hands and he was ready for Murray's attempt. Murray didn't kick it especially well or place it in a particularly difficult position. Calloway even seemed to have fielded it when—plunk—it bounced off his chest. Linebacker Corey Widmer had a shot at it. So did Ellsworth. Instead it squirted toward the Vikings' Chris Walsh. When the officials peeled back the pile near the left sideline, Walsh had the ball. "We practice the onside kick every week," Calloway lamented in the losing locker room. "No question, I should have had it. It came off low, it came to me, but it took a funny bounce, hit my chest, and went away."

And with it went the Giants' season. Sparks picked up a pass interference call. The defense continued its meltdown, arguing all the way into the offseason. Finally the 41-year-old Murray came through with a 24-yard field goal with 10 seconds left, bringing an eerie quiet to a once-boisterous Giants Stadium. It also left first-year coach Fassel nearly mute. "We lost our composure," the NFL's Coach of the Year said as he dejectedly looked off into space. "It's a very bitter pill to swallow."

Adding to the hurt was that the Giants bade farewell to two integral pieces of their organization that day. It was the last career game for Hampton, their then-record-setting running back who bowed out with just 18 yards, and general manager George Young, who made his anticipated retirement official shortly thereafter.

The Week That Was

Football teams go through stages of controversy, adversity, and transformation throughout a season. But rarely have all three come into play in one week unless that team was the New York Giants of 1999. From November 29 through December 5, the lives of five team members would change—Collins, Toomer, and quarterback coach Sean Payton for the better and Fassel and Strahan for the worse.

The worse came first. Only a month after Strahan had made his interception return for a touchdown in overtime against Philadelphia, the team's playoff hopes had almost vanished. The Giants lost three straight and Fassel, dealing with the loss of his mother, had put out an edict that team leader Armstead pipe down about criticizing the struggling offense.

That Monday, the day Fassel flew to Anaheim, California, for his mother's funeral, Strahan decided he'd had enough of that. The morning started off in surreal fashion. Strahan, regarded as the heart of the team to Armstead's soul, came off as uncaring about his team's fall to 5–6 with the previous day's setback against Arizona. "I'm not concerned about anything," he said. "It's not life and death. I've got a wife and three dogs at home. If we win, great. If we don't, I've got to deal with it. Put it aside, man. Smile. Be happy."

By the afternoon the defensive end's nonchalance had turned to outright anger. In an impromptu, unannounced, 80-minute rant in the Giants Stadium press room, Strahan proceeded to rip his absent and grieving coach about muzzling Armstead and by extension, himself. "You can't be a leader unless you can comment on the whole spectrum," Strahan said. "And we can't comment on the whole spectrum of this team. There's no leader right now. You have a guy [Armstead] who's a leader and a lion and you tell the lion to stop roaring? The lion's going to be quiet—period. He just ain't going to be the same lion in that den. And the locker room is the den."

Strahan also noted that the mental strain of watching the offense fail time and again, year after year under Brown, Graham, and Kanell: "It's frustrating when you've been here for seven years and it's kind of been the same old thing for seven years. We have a great defense here, but I think we're a little tired."

The comments in Tuesday's newspapers predictably spread with lightning speed across the continent to Fassel. Accorsi, attending the funeral, apprised his coach of Strahan's wayward thoughts. Fassel was not ecstatic with his mice playing while the cat buried its mother. When he arrived back at his Giants Stadium office that Wednesday, nearly sleepless after a 1 AM arrival from California, the first thing he did was summon Strahan for a visit. A good chewing out was more like it—45 minutes worth. "I was not happy with those comments," Fassel said, "not happy with any team member that makes those comments, and it angered me."

Strahan apologized, paid a $1,000 fine, blamed the media for twisting his words, and the issue passed to more important things like the Jets. That game brought the whole turbulent week to a positive end. Preparations started with a change in offensive play callers. Fassel, a former offensive coordinator with the Giants, Denver Broncos, and Arizona Cardinals, had handled those duties since he took over in 1997. But he didn't need Strahan's ill-timed tirade to tell him the offense needed something different than his conservative style. He had been considering dropping the play calling duties for a while. Quarterback coach Payton had made a positive impression when calling plays in the preseason opener in Minnesota when Fassel missed time to visit his ailing mom one final time in Phoenix.

With Brown demoted and the reign of Collins just one unsuccessful week old, Fassel realized the time had come to shift some things around. He couldn't have picked a better time. The offense exploded in a 41–28 win against Bill Parcells' Jets. So impressive was the onslaught that it left the former Giants leader red-faced. It was the last Giants-Jets game Parcells would ever coach. After the game Parcells admitted to being "out-coached," a high compliment to Fassel and Payton. "It's the first time in three years I've ever been ashamed," Parcells said.

Much of that had to do with Payton and how he used Collins and an up-and-coming veteran receiver in Toomer. Gone were the constant check downs. They were replaced with downfield throws and plenty of play-action. Collins finished the game with an astounding 134.4 rating on 17-of-29, 341-yard passing. It marked the Giants' first 300-yard passing effort in 96 games since Phil Simms against the Cardinals in 1993.

Toomer had a career day. The man who would post franchise receiving records was only in the midst of his first 1,000-yard season, and his 181 yards was a career high. He also scored three touchdowns, accounting for exactly half of his 1999 total. The big play officially became part of the Giants' repertoire that day, and Toomer had two of them on touchdown catches of 61 and 80 yards. Used primarily as a kick returner until that year, the second-round pick of 1996 had his coming-out party. From that point on, the receiver, who averaged four catches a game as a starter pre-Collins, caught an average of six passes per game with Collins. By the following season, he and Ike Hilliard would key Payton's passing philosophy that helped lead the Giants to Super Bowl XXXV against Baltimore.

At the time, though, the offensive breakout and the staff changes would only prove a temporary balm to the controversy earlier in the week. The Giants would beat the Bills the following week but then fall to the St. Louis Rams, Vikings, and Dallas Cowboys to finish up the 7–9 season. Payton would keep the play calling duties until 2002 when Fassel demoted him and eventually pushed him out of the organization. Ironically that embarrassment started the offensive guru on the road to his first head coaching job with the Saints. He would accomplish something Fassel never did. He won the Lombardi Trophy in Super Bowl XLIV.

Locker Room Hijinks

Locker room pranks usually affect only the prankees. But Rich Seubert, a guard who delighted in getting under everyone's skin, remembered one 2008 training camp joke that created some collateral casualties well after the fact. "Some of the rookies weren't behaving too well, so a bunch of us went to Walmart and bought those Super Soakers, the big water guns. Only we didn't fill them with water. We peed in them. Then we sprayed the rookies with them, and they weren't too happy about that."

But the story didn't end there. Somehow, Seubert said, the empty but unclean guns wound up in the trunk of punter Jeff Feagles' car where they stayed until the end of the season. "Like three months later, Feag's kids get ahold of them and they fill 'em up and start squirting each other, just having a good old time," Seubert said. "And they come in the house and they just smelled horrible. Feagles realized then what happened."

Rookies weren't the only targets. As laid-back as Manning was in public, he often pulled stunts on his teammates. In 2010 only their conscience and allegiance to the Maras prevented Seubert and Shaun O'Hara—no choirboy himself in the practical joke department—from getting him back in a big way. "We were gonna put a live turkey in his meeting room," Seubert said. "This guy was selling live turkeys around Thanksgiving, and we were gonna let it loose in the room. It would have pooped all over the place, made a real mess. So we get this thing, and I've got it in a dog crate in my house for like two weeks. We didn't do it only because we'd moved into our new Timex Performance Center by then. We didn't think Mr. Mara would like it if we dirtied up the new place. I wound up giving it to a friend, and the turkey lived for like six more years."

He only wished the prank Manning and backup Tim Hasselbeck pulled on him in 2005 was as easy to clean up as turkey droppings. They smeared Vaseline on his truck windshield. "You can't wash it off. You gotta scrape it off with a credit card," Seubert said. "I think that thing still has streaks from that."

PB&J

Three days after the Giants suffered one of their most shocking losses of the past 20 years, a 24-point, fourth-quarter meltdown in Tennessee in 2006, Strahan had a nuclear explosion. Or maybe call it a dirty bomb. Peanut butter and jelly can make quite a mess in the wrong hands or mouth. Strahan had called out wide receiver Plaxico Burress in a radio interview that Monday morning for allegedly giving up on tackling Adam "Pacman" Jones on Manning's first of two interceptions. "It's a shame," he said. "You can't give up. You can't quit because you're not quitting on yourself. You're quitting on everybody. I don't quite understand what his lack of motivation is in those types of situations."

The comments went right at Burress' pride and on-field work ethic. What made it worse was that he and Strahan, whose locker was just a few feet diagonally from the 6'5" receiver, had become good friends. But Strahan's comments threatened that bond. The two eventually settled their differences with Burress calmly telling Strahan that if he had something to tell him, he could just as easily have walked the 10 feet to his locker and said it. Strahan apologized and said his words didn't come out the way he intended.

The player crisis settled down, but not before Strahan brought a beef with the media, particularly with ESPN's Kelly Naqi, who was sent down specifically to question Strahan about the flap. Strahan initially rebuffed the reporter's question. But coming back from the lunch room with a peanut butter and jelly sandwich in hand, he consented to talk with the group of 15 or so media types. He called Naqi to the front of the group. "Come here!" he said, glowering and chewing a big bite of sandwich. "I want to see your face when you ask that question and the way you're gonna ask it. I know you're gonna ask it in a way that causes more division and more of a negative way. Look a man in the eye before you try to kill him!"

Throughout his tirade, the PB&J swirled sloppily inside his mouth. Tiny bits flew out the front of his famously gapped pearly whites. "I read papers every day," he continued. "You know the difference between reading your newspapers now and 10 years ago? Now I know [garbage] when I read it. Ten years ago, I didn't. It doesn't bother me because half is garbage. If you want to be negative, be negative. If you think it bothers me, I don't give a damn. I'm done talking. I'll see you guys tomorrow." For the rest of his career, Strahan ate either before or after he met with the media—never during.

Antagonizing the Rookie Receivers

Like any other team's locker room in the NFL, the Giants' proved no safe haven for rookies. Regardless of their drafted or undrafted status, the first-year players would pay their dues in service to the veterans. God help them if they slacked off or defied the unwritten code. Steve Smith learned all about that as a second-round pick in 2007. Before he became Manning's go-to receiver on third down, he first had to learn a lesson about waiting on his elders. Prof. Burress was happy to oblige.

Rookies were responsible for supplying their position groups with break-fast the morning of travel days and any other day the players had to fend for themselves. Smith had already shown his disdain of the rules when he thrice declined to supply the morning feed during training camp. Burress, to whom Smith announced his intentions to never, ever buy breakfast, let it go until the matter was forgotten by all. Almost all.

It wasn't until the Friday the team left for its first playoff game in Tampa that Burress exacted his punishment. Revenge, you see, isn't the only dish best served cold. Spying the brand new dress shirt Smith had in his bag, Burress took it out, neatly cut the sleeves off, refolded it, and put it back in its place. Then he put indelible ink, which the FBI uses to trace money, into Smith's socks. As the players boarded the bus to Newark's Liberty Airport, Smith pulled the shirt out of the bag and put it on. Off popped the arms, and his teammates roared. The dyed socks not only turned his feet purple but ruined a pair of $295 shoes so new they still bore the price tag. "The next time I tell you: 'you better have something,' you better have my sandwich," Burress warned.

Fellow rookie receiver Brandon London committed a similar sin and paid for it by having his travel suit doused in the visiting locker room shower. He had to wear his Giants sweats home.

"Next time y'all forget, I'm going to take your car keys," Burress said. "I'm going to take your girlfriend."

Smith and London learned. The receivers, according to Burress, ate what-ever they wanted the rest of the season—courtesy of the rookies. That included a steady diet of IHOP instead of the standard, cheaper fare of McDonald's and Dunkin Donuts.

Straightening Out Tooms

Even record-setting receivers need a little help from their friends every so often. Toomer was no different. When Burress arrived as a free agent in 2005, Toomer switched positions from the split end spot he had commanded since 1996 to flanker. That meant he had to learn a new set of plays, which, according to Burress, he kept forgetting.

Burress said he'd have to put him in position five or six times a game. The process became somewhat of a joke between the players and coaching staff, but few were laughing when the Giants' holder of the career marks for receptions (688), receiving yards (9,497), and touchdown catches (54) got mixed up during a two-minute drill in a 2007 primetime matchup in Atlanta. Burress had actually consulted Toomer on what play was called, utterly the wrong thing to do. "As soon as I took off, I knew it was the wrong play," Burress said. "He told me the wrong play."

The ball was at the Falcons 5. Had Toomer told his teammate the correct play, Burress would have been there near the goal line to throw a block that likely would have allowed Toomer to score. Instead Toomer was stopped at the 2, and the Giants settled for a field goal. When receivers coach Mike Sullivan asked Burress what happened, the lanky receiver said, "Coach, I don't even want to tell you." But he did. "Toom told me the wrong play."

"Why did you ask Toom?" Sullivan said.

"Because I didn't get the signal," Burress said. "I didn't get the call." Luckily for both receivers, the Giants cruised to a 31–10 victory.

Plax Ruins the Season

The 2008 Giants seemed poised to mount a successful defense of their 2007 Super Bowl championship season. That was before Burress hurt his team and himself by putting a bullet through his leg. Of all the sins Burress committed in his four seasons with the Giants—and there were many, ranging from tardiness to missing meetings outright to an irksome habit of not showing up and working with Manning during the voluntary offseason conditioning program—he finally committed a sin for which he could not be forgiven.

The end of the line for the recipient of Super Bowl XLII's game-winning touchdown came in the early morning hours of November 29 in the VIP section of the Latin Quarter nightclub. While partying with linebacker Antonio Pierce, Burress put a .40-caliber round into his right thigh. He had discharged the concealed Glock when he grabbed it after it slipped down his leg from the waistband of his pants. The Giants suspended him for the rest of the season, costing him more than $800,000 in salary.

If it wasn't bad enough that Burress had eliminated himself from a defending champion squad that started 10–1, the wide receiver eventually would be sentenced to two years in the Oneida Correctional Facility in Rome, New York, on a one-count plea to attempted criminal possession of a weapon. Though his teammates expressed sorrow over the general circumstances, their later actions toward Burress indicated their true feelings. Manning, who had developed a strong on-field and off-field rapport with his favorite receiver, never called, wrote, or visited Burress during his incarceration. Few of his teammates did either.

Coughlin was publicly non-committal over the prospects of signing him back after the team released him in April of 2009 but privately he dismissed any possibility of that happening. Besides all the trouble Burress gave him during more uncomplicated times, Coughlin worried about Burress heading back to jail if he violated his parole.

Burress wrote co-owners John Mara and Steve Tisch a letter of apology for "bringing all this bad publicity to such a stand-up organization." He vowed he would play again, which he did in 2011 and 2012 with the Jets and Steelers. But the Giants wanted no part of him. The gun incident had simply been the last straw. Coughlin had suspended him for 12 days in September and October and fined him $177,500 for missing a wide receivers meeting and dodging the front office's phone calls after that.

Smith chalked it up to "Plax being Plax," but Coughlin, who had tangled so frequently with the flighty Burress, was far less tolerant. "We have had success here because of the team concept," Coughlin said after meting out the suspension. "And the team concept means basically that everyone is accountable and responsible, and that we don't let the other guys down."

The NFL had suspended him for a game and fined him $45,000 for abusing an official and tossing a ball into the stands during an October 19 win in San Francisco. He was also fined $25,000 that offseason for refusing to practice at a mandatory minicamp. That came on top of the mountain of fines and suspensions Coughlin doled out in previous seasons.

It's one thing for Burress to shoot himself in the leg. It was quite another for Hanlon to manage the situation. The Giants' vice president of communications was awakened in his Westchester County, New York, home with the news early that Saturday morning, the same day the team was to catch their charter train to Washington. He didn't know it as he opened his eyes and answered his cell phone, but he was about to start his craziest day in his 20 years with the organization. "In this business nothing surprises you," Hanlon said. "But you don't expect on a Saturday morning to be awakened with that news. Aside from the birth of my children, it was the only time I didn't travel with the team. I wanted to be in one place to piece it all together. I went down in the evening."

Between early morning and late that night, Hanlon danced between phone lines, keeping Jerry Reese, John Mara, and others in the front-office hierarchy apprised of the early morning's events. He fielded calls from the police investigating the shooting. In his role as a publicist, whose main job is to spin news to put the franchise in the best possible light, he answered e-mail from media members who were all over the story. He quickly came to the realization that there was no positive light to be shed. This was a nightmare, and he was right in the middle of it, disseminating the whole, ugly mess. A lot of the leads he followed came straight from the reporters. "The first pieces you get come from the media," he said. "I'm fielding those calls and e-mails and trying to confirm or not confirm what's happening."

At that point there were no positives. Self-inflicted gunshot wounds tend to be harshly self-explanatory. "There's nothing to spin," Hanlon said. "I was just trying to figure out what happened and inform the appropriate people what was going on."

But his conversations with the often excitable Coughlin were anything but chaotic. "One of the attributes of a great leader is the maturity and poise and knowing what to do to achieve the objective, which in this case was to go down and beat the Redskins," Hanlon said. "He was poised and thinking. He wasn't excited. At that point he was just finding a way to conduct the final preparations for his team to play Washington."

The Giants defeated the Redskins 23–7. Toomer grabbed a 40-yard touchdown pass on the first possession, and the Redskins were never in it from there. Manning finished 21-of-34 for 305 yards with a touchdown and an interception. Brandon Jacobs ran for a touchdown, and John Carney kicked three field goals. The offense put up 404 yards as the Giants remained atop the NFC East at 11–1. "The fact that we went out and played as well as we played in Washington was unbelievable," Hanlon said, "considering the distraction and confusion the Burress thing caused."

After defeating Washington in a game that Burress—the team's receptions leader at the time—would have sat out anyway with a hamstring injury, the Giants then lost three of their last four games to Philadelphia, Dallas, and Minnesota. They needed overtime to beat the Carolina Panthers in the 15th game. And Coughlin's team lost its first playoff game 23–11 to the Eagles. All because Burress felt he needed a gun to protect himself in a nightclub.

Old School Ties

Eli Manning had no doubts about where he would spend part of his time during the 2011 NFL lockout. He went straight to the office of his former coach at Ole Miss, David Cutcliffe. More times than not, he'd find his older brother Peyton there, too.

A former quarterbacks coach and offensive coordinator at Tennessee—Peyton's alma mater—and Eli's head coach at Ole Miss, Cutcliffe stood as an important link to the two brothers. But Eli especially leaned on Cutcliffe after he incurred some heavy criticism for throwing 25 interceptions in 2010. The lockout gave him extra time to spend in Cutcliffe's film room and practice field at Duke, where the Manning coach had taken the head coaching job. For three days Cutcliffe put Eli through two-a-day practices. Turns out that amount is more than is now legal for NFL training camp under the collective bargaining agreement the league and players negotiated that summer.

Cuticliffe, who Eli's father, Archie, called "about as good with as I've ever seen at fundamentals" worked Manning through his footwork, agility, hand placement, and body mechanics. Manning took the hard-coaching lessons to heart and responded by cutting his interception total to 16 while throwing 29 touchdowns in a Super Bowl championship season.

His former coach is never farther than a cell phone call away. The two talked several times each season since Manning left Cutcliffe's immediate gaze in 2004. And no wonder. It was under Cutcliffe that Eli set or tied 45 Ole Miss passing records, most of which Archie set. "We have a great friendship and relationship that has carried on to this day," Manning said. "He's a great quarterback coach and someone who was a big help in developing me as a quarterback."

Cutcliffe loved working with both brothers. In past offseasons he had marveled at the competitiveness with each other in the film room that equaled their on-field fire against opponents. But he couldn't help but have an extra soft spot for Eli. "I've never understood why Eli wasn't as touted as Peyton was," Cutcliffe said. "I love both of them equally."

Chief Osi

When Accorsi selected Troy University's defensive end Osi Umenyiora in the 2003 NFL Draft's second round, a round earlier than most expected him to go, he knew he was getting a player whose chief role was to rush the passer. But an actual chief?

Four years after the Giants selected him, Umenyiora was indeed given that designation in his native tribal village of Ogbunike, Nigeria, for his humanitarian efforts toward educating the village's youth and building clean water wells. In addition to raising money, he returned each offseason to Nigeria to ensure the Changing Africa Through Education (CATE) funds were used properly. "Yes, I'm a chief, but it's no big deal," Umenyiora said. "It's been blown up too much and is kind of embarrassing to talk about. I'm just doing what I can to help."

Stateside, Umenyiora was just a football player, a pretty good one who made the strip-sack an art form. But along with the 75 sacks and 32 forced fumbles he recorded between 2003 and 2012—highlighted by 10 strips in an 11½-sack season in 2010—came some "chiefly," if not "princely" contract demands. And that is where Umenyiora might just as well have been a pauper in the eyes of management.

Giants defensive end Osi Umenyiora, designated a chief in his native Nigerian village, rushes the passer during a 26–3 victory against the San Francisco 49ers in 2012.

Reese never did bend on renegotiating Umenyiora's contract, which the defensive end turned into a real issue during the Super Bowl week following his 2010 season. Umenyiora launched a Radio Row tour in the Super Bowl press center, accusing Reese of going back on his word to renegotiate the seven-year, $41 million extension he signed in 2005. He told any sports show host who would listen that he'd quit football if he didn't get an extension or a trade. Then he added his name to the antitrust lawsuit during the 2011 lockout, accusing Reese of lying to him. He staged a one-day sit-out upon the opening of that season's abridged training camp. He called out Reese in the *New York Daily News* for making him look like a "greedy pig" for turning down two extensions the general manager claimed were offered. "Last year I was offered incentives," Umenyiora stated in an e-mail. "This year they offered me in guaranteed money HALF of what they just gave [Mathias Kiwanuka] guaranteed. HALF. I'm not making that up. Then Jerry tells the world they offered me an extension, and I turned it down. And I look like a greedy pig for turning it down. Hilarious."

The Giants had signed Kiwanuka to a three-year extension through 2015 worth $21.75 million with $10.95 guaranteed. Even his old teammate and mentor, Strahan, got into it, calling Umenyiora in 2011 "severely, severely underpaid" and imploring the Giants to "be fair." The GM publicly took most of the Chief's arrows calmly throughout the two-year ordeal. "Typical offseason chatter," he called it. But that didn't stop him from putting Umenyiora on the trade block. That was more for show, however, as the Giants demanded a first-round pick for a then-29-year-old defensive end who might have peaked.

The two finally came to terms—sort of—with Reese doubling the $3.5 million the two-time Pro Bowler was due to earn in 2012, the final year of his contract. As for his on-field behavior, Umenyiora never let his contract problems affect his performance. If anything, it was a laundry list of injuries from knee to hip that slowed him down from the double-digit sacker of 2005 (14½), 2007 (13), and 2010 (11½). He finished 2012 with six sacks. After that season Chief Osi became a free agent and signed with the Falcons.

Snowstorms and Hurricanes

The Giants' 10–6 record in 2010 was not playoff-worthy, but when Coughlin gathered his team after its season-ending, 17–14 win against Washington and proclaimed that all critics can "kiss my ass!" he might well have been referring to one particular obstacle the Giants hurdled that year. That would be the great mid-December snowstorm that swept the Midwest. Not only did it test the schedule-making ability and patience of a historically impatient coach, but also the mental flexibility of his players.

The weather forecasts had turned bleak in the days leading into the slated December 12, 1 PM kickoff in Minnesota. The storm was bearing straight toward Minneapolis and the huge swath of Teflon that covered the Metrodome. In an effort to beat the storm, they moved up the Saturday charter out of Newark's Liberty Airport by three and a half hours. It didn't matter. The plane never made it through as 17.1 inches of snow and 30 mph wind gusts closed down all the runways at Minneapolis International. It marked that city's fifth-largest snowfall since they started keeping such records in 1891.

The Giants were re-routed to Kansas City. Trapped for an overnight stay, they awaited news from the blizzard. The game was rescheduled for 8 PM Sunday night and then moved again to Monday night when workers sweeping the roof couldn't keep up with the snowfall. Coughlin, meticulously punctual and organized, began retooling the schedule. Meeting times were adjusted, and meal times were moved. So were the flight times. At first that didn't present much of a problem. Not until early Sunday morning, anyway. That's when the snow won.

Cameras inside the Metrodome showed the drama. It started as a small trickle of snow, and then the tearing increased. In seconds the Teflon membrane roof ripped wide open, pouring an avalanche of snow onto the field and rendering the Vikings' home unusable. The Giants got word of the collapse at 5 AM Sunday as they prepared to board the charter back to Minnesota. "This [game] probably presented more challenges than I can ever remember," president and CEO John Mara said. "We were stranded in the airport not knowing where to go, what to do."

The game was rescheduled for Monday night in Detroit. Back at the hotel, Manning kept the team loose and entertained by organizing an impromptu talent show featuring the rookies. Justin Tuck deemed guard Mitch Petrus the winner for his country performance. The song and dance entertainers and the rest of the squad finally arrived in Detroit that afternoon and held a walk-through in the hotel ballroom. It was hardly a good experience. Football players as a group define the term "creatures of habit." This change of routine went totally against that. "It's like recreating a bad Christmas movie," Tuck said.

But in the end, the Giants didn't let it affect them. They beat the Vikings 21–3. "Nobody panicked, nobody got upset," Coughlin wrote in his book *Earn the Right to Win*. "We just kept midstream adjusting. We keep detailed records of our midstream adjust schedule, and if the same issue occurs again, we'll be prepared."

Little did he know that more travel woes laid ahead. They got worse actually. Two games later another snowstorm stranded them Sunday night and Monday in the Radisson Paper Valley Hotel in Appleton, Wisconsin. The Giants licked their wounds from a 45–17 thrashing by the Packers among the throwback jerseys of Aaron Rodgers in the gift shop, giant pictures of Brett Favre, and a restaurant that bore Vince Lombardi's name. They finally got out of Wisconsin Tuesday, but not before rookie punter Matt Dodge had bought himself an "I Love Appleton" T-shirt.

The Giants must have figured they would never have to withstand another weather-related incident that so greatly affected their lives and schedule. Then came 2012's Hurricane Sandy.

The home game against Pittsburgh on November 4 went off as scheduled five days after the storm devastated the Jersey Shore and major parts of Long Island, Manhattan, Brooklyn, and Staten Island. MetLife Stadium was fully operational expect for the absence of the light rail line that brought fans from parking facilities in nearby Secaucus, New Jersey, and those who ordinarily would have come via the PATH train from Manhattan.

The Giants, however, had been disrupted. Several lived in Hoboken, New Jersey, a harbor-side town that Sandy smacked hard, and had to uproot themselves temporarily. Manning's building had water throughout the first floor, forcing the quarterback to find other living arrangements for him; his wife, Abby; and their baby daughter.

Tight end Martellus Bennett and his wife Siggi stayed at guard Kevin Boothe's house in Rutherford while they waited for the power to return. Boothe's two-year-old son, Dante, got the best of that deal. "My son loves him," Boothe said. "I think he thought Martellus was there solely to play with him, so they had a great time. They were painting and doing a whole bunch of other things." Victor Cruz lost cable and Internet, causing him to quip, "It just feels like 1990 all over again." Punter Steve Weatherford, his wife, and their three kids stayed with placekicker Lawrence Tynes.

The power outages put the Giants in catch-up mode as far as film study goes as many players would have taken home DVDs of Steelers game tapes to watch on their computers. Instead they had to conduct much of that at their training facility and were not fully caught up until that Wednesday afternoon.

None of the players suffered as much as the fans, many of whom lost loved ones and all or parts of their homes. The Giants were keenly aware that their task that Sunday was to entertain as well as keep their four-game winning streak alive. They accomplished neither. "We wanted emotionally so badly to win the game for obvious reasons, for all our neighbors who are struggling and who need some type of inspiration," Coughlin said. "Of course we didn't provide it for them."

The Giants filled the 24–20 loss with mistakes. The 6–3 squad had made plenty of the same miscues throughout the season, but the winning overshadowed them. This time the mistakes were out in the open. Manning was not himself, and the run defense was horrible as Pittsburgh's third running back, Isaac Redman, rushed for 147 yards.

It wasn't as if the Steelers came into the game in ideal fashion either. They traveled the day of the game, knowing that the hotel rooms they would have required were better used housing the many storm refugees. They even trailed 20–10 going into the fourth quarter. But their defense held the Giants to three three-and-outs on their final three possessions while they stormed back on touchdowns off Ben Roethlisberger's 51-yard pass to Mike Wallace and Redman's touchdown plunge from a yard out.

Manning went a lousy 10-of-24 for 125 yards and an interception. He followed up that performance the following week with his fifth straight sub-elite effort in a dreadful 31–13 loss in Cincinnati. He threw two third-quarter interceptions in a 1:16 span in that one. Whether Sandy facilitated the dive or not is debatable. The fact was the Giants continued their down-swing, and the defending Super Bowl champions finished out of the playoffs at 9–7.

Tittering Tweeters

The Twitter world did not exist when Jeremy Shockey came into the NFL in 2002. But by 2012 the innermost thoughts of teammates, ex-teammates, opponents, friends, and enemies were being spread all over the Internet in 140-character chunks. When Shockey was making noises about wanting to play for the Giants again after floating between the Saints and Panthers, Toomer told his followers why that should never happen. "Bad teammate," Toomer tweeted. "Worse person."

That triggered a vicious Twitter war between the two with Shockey bringing up Toomer's 2007 divorce. "Amani Toomer on Jeremy Shockey: Bad teammate, Haha," Shockey retorted. "Well he was the lazy one who broke my leg. Remember when his ex divorced him and he urinated on her clothes I guess he's the good person." In a follow-up tweet, Shockey said, "Go get a bucket of rocks and start throwing them at your glass house." To which Toomer replied, "Shockey thanks 4 proving my statement about u being a bad person. enough said. Have a nice day buddy."

Like many of his teammates, Toomer believed Shockey stood as one of the great impediments to Manning's development and shed few tears when that broken leg knocked him out of the 2007 Super Bowl championship season. After the tight end's own Super Bowl allegations that the Giants refused to fly him down to Arizona and allow him on the sidelines, he demanded a trade in an expletive-filled discussion with Reese.

The general manager granted his wish, setting fire to the frail bridge of tinder that once connected the Giants to their No. 1 draft pick of 2002. "I will never play4 you again! he yelled at Jerry Reese in '08," Toomer tweeted. "Let him keep his word."

"It's funny how the Ny media still try's to make money off me," Shockey concluded. "Can anyone find a quote from me on me wanting to play for the GAINTS?" It seems Shockey was as bad a speller and grammarian as he was a teammate.

CHAPTER 4
SEPTEMBER 11, 2001

A Day To Forget

A decade after the twin towers of the World Trade Center came down, the images of 9/11 remained as fresh in John Mara's mind as the day it happened.

The Giants had arrived back from their season-opening, 31–20 Monday night loss in Denver inconspicuously enough. They couldn't have known how close to the tragedy they really were when their United Airlines charter landed at about 6 AM at Newark Airport. At that point everything seemed normal— just business as usual after a typical road trip. Only weeks later did they learn that United Flight 93 was sitting at the adjacent gate. Four hours later the "Let's Roll" plane would go down with its 40 heroes and four hijackers in a field in Shanksville, Pennsylvania, some four hours, 20 flying minutes, and 130 miles short of the nefarious machine's Capitol Hill destination.

At 6 AM, though, the team's vice president had no idea the Giants' lives, and those of the rest of the nation, were about to change. He deboarded with the rest of the personnel and headed back to his Giants Stadium office to take a quick nap before starting the usual day-after-game schedule. Jim Fassel, who would learn later that his Anaheim (California) High School classmate Charles (Chic) Burlingame piloted the American Airlines Flight 77 out of Dulles that hijackers dove into the Pentagon, woke Mara a couple of hours later to relay some horrible news. A plane had gone into the World Trade Center. "I didn't think a lot of it except that it was a terrible accident," Mara said. "Then he came back and said a second plane went in, and the rest of the day was spent with the TV on. I remember walking to the top of the stadium, standing outside on one of the spiral ramps, and you could see the smoke and flames. It was a chilling experience."

Just as chilling was what happened in his office. While viewing the televised carnage, he received a call from Nick Kydes, a college friend who worked for Alliance Consulting, which was located on the 102nd floor of the North Tower. Kydes, who met Mara at Boston College, was one of the lucky ones. He had been called to a meeting in Princeton, New Jersey, that morning and was miles away when the planes hit. "He was driving in his car, listening to all this," Mara said. "He called me and said, 'Can I please stop by your office? I can't keep driving knowing all this is going on.' He came into my office, and we saw the second tower go down on TV. Everybody in that office he worked in perished. He was trying to call people to see if they got out. It was a really harrowing experience. I was just trying to comfort him, but what are you going to do? There's nothing you can do. And I was just trying to think of the people I worked with in those buildings."

Mara, an attorney at the high-powered law firm of Shea & Gould before he entered the family business in 1991, lost friends that day. He knew many of the brokers, analysts, and advisers in Cantor Fitzgerald's global investment offices between the 101st and 105th floors of the North Tower. The firm was the hardest hit of any single entity that day, losing 658 of its 960 New York employees.

While the son provided his friend with whatever aid and comfort he could, father Wellington Mara was busy lobbying commissioner Paul Tagliabue to postpone the games for the following Sunday. Fans still remembered—and many hadn't forgiven—Pete Rozelle's ill-advised decision in 1963 to play 48 hours after president John F. Kennedy's November 22 assassination. The venerable owner didn't want the league to make another mistake. Tagliabue listened and then heeded the wise man's advice. He moved the games of September 16 to the end of the season. "You still had families out there trying to find their loved ones," John Mara said. "It was just too early to play."

Some of those families' cars remained in the Giants Stadium parking lot. During the week the front section was used as a Park-and-Ride for buses to downtown Manhattan. The specter of empty vehicles sitting unclaimed for days would haunt Mara for weeks—and years—afterward. "To drive past that every day, to see those cars and know those people had perished, it was just a gut-wrenching scene," he said. "Especially those days immediately after because people weren't going into work those first few days. It was obvious to me that those had to belong to people working down there."

Coughlin's Anguish

Coughlin had gained a well-earned reputation by 1991 as an all-controlling head coach of the Jacksonville Jaguars. But the events of 9/11 left him powerless—save for a cell phone call—to help even his own family.

The second-eldest of Coughlin's four children, Tim, a 29-year-old-stock broker for Morgan Stanley, was at work on the 60th floor of the South Tower when the first plane went into the North Tower. Along with many others from his office, Tim had made his way down to the street despite a 44th floor security guard's assurance that the South Tower was safe and all could head back upstairs. Tim's wise disregard of that advice saved his life and those of many of his co-workers. Coughlin, of course, had no way of knowing any of the drama right off.

The coach was meeting with his Jaguars assistants when his daughter, Keli, called with the news of the first plane. For the next 45 agonizing minutes, he paced the floor and watched the horror unfold on TV as his secretary repeatedly tried Tim's cell phone. Tim had been on the phone with his brother, Brian, who talked him through the final 30 floors of his descent. Once Tim hit the street, he hung up with Brian, and Coughlin's call finally went through.

The father's message, delivered in typical calm and control, was firm and clear: "Do what you have to do to get away from that building as soon as possible." Tim had already done enough. As he waited in the 44th-floor lobby, the second plane hit the South Tower, sending a shudder down the whole building and throwing his colleagues into a stampede for the stairwell. He had blocked some of the mad-rushing crowd to keep others who had been knocked to the ground from being trampled, saving more than one life. But he was still in danger, and Coughlin knew it. "You need to get out of there *right now!*" Coughlin told him.

"Dad, this is like Beirut, man," Tim said. "It's just terrible, awful out here."

"Don't waste any time," Coughlin advised. "Just drop everything and go!"

Tim did get away by entering a subway tunnel that let out on Broadway a mile away. The South Tower collapsed 20 minutes after he went underground. "For Tim to be able to survive that, I just feel like the Holy Spirit took him by the hand in the second tower and guided him out of there," Coughlin said.

Tim told ESPN years later that phone call may have saved his life. "Looking back on that conversation, I think that was largely responsible for me kind of picking up my step and realizing that the important thing was to get out of there and get as far away from that place as possible," he said.

Although Coughlin doesn't like to rehash that story, he has gone out of his way to show his appreciation in other forms. He goes on the NFL's USO tour of foreign military outposts annually and hosts Wounded Warriors at practices and games. "What I want to dwell on is the incredible number of American heroes that died that day," Coughlin said. "I don't ever want the people of this great country to forget that."

Standing Guard

Jason Whittle didn't have a lot of time to digest the tragedy of 9/11. He had to get to Manhattan to the bedside of his friend, Randy Drake. Randy's brother and Whittle's best friend, Greg, had called the Giants lineman the night the towers went down with news that Randy, a Kansas City systems designer working on a special Port Authority project in the South Tower, was in bad shape. He had been hit by flying debris, undergone emergency surgery on his head, and lay in a coma in Bellevue Hospital. Doctors weren't sure he would make it through the night.

Drake was all alone as his wife, children, siblings, and parents sat anguished 1,200 miles away. Whittle had spent much of his childhood among Don and JoAnn Drake's 13 children and knew he had to get to the hospital to at least hold Randy's hand and offer support. It took him four hours for what was usually a 45-minute trip to get across the Hudson. The Lincoln Tunnel was closed. So was the Holland. The ferries were down. Finally he tried the George Washington Bridge, and even that almost didn't work. Whittle had to convince a policeman that he was Randy's brother, and that it was imperative he cross the bridge. "I kept telling him my story," Whittle said, never bothering to mention he was a professional football player. "He was nice enough to shuttle me down. It was unbelievable what the city looked like. It looked like a ghost town."

The officer got him to the hospital. Whittle got to the room. And then the 6'4", 305-pound guard held his friend's hand, alternately talking to him and crying. Whittle visited each day from his home in Ridgewood, New Jersey, until Randy was eventually transferred to a Kansas City hospital, where he died September 22, the night before the Giants beat the Chiefs in Kansas City area during the first football weekend after the attack.

Arrowhead Welcome

Regardless of whether the Kansas City Chiefs are winning or losing, Arrowhead Stadium, one of the loudest and toughest places any opponent will ever walk into, is a sea of red. But on September 23, 2001, Arrowhead Stadium turned blue. When the NFL reopened for business in this first game back from the horrors of 9/11, the Giants were welcomed with an incredible—and under any other circumstances incongruous—roar from the home crowd during pregame introductions.

Firemen's boots circulated through the stands for fan contributions. A tribute to the recovery workers flashed on the video screen. Jon Bon Jovi sang the national anthem as players and coaches, wearing the caps of the NYPD, NYFD, and the Port Authority, sang along, some crying openly. Even some of the crusty press had tears in their eyes.

For the first time since the towers fell, some sense of normalcy returned to the NFL. With the previous week's games canceled thanks to the urgings of Wellington Mara, the Giants players had spent that idle weekend floating over to Ground Zero on police boats. They went originally intending to help in removing the unfathomable amount of debris that created "the Pile," as the workers called it. But all the recovery people wanted were handshakes, some football talk, something to distract them from their grim tasks. Even in all the tragedy, the players saw the human spirit come out in the firemen who dug. "Nice to meet you," wide receiver Joe Jurevicius said to one of the dust-covered diggers.

"You cost me money in my fantasy league," the fireman said. "[If] you catch one of those passes Kerry Collins threw you Monday night, I win."

"Not his fault," the quarterback interjected. "I should have thrown it farther out there."

"You're right!" the fireman said. "You should have!"

By Monday the players had returned to the practice field—grudgingly at first. With smoke still rising from the scarred skyline, it seemed surreal that a sector of people should be worried about running slants and in-cuts. But guard Glenn Parker had come to realize after seeing Ground Zero that it was time to get back to work. "I knew it was the right time," he said. "Seeing the immense logistical problems those people were working through, it told me they don't need me over there. They need me working just like everybody else."

Not everyone, however, went into that day's practice with a settled mind. Left tackle Lomas Brown's 23-year-old stepson, Jeffrey Glover, was an Army infantryman stationed at Fort Benning, Georgia, and was preparing for eventual mobilization. "You know something's coming soon," Brown said. "And you worry."

The mounds of equipment next to the practice field—the parking lot had been turned into a staging area for the recovery effort—served as a constant, near reminder of the outside world. The Giants also continued making their pilgrimages to Ground Zero, creating long-lasting friendships in some cases. Collins became a firehouse favorite. Others visited shelters and other facilities. The letters came, too. Some suggested that the Giants might actually have saved some lives that fateful Tuesday. Because some fans stayed up late for the entire Monday night opener in Denver—a time slot the Giants likely occupied because they had gone to the Super Bowl the year before—they decided to skip work the next morning.

Another missive to coach Fassel reinforced the importance of diversion through sports. Fassel hung a note from a fan on the locker room bulletin board. Fullback Greg Comella reacted to those letters and the firefighter's pleas to go out and win that game. "Last week was the first time I questioned what I did for a living, what I contributed to society," Comella said. "But now I understand and I have this sense of purpose. We know entertainment's important."

Things, though, had changed. The vocabulary of football motivation had

Jim Fassel, the son of a fireman, and his team pause for a moment of silence in Arrowhead Stadium on September 23, 2001, which marked the Giants' first game after 9/11. *(AP Images)*

been altered somewhat. The man standing across the line had become the opponent—not the enemy. "The enemy showed up a week ago," Brown said. "The guy across from you is your opponent. And after it's all done, you shake hands and make sure he's all right. The things we used before to motivate us, they're not motivating factors anymore."

Whatever they used—the players' Saturday night speeches in the Westin Crown Center ballroom were said to cause some to cry—prefaced a 13–3 Giants win against the Chiefs. It wasn't an artistic triumph as Collins threw three interceptions. But they did bring some smiles to the people back home. "The first thing [the workers] said to us was, 'We're gonna be watching you,'" safety Sam Garnes said. "No way could we come out of this with a loss. It would have been devastating."

A Coach's New Friends

Even as coach of the United Football League's Las Vegas Locomotives, Fassel kept a slideshow of 9/11 on his office laptop to remind him of the horrors of that day. He really didn't have to. His charity never lets him forget what happened in downtown Manhattan. Over the 10-plus years since the towers fell, the Jim Fassel Foundation had raised more than $1 million to help families of those killed, including the 10 children of the late firefighter Frank Palombo.

Fassel, the son of a fireman, befriended the family shortly after 9/11 and made it a point to fund the firefighter's childrens' education. The family was often a guest at Giants practices and games. The charity also helped replace New York Fire Department vehicles that were destroyed on 9/11 and contributed heavily to the Wall of Remembrance at MCU Park in Brooklyn that memorializes the lost police and firemen of the towers.

But it started with the Palombo family. During one of Fassel's visits to Ground Zero, he had come upon a group of dirt-stained, discouraged firemen who had been digging for 10 hours. The firefighters recognized him and wanted to talk about football. But he wanted to know about them. "One of our guys lost his dad and his brother," the group's leader said. "Another one of our guys that we haven't found, Frank Palombo, had a wife and 10 kids."

Fassel leaned into the storyteller, Lt. John Atwell of Engine 219, Ladder 105 in Brooklyn, and said, "Give me a call, I'd like to do something." And then he pulled Atwell closer and said, "I really mean it. I'd like to do something." Fassel put together his foundation ostensibly to help the Palombos. But Palombo's wife, Jean, urged him to expand the focus. "Help a lot of people, not just us," Jean told him. "A lot of other people need help more than we do."

The foundation eventually made the biggest single contribution—$250,000—to first-responder groups. "We're all here for just a certain period of time, and you never know when it's all going to end," Fassel said. "That day changed my life."

CHAPTER 5
THE QUARTERBACKS

International Road Trips

The Giants have traveled across the Atlantic Ocean twice in their history. The trips to Berlin in 1994 and London in 2007 represented quite different experiences for Kent Graham and Eli Manning.

Graham always remembered his week-long sojourn to Germany as part of the league's since-abandoned American Bowl series as a bittersweet time. The old, once wall-divided city was fascinating, but the starting quarterback's focus was the battle he was waging with Dave Brown.

Graham looked good in the first two preseason games against the Miami Dolphins and Cleveland Browns, but Brown had played slightly better. Graham had hoped the game against the San Diego Chargers at Olympic Stadium that Saturday would settle the matter in his favor. As the plane touched down on the Berlin Airport runway the Monday before the August 13 game, Graham thought he had a legitimate chance.

After the next day's initial practice, however, Dan Reeves told reporters that Brown—picked in the first round of the supplemental draft two years before—had pulled "well ahead" of Graham, the eighth rounder, and would probably wrap up the Giants' quarterback competition with a good showing in the game. But then he said he spoke too soon. "I haven't had time to talk with either of them," Reeves said. "That was probably a mistake to say those things. They should hear it from me before they read it."

Reeves completely dashed all of Graham's hopes a day later. "Dave Brown is the starter," Reeves formally announced. "I know Kent's played well, but Dave's played better. He's a little ahead." Graham was crestfallen. "Between that and the time difference, I couldn't sleep at night," Graham said. "I was walking the streets at night because it just didn't sit well." Such an incongruous scene: An American football player walking around a foreign city in the dead of night not knowing the language or the way back to the hotel, only knowing that any chance of starting would depend strictly on Brown's health.

It could have made for a tense situation, but once Reeves broke the news to him, Graham congratulated Brown, and their relationship remained at least cordial throughout their time together. The two never really became friends, but they did co-exist. "I tried to support Dave as best I could," Graham said.

"Everybody likes to think there was some kind of animosity there, but there was none at all. We were both very professional in the meeting rooms."

Fourteen years later Manning was in a far different situation when the Giants took the finely cut soccer pitch at London's new Wembley Stadium for the first regular-season, transatlantic game in history. This time there were no tours of the city and countryside as there were in Berlin. Tom Coughlin locked his team into a schedule that had them practicing on Chelsea's training ground a few hours after their 6 AM Friday arrival from their overnight flight. By Saturday they were into their regular routine of meetings and meals in their hotel.

The home of England's national team drew just over 81,000 for the 13–10 win against the 0–7 Miami Dolphins and would host games every year after in the league's continued effort to globalize the game. The Brits were not exactly treated to a classic football game. The NFL's behemoths slipped and slid as clods of grass flew up from a rain-soaked field meant more for light, fleet soccer players. But Manning, a starting quarterback since the last six games of 2004, provided his 5–2 team's only touchdown with his legs.

Leading 3–0 in the second quarter, Manning took a shotgun snap at the Dolphins 10. Finding no one open, Manning tucked the ball in and started running for the left corner. Only slightly more mobile than his legendary older brother Peyton was with the Colts, Manning rumbled toward the end zone, seemingly fleeing for his life. He made it across the front corner a hair's breadth before getting tackled.

He threw for just 59 yards, but unbeknownst to him and the rest of the Giants, a Super Bowl title lay in their future.

Beating the Broncos

Graham didn't have a lot of highlights during a five-year career under Ray Handley, Reeves, and then Jim Fassel. The Ohio State product was an affable, tough quarterback who nevertheless had a small chip on his shoulder as he worked in the shadow of Brown, the team's golden boy. So imagine the celebration the eighth-round pick of the 1992 draft threw himself the night of December 13, 1998 when his 20–16 comeback victory against the 13–0 Denver Broncos went down as one of the most improbable regular-season wins in football history.

Actually it was anything but a big whoop-dee-do. The 6'5", 231-pound father of three went straight home that night to tend to his seven-year-old son Taylor. "He's got the chicken pox, so I'm into the realities of life," Graham said. "Now we're hoping the other two kids get it."

Graham also spent part of that night calling back friends, who left congratulatory messages on his answering machine; talking to his father, who had watched from the sideline; and viewing ESPN highlights of the game. "It was a great night," he said.

It was great for the Giants, too, who were mired in a dreary 8–8 season. With the departure before the season of the ineffective Brown, Graham was left in competition with Florida State product Danny Kanell. The Giants' fourth-round pick of 1996, Kanell originally won the job and then lost it after going 3–7 in the first 10 games. Graham came in and eventually finished the season with a 5–1 mark.

He already had sandwiched his lone loss in San Francisco with wins against the Philadelphia Eagles and Arizona Cardinals. But few gave the Giants even a puncher's chance against the undefeated, John Elway-led Broncos. Denver had actually won 18 straight, counting their Super Bowl run in 1997. The Broncos were averaging 34 points per game and were being regarded as one of football's greatest teams ever. Only the perfect Miami Dolphins of 1972 had gone into their 14th game undefeated, and the veterans of that team had been planning an emotional sideline stand for the Denver-Miami game the following week.

The betting line looked more like a cumulative score between two up-tempo basketball teams. Graham played his weekday part perfectly. "We'll be lucky to stay within 10 points," he whispered to a reporter four days before kickoff.

Come game day, he did more than that. He out-Elwayed Elway.

With New York down 16–13 late in the fourth quarter, the most unlikely of heroes took over. Graham found Chris Calloway for 15 yards and then

Quarterback Kent Graham acknowledges the crowd after his 21-of-33, 265-yard performance to help the Giants upset the previously undefeated Denver Broncos on December 13, 1998.

scrambled for 23 to the Broncos 48. Joe Jurevicius caught a pass for 11 yards to the 37. Finally the Giants lined up in a four-wide set, and Graham sent all the receivers deep. Scrambling again he spotted Amani Toomer, who had muffed a previous punt, matched up one-on-one against nickel cornerback Tito Paul in the back of the end zone and let fly. Toomer cut underneath the defender, leapt, and came down with both feet inbounds as the pair fell over the end line. "The ball looked really big like the Hindenburg balloon," Toomer said. "I knew I'd catch it. I knew I scored."

Elway had made a career of those kinds of fourth-quarter comebacks, but Graham outdueled him this time. Fassel, who received a Gatorade bath at game's end, called Graham's 21-of-33, 265-yard performance "unbelievable." The players received a case of champagne from the old, grateful Dolphins warriors, toasting a victory, which represented Graham's career highlight by far.

Danny's Boy

When George Henshaw served as offensive coordinator throughout the four-year Giants career of Dan Reeves, he always spoke publicly in the gentlest of tones as befitted a southern gentleman. The easy lilt rolled off the tongue of the Richmond-born assistant as sweet as honey-baked Virginia ham. Never coarse, always refined, Henshaw rarely had a bad word to say about anyone—except when it came to Tommy Maddox.

That well-mannered, otherwise well-liked quarterback actually moved Henshaw to profanity during a one-season stay in 1995. When asked what he thought of Maddox after one particularly bad performance, Henshaw glared at the questioner. "The sum-bitch cain't play footbo-o-w-w," Henshaw growled. "Nahce boy, but the sum-bitch cain't play!"

It took some time to convince Reeves of that, however. The coach had a soft spot for the 6'4", 219-pound thrower out of UCLA. He had used the Broncos' first-round pick on him in 1992, thinking he'd just landed Elway's successor. Doomed Coach Handley helped bolster that feeling during Maddox's rookie season when he inexplicably failed to blitz the kid after the defense knocked Elway out of the game. Given plenty of time to find his receivers, Maddox picked the secondary apart to finish up a 27–13 victory at Mile High Stadium.

Teams soon found out a little pressure was all that was needed to turn Maddox from an effective quarterback to a turnover machine. He started the next four games, losing them all while piling up the interceptions, fumbles, and fumbled snaps. The Broncos cut him after the 1993 season, Reeves' first with the Giants, and he spent the next season with the Rams as a third-stringer behind Chris Miller and Chris Chandler. Three days after the Rams released Maddox in the final cut of the 1995 training camp, the Giants picked him up to serve as Dave Brown's backup.

But it was apparent from the outset that Maddox was not going to work. Primarily a holder for placements, he went under center for three games as Brown nursed injuries. Taking over in the second half of an October 15 loss to the Eagles, Maddox completed his first pass but then went 6-for-23 for 49 yards and three interceptions. He stepped in late in the fourth quarter of the Eagles rematch on November 19 and lost a fumble.

Maddox was back for the start of the 1996 training camp, but his appearance in two preseason games did nothing to enhance his value. Against the Jacksonville Jaguars, he fumbled away his first snap and lost two other fumbles. But he did lead the game-winning drive. By the time Maddox's start against the Baltimore Ravens in the second preseason game ended with 5-of-10 passes for 42 yards, a touchdown, an interception, and two fumbles, the Giants had seen enough. They cut him on August 20. Forced into the move by co-owners Wellington Mara and Bob Tisch, Reeves was none too happy about it and he blamed a lot of Maddox's issues on the unforgiving fans and the media. "Maybe they're trying to get rid of us both," Reeves said. "They're 50 percent of the way there. They ought to be happy because they're getting closer to 100 percent."

The Giants might have been done with Maddox, but believe it or not, Maddox wasn't done with the league. After some bouncing around in Arena Football and the short-lived XFL where he became a star, Maddox launched a comeback, starting for the Pittsburgh Steelers before eventually earning a Super Bowl ring as Ben Roethlisberger's backup in 2005. A Week 11 start against the Ravens that year marked his final career game. In keeping with his past, he threw an interception on the Steelers' final drive of regulation in that 16–13 overtime loss.

Reclamation Project

Ernie Accorsi knew he needed a quarterback to breathe life into the sleepy, boring offense of the Brown/Graham/Kanell era. He also knew good quarterbacks were hard to come by. So he looked to the scrap heap. On February 19, 1999, he set the football world's collective head to scratching by signing— for $16.9 million over four years—the scrappiest of the scrap, Kerry Collins.

The big right arm was about all Collins had going for him at that point. The rest of him amounted to one Mount Everest-sized pile of problems on and off the field. But Accorsi had consulted with Collins' coach at Penn State, and Joe Paterno told him the 6'5", 240-pound quarterback thrived in big games. That and all the other research he and his scouts conducted was good enough for Accorsi. "What we concluded was this is a very talented quarterback and a good kid who got off track," Accorsi said.

It was really no surprise Accorsi took an interest in this particular player. Collins was brought up in Lebanon, Pennsylvania, a flare pass from the general manager's hometown of Hershey. And Accorsi had spent the late 1960s serving as an assistant public relations director at Penn State, where he came to regard Paterno almost as family. If Joe Pa vouched for the kid, Collins couldn't be all that risky.

But signing Collins represented the biggest chance he ever took as a general manager until his engineering of the draft-day trade for Manning five years later. In a few short years, Collins had earned tags as a racist for a drunken slur he threw out at Panthers receiver Muhsin Muhammad in 1997; a quitter for a conversation he had with coach Dom Capers that got him pulled from the Panthers' lineup after an 0–4 start in 1998; and a lush for a DUI arrest in Charlotte after the Panthers cut him.

Only after a photo went nationwide of a defiant Collins, cigar hanging from his mouth as he walked out of the precinct station, did the light go on. Collins wound up in alcohol rehab after the arrest. "That transcended the 'Okay, I've got personal problems and I've got problems with alcohol,' to 'Now I've got problems with the law,'" Collins told a rapt Super Bowl XXXV-week media audience. "The NFL ordered me to rehab, and that first day there was the realization that I have to go somewhere in a structured environment to get help. It was very shocking to me."

On top of Collins' existing troubles, signing with the Giants brought the temptations of New York City—not exactly an ideal place for a recovering alcoholic. But Accorsi made sure to include a clause that voided the deal and put Collins' $5 million signing bonus at risk if he stepped out of line. "The Giants have given me an opportunity to develop as a person and a player," Collins said. "It's up to me to take advantage of that opportunity."

When Collins' opportunity in New York came, Fassel didn't know a lot about him—just enough to make him skeptical. He recognized the off-field problems. Those were all over the papers. But when he looked at the tapes, the quarterback specialist saw mechanical problems, too. Correcting those, however, would be the easy part. "I knew I could change that," Fassel said. "I got all sorts of film and studied him. He had this long release. I said we can shorten his release, and that'll lead to more accurate throwing."

The question was, how Collins would take to all of this? Fassel prepared to throw some hard coaching at him, drilling him to cock his arm to eliminate what the scouts called a hitch. Collins would loop his powerful right arm back past his head in a circular motion, allowing another split second for defenders to close on his passing targets. His sheer arm strength allowed him to get away with it at Penn State and his early pro years. But teams had picked up on it a long time ago, and it had to change.

On top of that, Collins by necessity of his past would have to heel to the Giants' short-leash dictum. One screwup and out he'd go, along with his incentive-laden $16.9 million, four-year contract. Fassel needed a lot of reassurance before he signed off on such a flawed entity. He had to know where Collins' head was at. He found out in a clandestine meeting in the office of team psychologist Dr. Joel Goldberg. "I'd done my homework," Fassel said. "I started questioning him and I purposely opened the door for him to make excuses and blame other people for his problems. You know, bad coaches, bad system. Well, he said the racist thing was wrong, and I believed him. These guys say everything to each other in the locker room. It's really unbelievable what comes out of their mouths, and nothing means anything. So I believed him on that. We went on, and at the end of the day, I thought he was very up-front with me. What was more important was that he accepted responsibility for everything, and he wanted to make changes."

Fassel and quarterback coach Sean Payton went to work on the mechanics immediately. They focused on footwork. They emphasized holding the ball with two hands at the helmet's earhole and then throwing. They never eliminated the hitch completely, but the motion became quicker and more compact in a relatively short time. "He accepted the coaching and improved his play," Fassel said. "He was comfortable with everything. The guys looked at him and said, 'Hey, this guy's playing pretty good.' The rest was up to Kerry."

Twice-weekly Alcoholics Anonymous meetings at a New Jersey facility called "Honesty House" kept him on the straight and narrow. He mingled easily with his teammates and they with him. "I know they're watching me," Collins said. "If I go out and get drunk, I'm done. I'm very clear on what I have to do."

Collins became a starter-in-waiting as Graham struggled through the early part of the schedule. He finally replaced Graham permanently in the 11th game against Arizona and kept the job the next four years. And he became a much-valued team leader. "Along with Michael Strahan and Jessie Armstead, Kerry has to be right up there," Fassel said. "They were the foundation of everything great that we did."

The Giants underwent almost immediate change as long, downfield throws became common sights around Giants Stadium. Collins evolved personally, too, eschewing bars for visits to children's hospitals, trips to the supermarket to buy groceries for the underprivileged, and frequent post-9/11 stops at firehouses to chat with first-responders. He set up charities and became a New York-area jewel.

The Giants' record in 1999 sat at a disappointing 7–9, but Collins soon rewarded Accorsi's faith in him. The Giants went 12–4 in 2000, advancing to the Super Bowl after beating both the Eagles and Minnesota Vikings at home during the playoffs. The man who thrived in big games had one of his worst ever in that Super Bowl. Collins threw four interceptions in a 15-of-39, 112-yard performance. He produced exactly zero offensive points in the 34–7 loss.

Collins returned to the postseason in 2002, but his team's infamous melt-down in a 39–38 wild-card loss in San Francisco, a setback that could be laid on any number of factors except his quarterbacking, deprived him of a shot at a redemptive Super Bowl. The Giants cut him shortly after Accorsi acquired Manning in 2004 as Collins stormed into the general manager's office demanding his release.

Collins never got that Super Bowl ring, but he did turn his life around. He spent the next seven years as a clean, sober starter with the Oakland Raiders and Tennessee Titans before ending a 17-year career as a Colts backup in 2011.

Reality Bytes

Well before active players started tangoing on *Dancing with the Stars* and long before Terrell Owens bared his videotaped life to the world, backup quarterbacks Jesse Palmer and Tim Hasselbeck immersed themselves in reality television in two very different ways.

The Toronto-born Palmer spent most of his four-year Giants career back-ing up Collins. But during the spring of 2004 and just months after an injury to Collins allowed him to join Mark Rypien as the only Canadian quarter-backs to start an NFL game, he became the only pro football player to be fea-tured on *The Bachelor.*

Then in its fifth season, the show's producers approached the handsome, 6'2", 219-pound professional athlete. Not that he needed a reality show to meet girls. He had his pick of a number of women. Palmer had only recently gone though an amicable breakup with University of Connecticut women's basketball star and eventual three-time Olympic gold medal win-ner Sue Bird.

But Palmer was game despite never having seen the show. Using a month-long trip to Australia as a cover story for family, friends, and teammates, he taped the show over six weeks of the offseason. When the network released the news that Palmer was that season's bachelor, his phone lit up with calls and messages. Messages like, "Wait 'til you get your ass back here in the locker room."

As one might imagine, the razzing increased as the show aired. Teammates cut out pictures of him from newspapers and hung them in his locker. His dressing stall, adjacent to Collins', offered zero protection from the starter's barbs or those of any other player. They howled when in one episode the quarterback got confused and handed the wrong woman the rose that would have advanced her to the next round. Later that year Manning, the rookie first-round pick, took it a step further as he hosted a Halloween party. Manning dressed up in one of Palmer's suits, gelled back his hair in Palmer's style, and handed out an armful of roses to all the women.

In the end Palmer wound up picking a young lady named Jessica Bowlin. The relationship didn't last. Distance and absence—they were not allowed to see each other until the show finished airing—led to them breaking up shortly after the finale.

Hasselbeck, the son of former Giants tight end Don and brother of NFL starting quarterback Matt Hasselbeck, actually became part of that reality world by extension when he married his Boston College sweetheart, Elisabeth Filarski, in 2002. She's better known today as Elisabeth Hasselbeck on *The View*. Back then her greatest claim to fame was her fourth-place finish on 2001's *Survivor: The Australian Outback* as a member of the Kucha tribe.

Both players benefitted from their increase in exposure, landing jobs with ESPN. Palmer covers college football, and Hasselbeck serves as an NFL analyst.

The Savior Arrives

Just 13 days before, Accorsi had engineered a draft-day trade with the Chargers to bring Manning—a quarterback Accorsi was convinced possessed the same incredible stuff as his brother, Peyton—to the Giants with the first overall pick. Now on May 7, 2004, Manning took the practice field for the first time. This was the time for first impressions, and Manning certainly made one in his first workout.

The first pass of his first minicamp was a strike—right to the head of a tackling dummy stationed not five yards in front of him for the seven-on-seven drill! Keep in mind: dummies represent defensive linemen, not wide receivers in those drills. And they're inanimate objects. They don't move. They don't pop into passing lanes. The media snickered, and more than one player wore a smirk as the blue dummy wobbled like a kid's toy. Things didn't get much better for Manning that day. Passes fluttered. Passes wobbled. Defensive backs intercepted them, knocked them down. Manning dropped snaps. His first completion was a little flare pass to running back Tiki Barber against air, meaning the defense was not involved in that particular drill.

After the carnage the cameras lined up in the back of the end zone, prompting the Ole Miss passer to quip that there was more media there than in the entire state of Mississippi. At least he was already savvy to the realities of life in New York. "The media's going to be on you," Manning said. "They're going to be around you wherever you go. You're going to be in the paper, so you better watch out. I think I'll be fine. I'm going to be myself."

He never lost sight of that. Not even after the press described him as "awful" after that first outing. Not even after star defensive end Michael Strahan said he had that "little deer in the headlights look in his eyes." Not even after Tom Coughlin, searching for something positive to say about the man upon whom the Giants had staked so much, commended him for his "excellent huddle command."

Manning started on the bench that year behind Kurt Warner, the veteran the Giants brought in to hold the fort and tutor their young, ersatz star. The lessons of the offseason and training camp were hard, especially for a player whose Pro Bowl brother became a starter from the second the Indianapolis Colts drafted him in 1998. But from the beginning, it was obvious Coughlin and offensive coordinator John Hufnagel were going to entrust him with a full slate of responsibilities, including the right to check out of plays almost at will.

Manning endured his slings and arrows—especially during his first training camp and especially from dreadlocked cornerback Frank Walker, a true character with an ever-chattering demeanor. Walker could get on a teammate's nerves but not Manning's. Walker rode the rookie quarterback relentlessly

97

during training camp, but Manning eventually got his revenge on the morning of August 22.

Manning abused him with short-range throws and then hit Toomer for a touchdown. He capped the team session by finding Ataveus Cash on a 55-yard touchdown catch that could have caused the deep-fried Walker's tail feathers to burst into flames. Manning was far from empathetic. "He came right up to me after practice," Walker said. "Wouldn't even let me finish my stretch to tell me he won today. I told him, 'It's about time you won!'"

"I think he started talking before I did," Manning said. "He picked on the rookie early in camp and made some plays, so I got him today."

0.0

Manning's development as a starting quarterback remained rocky throughout 2004. Like any young quarterback, he suffered the typical growing pains after taking over the final seven games for Warner, following a 17–14 loss in Arizona on November 14. The growth process of his 1–6 finish never seemed as rough as it did four games into that stretch, a 37–14 loss to Baltimore on December 12 when Manning flubbed his way to a 0.0 quarterback rating.

That's right. 0.0. 4-of-18, 27 yards, two interceptions, and no touchdowns. "Disastrous," Manning called it. "Probably the worst game I've ever played in any sport."

It was clear Coughlin was willing to throw in the rest of what became a 6–10 season when he switched from the Super Bowl XXXIV MVP winner to his rookie. The Giants still had an outside shot at a playoff spot, but the need to receive a quick return on the team's investment overrode any short-term benefits the veteran Warner offered. A lot of the players understood that.

But 0.0? That was almost impossibly bad. The Ravens' ever-shifting defense had confused Manning into total mental paralysis. It reached a point where Coughlin had to jump into the ring, so to speak, and end it. He pulled Manning for Warner with 6:07 remaining. The kid, now ashen, had gone 1-for-7 for six passing yards in the second half. To say there were a lot of worried faces around the Giants' locker room afterward would have served as a gross understatement. "It was an ugly feeling after that game," then-quarterbacks coach Kevin Gilbride said. "That was about as low as you could go. I don't think I had any question about his ability or what his future potential was, but I did worry about what was going to happen to him psychologically, emotionally, spiritually."

Manning had yet to attain the stoic demeanor he'd famously wear in good times and bad. Against the Ravens that day, he was befuddled to the point of despondency. "It was bad," Manning said. "They were confusing me. Even the simple throws I was missing. I hate saying it, but I was just kind of lost."

Coughlin wouldn't budge, though. Manning was still his quarterback. "The rookie player who has that kind of experience—it is a priceless experience," Coughlin said the Monday after the game. "It does not come without pain, and yesterday was a setback. But I'm not changing my opinion one iota. I think you've got to play through these things."

Manning's long talk with Gilbride on the train ride home and a half-hour meeting with Coughlin the next day—when the precocious 23-year-old quarterback aggressively sought to change the types of plays in the gameplans—helped restore some of his fast-fading confidence.

It took Manning three more games to get his first win, a 28–24 victory against the Dallas Cowboys on the last day of the season. He went 18-of-27 for 144 yards with three touchdowns and an interception and finished the day with a 101.5 quarterback rating. It took two more years of heavy criticism for him to ascend to Super Bowl MVP status.

Eli the Elite

On the wall of memorabilia collector Larry Greenberg's Staten Island, New York, living room hangs a picture of Manning dropping back to pass. At the bottom appears Manning's elegant signature with his No. 10 scripted onto the end of it. At an open spot near mid-frame, there appears another inscription in Manning's penmanship: *Elite!*

That was the quarterback having a little fun with a controversy he started all by himself during the 2011 training camp, one that raged straight through his second Super Bowl MVP performance in the 21–17 win against the New England Patriots in XLVI.

On August 18 Manning responded to ESPN-1050 radio host Michael Kay's question pertaining to his standing among the league's glitterati such as Tom Brady, Aaron Rodgers, and his brother Peyton Manning. Instead of taking his usual safe way out of the question, Manning put himself right up among them. "Yeah," he said. "I consider myself in that class, and Tom Brady is a great quarterback."

Ka-boom!

For the ever mild-mannered and diplomatic Manning, that was the equal of Patrick Henry telling King George to "Give me liberty or give me death!" The airwaves, newspaper columns, blogs, and tweets exploded, and suddenly the quarterback, whom some nicknamed "Aw Shucks," was the center of attention. Manning was never an avid listener of talk radio or reader of newspapers, so he didn't know of the debate until his father, Archie, apprised him of it.

Debates raged over his early years when he "managed" games at the cost of lofty passer ratings. Had he really done enough in the postseason? After all, the only playoff games he'd won were the ones in the run to Super Bowl XLII. But he did earn a Super Bowl MVP trophy. He had durability, having started 96 straight games to that point. There was that growing list of comebacks. But there were also those first-half miscues—he threw a career-high 25 interceptions in the 2010 non-playoff year alone—that created the circumstances of those comebacks.

Everyone had an opinion, including a couple of heavyweights. "He's just going to have to throw it better for them to become a big-time playoff factor," former Giants quarterback Phil Simms said. "I think Eli reading his words and all the other stuff, there's going to be a tremendous sense of determination to prove everyone wrong and shut them up." Former Bengals passer Boomer Esiason said he admired Manning for standing up for himself. "I love the fact that Eli said it because it's out of character," Esiason said. "The other thing he said that he has to reduce his interceptions…was the real key of any statement because he realized how many mistakes he made. If he's willing to accept that, then he'll be better and the team will be better for it."

By winning his second Super Bowl in dramatic fashion, quarterback Eli Manning proved himself to be an elite and clutch quarterback.

Whatever doubts arose outside the locker room, they didn't seep into it. "I feel like he's definitely top five as well," wide receiver Hakeem Nicks said. "I think he can break down a defense just as good as any quarterback in the league."

Manning said he was just answering a question, a contention Coughlin quickly backed up. That didn't dilute the coach's opinion on whether he had an "elite" quarterback on his hands. "I do, but what would you expect him to say?" Coughlin said. "He is for me."

Manning went out and proved it that year. The interception numbers fell from 25 to 16; the list of game-winning, fourth-quarter or overtime drives increased by six. That's actually eight if you count the overtime win in the NFC Championship Game in San Francisco and the late fourth-quarter touchdown drive in the Super Bowl.

The "Aw Shucks" quarterback was back to his old self by the end of a season despite a year's worth of questions surrounding that one, superlative adjective. "Well, the question was if I thought I was an elite quarterback, and basically I was just saying that I did," Manning said. "I'm usually not into the business of ranking and rating quarterbacks and comparing myself to other guys. Looking back, I thought I gave an honest answer and I don't regret anything."

CHAPTER 6
STAR TURNS

Hamp's Hand

Rodney Hampton came into the league with knee problems that never really improved by the time Dan Reeves took over in 1993. That didn't stop Hampton from producing for the former Broncos coach. He would have done anything for Reeves. What clinched it for Hampton was how the coach handled his star running back in the weeks after Hampton broke his right hand against the San Francisco 49ers in early October of 1995. He could have sat Hampton and used his considerable depth as a stopgap. Instead Reeves and the one-time franchise-leading rusher both made adjustments, and Hampton remained his featured back a week later against the Arizona Cardinals.

That relatively tiny segment of their four years together, albeit a key point in Hampton's fifth consecutive and final 1,000-yard season in his eight-year Giants career, earned Reeves his running back's undying admiration. "To this day I'll run through a wall for that man," Hampton said. "I had a broken right hand, and he told me to carry it in my left. I'd never done that before, and it's great that he still had that confidence to give it to me to get the tough yards, even though we had a veteran guy like Herschel Walker and [rookie] Tyrone Wheatley on the team."

It didn't start quite that way. Reeves was at first convinced he'd lose his featured back for several weeks after numbness in Hampton's right hand forced doctors to remove him from the 20–6, October 1 loss in Candlestick Park. "I squeezed the ball and felt it pop out," Hampton said. "There was no feeling in my hand. I knew it was bad."

The situation looked a bit brighter by that Wednesday. Doctors deemed surgery was unnecessary on the damaged fourth metacarpal. With Hampton still 101 yards short of Joe Morris' franchise rushing record of 5,296 yards, wasting time on the bench wasn't exactly in his plans. But he still had to do a major sales job on Reeves to get back into the lineup in time for Arizona. Once he proved he could catch the ball with a protective pad the equipment men rigged up for him, he went back to work. The Giants, 1–4 at that point, indeed needed him.

Linebacker Jessie Armstead would provide the ultimate highlight in the 27–21 overtime win against the Cardinals with his 58-yard touchdown return of an interception. Playing this one in a secondary role as Wheatley made his first career start, Hampton carried nine times for 47 violent yards.

Hampton would get his record two games later on his third carry in a 24–15 win at Washington. He also suffered his fourth fumble in four games and third inside the opponent's 5. But Reeves' faith in his running back's pluckiness never wavered even if it came at the cost of Hampton's usual sure-handedness. He ordered the ball into Hampton's hands 17 times, and his running back responded with 83 total yards.

Hampton completed 1995 with a career-high 1,182 yards on 306 carries. It marked one of only two seasons where he didn't miss a game because of injury. But even in the seasons he did, he still credits Reeves with getting him through them all. "I always had problems with my knees even coming out of college as a junior," Hampton said. "But Dan took care of me. He'd put me on the sidelines during practice and tell me to just take mental reps. Then he'd put me in the game on Sunday and give me the ball 20 times."

The playoff season of 1993 illustrated that perfectly. Despite rare practice field appearances at the end of that 11–5 season, Hampton buried the Minnesota Vikings, New York's first-round playoff opponent, under 33 carries for 161 yards. The rushing attempts and rushing yards still stand as Giants postseason records shared with Rob Carpenter. Hampton exploded in the third quarter, scoring touchdowns on runs of 51 and 2 yards.

The man who came into the NFL in 1990 under Hall of Famer Bill Parcells holds Reeves in the highest regard. "Dan's my favorite coach," Hampton said. "He was a classic coach. You did it Dan's way, and if you left it all on the field, he never had a problem with you. But if you didn't, he'd get all over you."

Jessie's List

Armstead had a list.

In his rise from special teams standout to the leader of Reeves' and Jim Fassel's defenses, the five-time Pro Bowler kept a list of every linebacker who was drafted before the Giants called his name in the eighth round of the 1993 Draft. Whenever one of them retired, he crossed him off. That list, a self-inflicted insult of sorts, created a fire that constantly burned inside Armstead until his retirement after 2003. The draft already had shrunk from 12 rounds to eight in 1993. A year later it contracted again to seven. Had Armstead appeared in the 1994 talent pool, he would have gone undrafted, and that never would have sat well with a weak-side linebacker who considered himself "a hunter" and "a warrior."

Every linebacker in the league deemed more worthy of an investment than the undersized but gritty University of Miami product with bum knees had their spot on the list. They were all there: Marvin Jones, Wayne Simmons, Chad Brown, Darrin Smith, and future teammate Michael Barrow. And those were just from the first two rounds. A total of 32 linebackers went before the Giants took the 6'11", 230-pound Armstead with the 207th pick of the draft. One by one, year by year, Armstead crossed them off. Some went early—straight out of their first training camp. Others lasted.

But none played as long as Armstead, which was saying something for a player who originally got lost in the draft shuffle because of knee reconstruction as a Hurricane sophomore. And none possessed the mental toughness that allowed Armstead to play in every game of every year despite several close calls involving a high ankle sprain in 1998 and a combination knee and calf injury in his final season. Armstead's longevity had motivational fuel. "I always played with a chip," Armstead said. "I always carried that. I never backed down from nobody and I was never scared of a fight. That's my attitude, and I always carried that."

"Jessie was one of the greatest linebackers in the history of the franchise," president and CEO John Mara said. "He was a team leader who always gave 100 percent. We could always count on him to make a big play at a crucial moment of the game."

After New York released Armstead following the 2001 season, he signed on with Washington for two more seasons and continued his streak of perfect gameday attendance. He had little choice. He had to make sure his name was the last one on the list.

Thunder and Lightning

Fassel and his offensive staff knew they had something special when Heisman Trophy winner Ron Dayne arrived at the 2000 training camp. Along with the agile, fast Tiki Barber itching to get started full-time in the backfield, the coaches had the 255-pound bruiser out of Wisconsin, an ideal change-of-pace back in the first round. They realized immediately that working the two as a backfield tandem would improve the sluggishness of 1999, when Joe Montgomery's rushing yards marked the lowest total ever for a Giants starting running back since the 16-game schedule came about in 1978.

New York hit that one square on the head. If the Super Bowl Giants did anything well offensively that year, it was run the ball. And the bulk of the yardage came from Barber and Dayne or "Thunder and Lightning" as history came to know them. Barber was Lightning. Having lost 10 pounds from the year before, he put together his first of six 1,000-yard seasons. He might even have produced more than the 1,006 yards on 213 carries had the Thunder-ing Dayne not carried 228 times for 770 yards. The total represented his second-most productive season next to the 773 he recorded as a Houston Texan in 2007, his final year.

Only a fool would have shied away from giving them an almost even split of the workload. Fassel and his offensive assistants were no fools. "We had certain plays we thought Tiki ran real well. We had certain plays we thought Ron would do real well," running backs coach Mike Gillhamer said. "We just labeled the personnel groups. One was Thunder. One was Lightning. It kind of took off."

It got Barber plenty excited. "It's perfect because we're so different. Thunder and Lightning," Barber said just before the season. Dayne wasn't at all preoccupied over whether the order of the nickname would mirror the order of battle. "So long as I get to play," he said.

Fassel played it up. He had them introduced together as offensive starters in the September 3 opener against Arizona. Mother Nature put her stamp on it 90 minutes later, interrupting the already rainy third-quarter proceedings with a different kind of thunder and lightning that sent players, coaches, support personnel, and officials scurrying for the Giants Stadium tunnel in the franchise's first weather delay. Wide receiver Ron Dixon—not Barber or Dayne—happened to be the fastest man on the field as the 22-minute, 50-second delay began, racing from his split right spot to sanctuary in world record time.

The on-field manifestation was just as impressive. Barber rushed for 144 yards that day, including touchdowns of 10 and 78 yards. The latter went as the longest touchdown run since Frank Gifford's 79 against Washington in 1959. Dayne took it 23 times for 78 yards and a touchdown.

As the running game usually does, it created space for Kerry Collins to throw. But mostly the Giants won that year by controlling the clock. Thunder and Lightning jumped the rushing ranking to 11th overall, improving the ground game 37.5 yards from the previous season to 125.6 yards per game. All that happened despite Dayne notching 100 yards only once, a 108-yard, one-touchdown effort on 21 carries in a 19–14 win against the Cowboys on October 15. He followed that up after the bye with 25 carries for 93 yards and a touchdown in beating the Eagles 24–7.

The Giants owed much of their 12–4 overall record and their impressive 7–1 road record to "Thunder and Lightning." By the time they hit Super Bowl XXXV, Dayne (255) and Barber (240) stood amazingly close in combined regular and postseason carries. Used as both a runner and receiver out of the backfield as well as a punt returner, Barber came away with the franchise record for 2,089 all-purpose yards.

In their four years together, the duo would never rack up the balanced numbers it did in 2000 when they combined for 1,555 yards. Barber would step forward as the premier back, and they would never lead the Giants to another Super Bowl. But the two-headed monster of Barber and Dayne became the league's foremost rushing duo in an age where backfield duties usually rested on one running back's shoulders.

Caught With His Pants Down

It can be argued that no Giant of the last 20 years has taken his shirt off for the camera more than Jason Sehorn. Handsome and chiseled, he cut a fine figure on the pages of countless sports and men's fashion magazines. But he never dropped his trousers, not even for *GQ*.

It did, though, nearly happen against Detroit in 2000. As if a 31–21 loss at Giants Stadium that dropped the Giants to 7–4 wasn't embarrassing enough, Sehorn darned near lost his britches on Johnnie Morton's 32-yard touchdown catch in the third quarter. As Sehorn chased Morton across the middle, he had to pull up just short of the goal line to yank up his pants. "The pants are just so tight," he said.

The Giants had a good chuckle over that one, but Sehorn ultimately had the last laugh. Shortly after his team's Super Bowl appearance, the cornerback married gorgeous *Law and Order* actress Angie Harmon, to whom he famously proposed while Harmon taped a spot on *The Tonight Show with Jay Leno* in March of 2000. His tuxedo pants reportedly stayed in place through the entire wedding ceremony.

The Sack Record

Michael Strahan went into the last minutes of a 34–25 game against Green Bay Packers half a sack behind former New York Jet Mark Gastineau's single-season record, and time was running out. The Packers were clearly in run mode, looking to kill out the clock to a game the league transplanted from Week 2 of 2001 to season's end in the aftermath of 9/11. Little did Strahan know that he was about to get a little help from a friend to nab that record.

Quarterback Brett Favre took the snap and inexplicably began to drop back. A fake handoff, three quick steps to the right where the defensive end had broken through, and then…down! Favre hit the dirt at his good buddy Strahan's feet before the defender could even breathe on him much less touch him. But once Strahan did, he passed Gastineau on the all-time list with 22½ sacks, a record which still stands.

So does the debate. Did Favre take a dive for his pal? Did the quarterbacking great set up a scenario for Strahan to set the record? Was Favre a flopper?

Both players denied the accusations. Strahan, of course, had little to do with it. But Favre had everything to do with it, and his coach and teammates were none too happy with him. The Packers' offensive line had pitched a shut-out up to that point, keeping Favre's uniform perfectly clean, and the sack ruined an achievement offensive linemen relish. Making matters worse, players in the huddle said Favre originally had called for a run and never checked out of it.

Favre gave the ball to Strahan as he walked off the field, fueling further speculation that the record was set up. Strahan always denied it, saying "What am I supposed to do, get up and say, 'Brett, why didn't you throw it?'"

Strahan bristled at the controversy for good reason. Though the record-breaking sack may have been tainted, what could not be doubted was Strahan's efforts to get to that point. He had a phenomenal season. After the Denver Broncos and Kansas City Chiefs shut him out the first two games, he only played one more game where he failed to at least share a sack. Along the way he had a three-sack game against the New Orleans Saints on September 30, four against the St. Louis Cardinals on October 14, and two each in the following weeks against the Philadelphia Eagles and Washington Redskins. He also racked up three-and-a-half sacks in Philadelphia in the second to last week of the season. But during that latter contest, the inability of the Giants secondary to cover Donovan McNabb's receivers and the absence of a second-half pass rush led to a 10-point deluge in the final 2:43 and the extinguishing of the Giants' playoff hopes in a 24–21 loss.

But there was no denying Strahan had earned his sack record whether tainted or not. Even Gastineau, who saw his record fall in person, had to admit that. "No sack is a gimme in the NFL," he said.

Tiki's Hill

By the time Barber ended his 10-year career in 2006, he held team rushing records in five categories, including single-season rushes, yards, and career rushing yards as well as ranking among the top five in several other areas. He didn't get there by accident.

Barber was a conditioning freak who actually evolved physically over the years. As a younger player, he concentrated on pure speed. As he entered the middle of his career, speed and endurance became paramount. In his final seasons, strength became the focus as he looked to ward off injuries.

The Hill became his most famous and admired workout regimen because of its torturous nature. Working with fullback Greg Comella, the two attacked a steep hill that sat among a clump of trees in New Jersey's Ramapo Valley County Reservation. Winding for 2½ miles at what seemed like a 90-degree grade, the trail proved a tough hike for even a well-conditioned human.

Barber and Comella ran it every day. At 7 AM.

"The first time I ran it, it was hell," Barber said. "It kicked my ass. I almost passed out. But I can honestly say this hill has made me a better player. The hill has no weaknesses, and if you can consistently beat it, then in your mind you have no weaknesses."

Found by teammate Comella in 1999 after an unsuccessful search of ski facilities for a hill to run and adopted by Barber as his preferred offseason workout shortly thereafter, the runs built up cardiovascular endurance. It got Barber to the point where he never became fatigued in the latter stages of games. And that resulted in the running back jumping his rushing totals from 258 yards in 1999 to a then-career high 1,006 yards in the Super Bowl season of 2000.

The low-tech training actually consisted of three levels of increasing mental and physical difficulty up Rocky Mountain (1,063 feet high) and Drag Hill (1,074 feet). The first involved steep climbs. The second had a more gradual ascent but was dotted with small creeks to leap and thick underbrush to negotiate—not to mention a preponderance of gnats and other insects to add to the discomfort. The third was the nastiest. Just when fatigue began burning the lungs and lactic acid buildup started cramping the legs, the runners encountered steeper inclines and large rocks jutting out of the ground. The home stretch was a gravel trail that led to the summit, their daily Super Bowl. The Hill became a metaphor for Barber's career. "The first stage was really tough," he said. "That's how it was for me my first couple of years in the league. Then it gets a little bit easier, and that's when I thought I had it, but that's when I fell off. That was the second stage. And suddenly you have another hill, the third part, another tough part of your career, but you keep pushing until you reach the summit."

Barber didn't know it then, but he had yet reach his own football summit. The improvement in 2000 marked only the first of six 1,000-yard rushing seasons, which were capped by his single-season record of 1,860 in 2005 when he also set the franchise mark of 357 carries. By then his training had evolved into pure strength workouts with former power-lifting champion Joe Carini. Noting how his body had become more susceptible to injury due to the beatings of seven years as a three-down back—his pass-blocking skills were outstanding, considering his 5-foot-10, 210-pound stature—Barber decided in 2004 that muscle mass was the way to go.

Carini devised a workout far different than the ones he endured in the Giants' weight room or the Ramapo Reservation. Concentrating more on quantity of iron rather than quality of reps, Barber found himself doing sets of low-rep lifts in various contraptions of torture Carini developed himself, including a 400-pound cage called "The Yoke" the running back would shoulder-carry for 20 yards back and forth across the West Paterson, New Jersey, facility's floor. He also would do six sets of two reps on an upright leg press with 950 pounds of metal plates on it, one squat per set of 750 pounds off an overhead safety bar, and four sets of three deadlift reps of 405 pounds.

It was agonizing, but the pain was worth it. Combined with running backs coach Jerald Ingram's high-and-tight adjustment to his ball-handling style that cured a chronic fumbling problem, Barber put up his three best years, chewing up 5,040 yards of real estate. He didn't miss a game from 2002 to 2006 and gained 1,662 yards in his final year.

Carson's Canton Arrival

No two ways about it, former Giants middle linebacker Harry Carson had grown bitter. The solid rock to Lawrence Taylor's dervish both on and off the field, he made the Pro Bowl nine times in a career spanning 1976 to 1988, became the youngest Giants captain ever at age 25, and helped Bill Parcells win his first of two Super Bowl titles. And he was tired of waiting, tired of being disappointed the day before 13 Super Bowls when the Pro Football Hall of Fame voting board would find somebody flashier and more prestigious to reserve a spot for a bust in Canton, Ohio.

Carson had grown so sick of the wait that on February 5, 2006 he hadn't even bothered to power up his phone when he landed in Hawaii for some sun and golf with the family. He put it all out of his mind, going so far as to rebuke an inquiring gentleman sitting next to him on the plane. "I said, 'Listen, we're not going to talk about that,'" Carson said. Anyone remotely familiar with Carson's forceful demeanor would know that was the final word, too. "It had become a no-no subject for me. People who were close to me knew not to talk about it. We weren't going to go there."

It all changed after some kid came up to him in the Honolulu International Airport baggage claim with a piece of news from the mainland. Another premature congratulations, he thought. Carson had received a lot of those from radio stations and newspapers in previous years, jumping the gun to get ahead of the news and resulting in a failed investment of a phone call. "So when the kid told me that, I really didn't think anything," Carson said. "Then about five or six people came up, and they started congratulating me. I had a sense that something was up. Then I turned my phone on and got the news."

Carson was finally going to Canton, joining quarterbacks Troy Aikman and Warren Moon, coach John Madden, defensive end Reggie White, and offensive tackle Rayfield Wright in the same class. Great company. It was certainly a group the former lightly regarded fourth-round draft pick out of South Carolina State was proud to be part of.

But Carson always thought he should have gone sooner. As his years in waiting turned into a decade and beyond and as the panel snubbed him seven times as a finalist, he had grown so soured by the process that in 2004 he had asked the Hall to take his name out of consideration. The Hall of Fame refused. When the board denied him for a sixth time in 2005, Carson said he was done with it all. "I've been through this long enough," he said. "It has to do with my own pride, and what I think about myself. What was an honor is now a burden."

Wellington Mara, a huge supporter of the man who could quiet a locker room simply by walking through it, died that October. Right then and there, Carson's outlook changed. "There were so many things that went through my

After enduring a long wait, linebacker Harry Carson finally receives induction into the Pro Football Hall of Fame in August of 2006.

mind during that time," Carson said. "I knew how strongly he felt about me being a Hall of Famer. I knew that if it did come, that I couldn't tarnish his memory because it was something that he wanted for me, and I could never embarrass his memory, embarrass the Giants organization, or embarrass the National Football League. For me not to show up would have been disrespecting those people who really went to bat for me."

By the time he received the official news, his voice mailbox was full, and the Hall of Fame press conference—where the media gets to interview the new inductees—was over. TV, radio, and print never did get his initial reaction. "It's only fitting that he puts the Hall of Fame on hold for a little bit," press conference master of ceremonies and NFL Network anchor Rich Eisen said.

What the reporters missed that late afternoon in February, they received in surplus on induction day. Presented by his son, Donald, who suffered from a severe bone marrow disease called aplastic anemia, Carson issued a 15-minute stream-of-consciousness acceptance speech. "I'm here," he started. "Maybe a little late, but I'm here. I don't care how long it's taken, I feel great about being here. Well, I can't be happy about it until I get one or two things off my chest."

And then to no one's surprise, he turned his speech into a referendum on player health and minority hiring. He challenged the NFL to take better care of the retired players, many of whom suffer from debilitating conditions caused by the constant collisions on the gridiron. "If we made the league what it is," he said, "you have to take better care of your own."

He pushed for more black executives and coaches. It was a time when somebody had to say something. Carson, an activist on both fronts, used his speech to deliver that message. He never mentioned Taylor, George Martin, Brad Van Pelt, or any of his former teammates. They knew how he felt about them, he said. They all received thank you notes.

Good Eats

Sometimes, the most erudite humans are found in the most unlikely of places. Take Plaxico Burress and Glenn Parker for instance. For all his many foibles and issues with authority figures, Burress was one of the most well-rounded and intelligent people in the locker room. Hard to believe that the man whose Giants career would end ignominiously in 2008 with a bullet in his thigh could bear that tag, but Burress was indeed well-read with a preference for self-help books. His wife, Tiffany, was a corporate lawyer.

In addition to all that, his palate went beyond the massive servings of steak and potatoes football players are known to scarf down. Burress was particularly fond of the spicy Cajun dishes. "When you're eating and your nose is runnin', that's good eatin'," he once waxed whimsically over red beans and rice.

Burress wasn't the only one with advanced culinary tastes. Few might have guessed that Parker was a connoisseur of the grape. Heavily tattooed and standing 6'6", 315, the old guard cut an incongruous figure as he held a wine glass by the stem, swirled, sniffed, and tasted. But he knew his stuff. Parker had the collection to prove it. His 2,000-bottle stash featured high-end California Cabernet Sauvignons and Bordeaux. The magazine *Wine Spectator* thought enough of his taste buds to turn Parker into a feature subject in 2000. In the article he traced his enophilia back to his days with the Buffalo Bills where he became friendly with wine-loving French Canadians.

He even carried wine conversations over to the field. "I was playing against Chris Doleman," he told *Wine Spectator*. "And in the heat of the battle, most people are talking trash. He just looks at me and says, 'Hey, I hear you collect wine.' I said, 'I sure do.'" For the next three quarters, the two exchanged quick thoughts about vintages and tastes. "The guys in my huddle were saying, 'Would you shut up about the wine! We're trying to play a game here!'"

Parker would have no trouble doubling a dinner bill to make sure his guests were drinking an appropriately matched wine.

The Son-in-Law Also Rises

The Giants' second-round draft pick of 2004 was a good-looking guard from Boston College. Tom Coughlin originally noticed Chris Snee during Snee's redshirt freshman season while the Jacksonville Jaguars and former BC coach scouted one of the school's running backs.

Coughlin liked everything about him—his toughness, competitiveness, and build. The fact that Snee and the coach's daughter, Kate, had Coughlin's grandson, Dylan, had nothing to do with it, of course. A guy who gets drafted with the 34th pick overall by anyone has great potential. That's why Coughlin signed off on the move after the Giants asked him repeatedly if he could handle coaching the father of his grandchild.

Players are players, and family is family in Coughlin's mind, and the two should remain separate. "He wouldn't want it any other way, and it's never been an issue," Coughlin said. "I never think twice about it. We've been able to keep business *business* and family *family*. He does a great job of making sure of that."

Snee might never have made it to the Giants had Ernie Accorsi rolled over for the San Diego Chargers after they picked Manning with the top overall pick. Chargers general manager A.J. Smith had wanted defensive end Osi Umenyiora and the first, second, and third-round pick of 2004 for Manning. Instead as the clock on the Giants' No. 4 overall position wound down and with tension growing in the Giants' draft room, Accorsi convinced Smith that he would take Philip Rivers and ship the quarterback to San Diego with the 2004 third-round pick and the first and fifth-round pick of 2005 for Manning. That kept Umenyiora in Giants Blue and opened the way to take Snee with the second pick.

There was just one more obstacle: Coughlin's wife, Judy. The whole family had been stunned in 2003—and not in a good way—to find out that Snee and their unwed daughter were having a baby. But Chris and Kate grew up fast after Dylan arrived, and by April of 2004, the guard had won his in-laws' hearts. So when Coughlin called on draft day and asked Judy, "Do you mind if we draft this kid?" Judy gave her consent. "Chris had already been through the worst of my husband," she said. "He had to earn his way into our family."

Aside from the ceaseless ribbing he took from his linemates during his rookie season, Snee had no problems adjusting to the football/family duality. Always hard-working and looking to excel, the son-in-law has helped the father-in-law win two Lombardi Trophies and had earned spots on four Pro Bowl teams.

Snee—now the father of three with sons, Cooper and Walker, coming after his 2004 marriage to Kate—once described his off-field relationship with Coughlin. "We come to the door for dinner and he says, 'Hi, Chris. How are you?' and then he turns around and plays with the grandkids," Snee said. "That's why it works. We've been able to separate the two things."

Through the Snowflakes and to the Super Bowl

When the Giants released Ahmad Bradshaw in February of 2013, general manager Jerry Reese said, "Pound for pound Bradshaw is one of the toughest football players I've ever been around. Ahmad played football the way Giants football should be played."

That was never more true than on December 23, 2007, before all the foot and knee injuries turned a hard-nosed, 26-year-old running back into too big of a salary cap risk. He was a rookie backup to Brandon Jacobs back then, a seventh-round compensatory draft pick with mid-round talent and a troubled past. Bradshaw came to the Giants off two college arrests. The first for underage possession of alcohol and resisting arrest got him thrown off Virginia's team before he even started his freshman year. He walked on at Marshall, but in January of 2006, he was pinched for stealing a PlayStation 2 video game from another student's dorm room. That one led to two years probation for a plea bargain from felony burglary down to misdemeanor petty larceny. He had also run afoul of the law as a juvenile and wound up splitting a 60-day jail sentence for a parole violation on that incident during the offseasons of 2008 and 2009.

The Giants knew that was coming, but they decided to take a chance on him given his solid 5'10", 214-pound frame, his speed, and his elusiveness. At the same time, Reese and player development director Charles Way, a former Giants fullback, told Bradshaw in no uncertain terms that further transgressions would not be tolerated. Bradshaw promised and became a model citizen throughout his six-year Meadowlands career. But on this snowy day in Buffalo, he would justify Reese's faith in him as a running back.

With a playoff berth at stake, the Giants had battled back from a 14–0, first-quarter deficit to take a tenuous 24–21 lead in the fourth quarter. Jacobs,

After trying to grind out the rest of the clock, running back Ahmad Bradshaw stumbles into the end zone, accidentally scoring a touchdown to give the Giants a 21–17 lead with 57 seconds remaining in Super Bowl XLVI. *(AP Images)*

the Giants' bellcow rusher who had burst forth after Barber's retirement, had left the game with a sprained ankle. By then the cold rain of the first half had turned into a blizzard. On first-and-10 from the 12 with 6:27 remaining, Bradshaw broke the game open with his first career touchdown. Cutting right, then back left, he nearly stumbled going through the hole Rich Seubert and fullback Madison Hedgecock opened. Bills defensive end Chris Kelsay missed the ankle tackle as Bradshaw headed into the second level. And then the runner threw it into a higher gear to outrun defensive backs Donte Whitner and

Terrence McGee to complete an 88-yard journey to the end zone. It was the league's longest run from scrimmage that year. "I was just waiting my turn," Bradshaw said.

Corey Webster's touchdown return of an interception sealed the 38–21 victory, clinching the No. 5 playoff seed. For Bradshaw, whose 151 rushing yards went along nicely with Jacobs' 143 and two touchdowns, it proved a jumping off point. He would provide more key moments over the years. His recovery of his own fumble in the second quarter of Super Bowl XLII kept New England from potentially adding to a 7–3 second-quarter lead. He overcame foot problems to rush for a career-high 200-yard effort against the Cleveland Browns in 2012.

Bradshaw sped, bulled, and cut his way to 34 career rushing touchdowns with the Giants, and one of them came by accident. It happened in the closing seconds of Super Bowl XLVI as the Giants trailed the Patriots 17–15. With 1:04 remaining and the ball on the New England 6, the Giants wanted to work the clock down to almost nothing and put the game on the foot of Lawrence Tynes, who hadn't missed a kick inside 30 yards in four years. The Patriots had other ideas. Out of timeouts and knowing Tom Brady could move the ball in short order from anywhere on the field, they were going to intentionally let Bradshaw score as he took a centering handoff. He broke through the line untouched. Clued in by Eli Manning's screaming to "Get down," Bradshaw realized the Pats were going to lie down. "I thought I heard Eli yelling," Bradshaw said. "I tried." He turned away from the goal line, attempting to go down and churn out more clock but stumbled into the end zone—butt first—with 57 seconds remaining on the clock.

Call it the Reluctant Touchdown.

The two-point conversion failed, leaving the lead at 21–17. Brady indeed did get his last shot but failed because Rob Gronkowski could not make what would have been a legendary grab of a deflected Hail Mary pass as time ran out. "It was the happiest moment of my entire life, man," Bradshaw said.

Earth, Wind, and Fire

Though neither Jacobs, Bradshaw, nor Derrick Ward could carry a proper musical note if their lives depended on it, that rushing trio of Earth, Wind, and Fire made beautiful music together in the Giants' 2008 backfield. By the time Jacobs (Earth), Bradshaw (Wind), and Ward (Fire) finished running all over opponents in that 12–4 season, the NFL's top-ranked rushing group sported two 1,000-yard rushers in Jacobs and Ward and set team records with 2,518 rushing yards and a 5-yard average.

At the same time, they took accepted procedure a step further. Teams had become leery of overusing a single featured back and had started going to two-headed attacks. The Thunder and Lightning setup of Dayne and Barber that appeared revolutionary at the turn of the century was no longer a novelty. But the Giants had drafted a real sleeper in Bradshaw in 2007. His productivity in running for a playoff-clinching, 88-yard touchdown in the snows of Buffalo, and his work in Ice Bowl II indicated that he, too, belonged with the brutalizing Jacobs and the slashing Ward.

Thus evolved the three-headed attack aptly nicknamed by defensive end Justin Tuck as natural manifestations working in harmony. "Everybody goes 'Thunder and Lightning,'" Tuck said. "But we've got three of them. So I call them, 'Earth, Wind, and Fire.' I think Earth is Brandon. I think Fire is Ward. I think Wind is Bradshaw."

The band began their tour in the second game of the season, a 41–13 win over the St. Louis Rams. After watching Bradshaw score his second touchdown of the fourth quarter against a defense worn to exhaustion from three quarters of cutting and banging, Tuck wandered over to the trio during a timeout and said they reminded him of the 1970s musical group.

A nickname was born. But a nickname doesn't stick unless the subjects produce, which they certainly did. Jacobs, Ward, and Bradshaw produced 203 rushing yards against the Rams, though none of the three had a 100-yard game. The 264-pound Jacobs had 93 yards on 15 carries while the 228-pound Ward rushed for 58 yards on eight carries. Bradshaw, the nimble cutback specialist, brought his 198-pound frame to the field late and rushed for 52 yards on five carries with touchdowns on an 18-yard reception and a 31-yard run.

The theory was simple. Bang away with Jacobs and Ward and then turn it over to the fast second-year player. Bradshaw was still a year away from the foot problems that would dog him through 2012 and cause his release after that season. "Me and Derrick pound them, pound them, and pound them the whole game, and guys' legs are tired," Jacobs said. "Guys are gassed, and here's Bradshaw coming off the sidelines with all his quick moves and things like that, and guys aren't ready for that."

"All three of us, we complement each other," Bradshaw said. "We tell each other every day we can be the best group in the league. We give each other different advice and take advantage of it."

The year proceeded well. Jacobs topped a 254-yard effort against the Seattle Seahawks in the fourth game with 136 yards, his second of four 100-yard performances. Ward went 101 yards in a loss to Cleveland a week later and would eventually carry for 215 yards against the Carolina Panthers in the 15th game. Bradshaw neared the 100-yard mark with 96 against the Baltimore Ravens in the 10th game but never actually reached it.

Pulverize early and run them ragged late. It worked. Jacobs finished the season with 1,089 yards and 15 rushing touchdowns. Ward went for 1,025 with two touchdowns. And Bradshaw finished with 335 yards and one touchdown. Earth, Wind, and Fire didn't stop in the playoff game either. Though the Giants lost 23–11 to the Eagles in a season marred by the Plaxico Burress shooting incident, Jacobs and Ward rushed for 138 yards while Bradshaw handled kickoff return duties.

The trio would never harmonize again. Jacobs and Bradshaw formed a duet for the next three seasons as Ward migrated to Tampa Bay in free agency after 2008. Unhappy about losing his starting job to Bradshaw, Jacobs left after 2011 for San Francisco. Game but unable to participate in full practice weeks because of chronic foot and knee injuries, Bradshaw was released after 2012. The old band had been split up.

Live from New York...

When does a two-time Super Bowl MVP know he's arrived? When he hosts *Saturday Night Live,* of course. So on May 5, 2012, smack in the middle of sweeps season, baby-faced, laid-back "Easy" Eli came to follow in brother Peyton's footsteps as host of television's longest-running show.

Usually known for his bland though respectful manner, Manning showed both charm and acting chops in what really amounted to his second appearance on the show. The first came five years before when he offered a wave from the audience during the monologue of Peyton's bravura host turn in 2007. Unlike Peyton, who had acted in high school productions, Eli had never trod the boards except for a couple of awkward appearances in commercials. Those never put him in danger of earning a CLIO Award nomination. But SNL? That was breakout stuff especially as he lampooned big brother Peyton, his foil-in-absentia.

The highlight came in a sketch playing off Peyton's United Way spoof when the then-Colts quarterback spent his time with his young charges, alternately insulting them and abusing them with footballs. Peyton was seen giving one kid a prison-style tattoo before teaching the whole lot of them how to break into a car. Eli's spot used the Little Brothers sketch as a premise to help younger siblings strike back at the bullying of older brothers. The end sees him throwing cast member Andy Samberg, playing an older brother, into a car trunk. "And now you'll learn to treat your younger brother with respect, Peyton!" Manning yells.

"I'm not Peyton," Samberg responds.

"Whatever," Eli said, sneering.

He dressed in drag as "Miss Chicken-Fried Steak" for another skit and devised a lame touchdown celebration—dropping a sandwich to the ground and picking it up and eating it—for another.

Reviews were mixed. "Considering how the clean-cut Manning is so politically correct and safe during media interviews with reporters, it was interesting to see the quarterback in a different light on 'SNL,'" wrote ESPNNew York's Ohm Youngmisuk.

ESPNW's Jane McManus said his performance "wasn't terrible; he was a bit wooden but pretty good-natured." *Entertainment Weekly's* Marc Snetiker said he "may not have completely scored, but at the very least, he was a good sport." NFL.com's Greg Rosenthal gave him a B+. "It was a lot like Eli's career," Rosenthal wrote. "We had low expectations, but he wound up looking cool under pressure."

The Ultimate Survivor

Mark Herzlich stood on the sidelines in street clothes during Super Bowl XLVI, watching his teammates accomplish their 21–17 win against the Patriots. He'd have given anything to be on the field with them. Well, almost anything. The former Boston College linebacker had already achieved so much more than a Lombardi Trophy just by making that 2011 team.

He beat cancer.

Signed as an undrafted rookie on the urging of John Mara, Herzlich was a long shot to even continue his football career much less play on a pro squad. A pain in his left thigh in the spring of 2009 turned out to be a rare form of bone cancer. It started as a twinge, but it became a screaming, searing, sleep-depriving agony. Doctors identified it as Ewing's Sarcoma, a rare and potentially deadly cancer. Fewer than 400 patients contract it every year in the U.S., and 30 percent of them don't make it.

Suddenly, Herzlich went from a potential first-round draft pick to just a 21-year-old wondering if he'd ever see 22. "It's a feeling where your whole world is taken away in 20 seconds," Herzlich said.

The only thing Herzlich knew was this: If he did make it to the other side, the 6'4", 240-pound All-America linebacker was determined to continue his football career. "That was my end goal," he told ESPN. "Whenever I had a bad day in chemo, when I was in chemo and sitting in that chair for six hours, a one-inch needle in my chest, bag dripping over my head, that's what I thought about."

He took a huge risk to ensure that possibility. Instead of undergoing a traditional treatment that would have ended his career—replacing the femur with that of a cadaver—Herzlich opted for an experimental course. The original femur was left intact, and they attacked the cancer with intensive chemotherapy and radiation. *Major radiation.* Fifty rounds. Twice a day for five weeks.

After that surgeons ran a titanium rod down the inside of the bone to reinforce it. Two bolts held it in place. It worked. On the day doctors declared him cancer free, Herzlich received a call from Patriots linebacker Tedy Bruschi, who had come back from a potentially career-ending stroke. Of his many pieces of advice, one in particular stuck out in Herzlich's mind. "He said, 'Mark, be proud of being a survivor,'" Herzlich said.

Five months after his diagnosis, Herzlich led his Boston College teammates onto the field for the 2009 opener. He missed that season but returned in 2010, though a bit weaker and certainly not as explosive as he once was. The scouts noticed. He was no longer a potential first-round pick. In fact he wasn't even considered draftable.

The Eagles, Ravens, and Giants, however, stood at the top of a list of teams who thought he was still worth a risk. A call from Coughlin on the day the 2011 lockout was lifted cinched it. He'd try to become a Giant. "They asked me to come here because they wanted to see if I could play football and not to see if I was over my cancer," Herzlich told *60 Minutes*.

He showed them enough. Herzlich made the team primarily on kick coverage where he made six special teams tackles. But he started two games when injuries hit the linebacking corps and made a total of six tackles. Herzlich didn't make the active Super Bowl roster. A sprained ankle knocked him out for the last five games of the regular season and the whole postseason. But he did compete for a starting job in 2012.

Though Chase Blackburn won that battle, Herzlich became part of the linebacker rotation and started two games when Blackburn sat out with a strained hamstring. A November 4 start against the Pittsburgh Steelers produced a career-high nine tackles. He didn't need the stats to become a true survivor. Herzlich had already won his greatest battle. "It was a gamble," he said. "I guess I was gambling with my own life. But in the end, it was my choice."

Cruz-ing Through the Air

Between the Giants' MetLife Stadium co-inhabitants and a single-wing airplane, Victor Cruz can honestly say that the Age of Flight helped him become a Pro Bowl player in 2012. The Jets helped him earn a spot on the roster as an undrafted rookie out of UMass in 2010 and enhanced his legend the following year when he took Manning's pass 99 yards in a huge win for the Super Bowl-bound squad. But it was in 2012 that a single-engine Cessna, flying high over Red Bull Stadium in Harrison, New Jersey, helped him land his first Pro Bowl spot.

Sort of.

Cruz had actually campaigned for himself, following the practice of several other past candidates who YouTubed their workouts and other football activities. Cruz's fiancée/manager/baby mama, Elaina Watley, came up with an imaginative twist: have Cruz catch a football dropped from a plane. "I've seen some different videos where guys promoted themselves for the Pro Bowl," Cruz said. "Just little things like how some guys train and things like that. I just wanted to do something cool. It keeps people interested and maybe gets some traffic toward the Pro Bowl. It was a good idea."

It wasn't the easiest stunt to pull off. Flying at 1,000 feet, the pilot had to gauge airplane speed, wind speed, and altitude in order to get the football to fall to Cruz' approximate position in the soccer stadium's parking lot. It turned out to be a perfect drop as seen on the video—or so it seemed. There was this little matter of veracity. Would viewers believe it or simply consider it a piece of camera magic? "[It] felt pretty real when I caught it," Cruz said coyly.

Coy indeed. The Federal Aviation Administration tends to frown on people throwing objects out of planes in the middle of cities. They looked into it and quickly debunked the stunt. "Our inspectors interviewed the Giants' promotions staff," an FAA spokesman told AVweb, an independent aviation website. The agency told the site the Giants immediately "fessed up" to it being imaginative video trickery.

Several of the website's readers, however, had figured that out well before the FAA got into it. Some noted that the airplane's altitude and speed and wind factors could not possibly have produced as near-perfect a drop as what appeared on the video. "Looks fabricated, as there is no trajectory to the inbound path of the ball," Cary Alburn wrote. "If the plane is moving 70-to-70 knots, then so is the ball as it's on its way down. The ball seems to drop straight down to the receiver with a forward speed of zero."

Yet another reader, Ron Harger, figured out mathematically that the less-than-four-second drop would have warranted a height of just 256 feet, and that was if it was performed in a vacuum. Real or not, the gambit didn't hurt the campaign, though his stats told a better, more genuine story. Cruz made his first Pro Bowl squad with 86 catches for 1,092 yards and 10 touchdowns, one year after he broke Amani Toomer's team receiving yardage record of 1,536 yards on 82 catches with nine touchdowns.

One of those scores came in a must-win against the Jets in the penultimate game of the season. It was a Christmas Eve gift as Cruz turned a short, second-quarter throw from Manning into a 99-yard touchdown catch. It replaced Earl Morrall's 98-yard connection with Homer Jones in 1966 as the Giants' longest play from scrimmage.

Records aside, the catch saved the Giants' season and ultimately allowed their entry into the playoffs and a Super Bowl XLVI victory. As the designated home team at MetLife Stadium, the Jets were up 7–3 and controlling the action, but Cruz's catch-and-run turned around that 29–14 win and in fact the whole season. "You could see the look in the Jets' faces how they became drained," Cruz said after catching three balls for 164 yards and a touchdown.

Why wouldn't they? The Jets were the people who all but gave Cruz his spot in the NFL to begin with. A longshot at best to earn a roster spot in 2010, Cruz burst forth in his first game ever—the football christening of MetLife Stadium against—you got it—the Jets. Cruz went for three touchdowns to go along with six catches for 145 yards.

The Salsa and the Hynoserous

The Giants have never had a Lambeau Leap or a Mile-High Salute as part of their post-touchdown repertoire. They've never even pulled out a cell phone from the goalpost padding as Saints receiver Joe Horn did during his

Wide receiver Victor Cruz performs his post-touchdown salsa dance in honor of his grandmother, Lucy Molina, during a 2012 game against the Tampa Bay Buccaneers.

Superdome touchdown celebration in 2003. But that doesn't mean an organization more known for its steady consistency and conservative attitudes hasn't had its spicier moments. The Giants, too, can dance.

Since Cruz started making regular visits to pay dirt in 2010, fans at MetLife Stadium began roaring "Cru-u-uz-z-z." Their excitement built because they knew Cruz would spread a little salsa in that end zone afterward.

But on September 16, 2012, Cruz heard none of the sellout crowd as he danced after an 80-yard catch-and-run in the fourth quarter. There were no spectators, no Tampa Bay Buccaneers defenders, no teammates. Just Cruz and his grandmother, Lucy Molina, the woman who helped raise him while his mother, Blanca Cruz, worked. She was the woman who taught him how to swing his hips and do the salsa dance the right way. Cruz went into that game with a heavy heart. Lucy, 77, had died that Monday, and this salsa was for her. "It was almost like the place kind of went silent," Cruz said. "I was just there dancing with her. Right as I was done, I kind of looked up to her and held my hands up to her, letting her know that one was for her."

Cruz's dance, one of 10 he would do in the Giants' 9–7 non-playoff season, went down as the year's most touching moment. But it wasn't the only touchdown dance. The season saw the unveiling of the Hynoserous, concocted by congenial fullback Henry Hynoski after his first career touchdown in the season-ending 42–7 win against Philadelphia. Here's how he performed that signature dance: He put his thumb at the top of the facemask with his middle finger bent and the others extended; shuffled his feet three times to imitate a rhino's charge; and then swayed to the right, then to the left, then to the right again, then to the left again, and then to the right one more time. Then he stood back and absorbed the MetLife Stadium cheers.

Not every player, however, busted moves that brought the world to its feet. Coughlin and several teammates of running back David Wilson, then a first-round draft pick, became irate when he started doing backflips in the end zone. Defensive captain Tuck actually had a talk with him, reminding the speedy back that his services were better rendered on the field than in traction in some hospital, which is where he could have ended up with a mistimed leap. Cruz said his stomach would get tied up in knots whenever Wilson went airborne. "It scares me every time he does it because you never know what can happen," Cruz said. "You don't want to see him get hurt."

But Wilson always regarded the criticism as a bit of overcautiousness. "I've been doing 'em since I was three years old," Wilson said. "It's like easy. It's almost like running for me to jump and turn backward. I've been doing it for a while, so I think people can relax a little."

The defensive side of the ball wasn't immune to celebrating. Modeled after Korean pop star PSY's Gangnam Style rodeo step, defensive end Jason Pierre-Paul's sack dance received only a lukewarm reception. And fellow defensive end Osi Umenyiora has suffered through the artistic critiques of both Tuck and Strahan for a sack dance where he makes like an airplane, flying around the field with arms extended hip-high in wing-like position. Strahan had no room to talk. He was no Baryshnikov himself; his sack dances consisted of him beating his chest once and striking a strong-man pose.

CHAPTER 7
OF GODS, GENERALS, AND FULL-BIRD CAPTAINS

The Last Man Standing

For all the ups and downs Dan Reeves had during his four years at the Meadowlands, he could not have been more grateful to land the Giants' head coaching job in late January 1993. The search for the successor to the inept Ray Handley had taken a month, and George Young already had been turned down by Bill Parcells' wide receiver coach Tom Coughlin, who wanted to stay at Boston College to finish the rebuilding job he'd started two years before. Another candidate, Dallas Cowboys assistant Dave Wannstedt, had accepted the Chicago Bears job.

Reeves' name came into the equation late. As it turned out, he was the right man at the right time. The Giants were looking as much for a personality shift from the humorless, paranoid, and combative Handley as for real coaching know-how. With his Georgia drawl and bottomless reservoir of stories told in entertaining, down-home style, Reeves proved ideal. Plus Denver had just released him after a 12-year run in which Reeves led the Broncos to three Super Bowl appearances behind John Elway, the Hall of Fame quarterback who developed under his guidance. During Super Bowl XXI after the 1986 season, Reeves was on the other sideline when Phil Simms took his defense apart.

Despite his vast experience and coaching accomplishments, Reeves didn't mind his status as a third option and signed a five-year deal for $4 million. "I was my mother's third choice," he said. "I don't feel I was any less loved than the rest of them. It doesn't make a difference with me. The main thing is—I'm their last choice."

It didn't take Reeves long to set a tone. The very first day of training camp, he put his team through the physically taxing Oklahoma drill, which he used yearly in Denver. His version involved a single defensive back shedding a wide receiver's block in order to tackle a running back, who lined up stacked behind the receiver. Little veteran wideout Stephen Baker caught the staff's attention by flattening Willie Beamon. "You have to hit a great deal to get ready," Reeves said in giving his nutshell philosophy that would also include three-hour practices during losing streaks. "We'll always have that kind of tempo where it's pretty much live."

After the two previous years, Simms welcomed the change. "It's a chance to start over, to forget the bad things that happened to us the past two years, and get us going the right way," Simms said. The rest of the Giants agreed. Their 11–5 record marked the best a Giants team ever compiled for a first-year coach.

Learning from the Best

Dan Reeves' offensive coordinator George Henshaw once said in 1993 that watching Simms, Dave Brown, and Kent Graham walk into a meeting room was kind of like watching a mother duck and her two ducklings waddling by a pond. As soon as Simms rose, Graham and Brown followed in close pursuit.

That's not surprising. The lessons Simms taught Graham, an eighth-round pick in 1992, during those two years of meetings lasted a lifetime right through the tutoring of his own son into a starting quarterback at the University of Hawaii in 2013. "Phil was excellent," Graham said. "I always think of him as a mentor for me. He was gracious to both Dave and myself, a real man's man."

Simms would be gone after the '93 playoff season. But his presence remained with Graham and Brown in their huddle command, including the way Simms might lay into teammates who messed up their assignments. Keith Elias, an intelligent but undersized rookie running back in 1994, got a taste of that when he lined up wrong during the final minutes of a preseason loss to Cleveland. Brown let him have it, just about sending the Princeton product into shock. "I chewed out Keith Elias for the first time," Brown said. "He walked back to the huddle in the two-minute drill, and I yelled at him. He told me later that was the first time in three years he'd been yelled at because he was always the man at Princeton. Before I might have gone up to him and said 'I'm sorry' after the game. But now I don't feel like I have to say 'I'm sorry.'"

Brown had been named the Giants' starting quarterback by that time, but Graham didn't let the lessons go to waste. He fashioned his own career between the Giants, the Arizona Cardinals, and then the Giants again before finishing his career with the Pittsburgh Steelers and Washington Redskins. Graham now helps instruct student-athletes in Wheaton, Illinois. "He taught us how to be a pro and what being a pro meant," Graham said. "I help a lot of high school quarterbacks now, and a lot of the things I teach them are things I learned from Phil. His lessons are very instrumental in what I teach. I'll never forget my rookie year. He asked me to play golf with him at Ridgeway Country Club [in Westchester, New York]. First tee, I take a swing and I don't think I hit the ball at all. I took this huge divot. I was so nervous. Here I am, a rookie playing golf with Phil Simms. But he said, 'Relax. Take it easy.' That set the tone.

"He was just great like that with the social skills and the way he handled people—a real leader with integrity."

Coach Landry

As most any coach in the NFL would, Dan Reeves referred to most of his brethren by their first names. But there was one he refused to call by any other name but "Coach"—Tom Landry. In Reeves' many references to the man who made him an All-Pro halfback and started him on a coaching career that would include four Super Bowl appearances with Denver and the Atlanta Falcons, it was always "Coach Landry." To Reeves it was a term of honor as much as one of endearment.

As the player his coach called "Danny," Reeves learned about Landry's calm but calculating demeanor. He carried over Landry's wordy play calls, which accounted for every position's responsibilities, even though some of them approached 20 words. The Landry philosophy, where executing plays right took a back seat to executing things *exactly* right, became as much a part of Reeves as breathing.

He also adopted Landry's competitiveness. He became intimately acquainted with that from serving as his old coach's offensive coordinator in the late 1970s. He, fellow assistant Mike Ditka—the great tight end and future Super Bowl-winning coach of the Bears—and Landry engaged in some vicious racquetball games after hours in the Cowboys' training facilities. "You could see [Landry] was ready to whip us," Reeves said. "He had that square-jawed look. He was under control, but you could see he was burning up inside.

Beat you? Heck yeah, he'd beat you. He wasn't going to meet us out there just to get exercise."

Landry never raised his voice on the gameday sidelines or practice. Reeves rarely did. He didn't yell or scream. He just worked his players. When practice drills were not run to Reeves' satisfaction, he simply ordered, "Run it again." When the team needed post-practice punishment, Reeves simply gathered the players, stood before them, and calmly ordered them through the up-and-down drills: "Get 'em up, get 'em up, get'em up. Down. Up," he'd command as the players pumped their legs, hit the dirt, and rose again for more.

Reeves inherited a lot of Landry's stubbornness, too. He sometimes stuck with strategies too long, including his reluctance to allow Brown to throw the ball downfield with any great frequency. He added a twist of his own during his final two seasons at the Meadowlands, sparring with management over his desire for the same control of the roster he had in Denver.

When Wellington Mara returned a firm "No" to Reeves' demand for more control of player acquisitions at the end of 1995, it marked the beginning of a downhill slide to his firing. Mara was not going to change a coach/general manager system that worked. He would not cut into George Young's powers. Reeves thought about walking away from the final two years of his contract. That didn't happen, but going 6–10 in 1996 combined with the hubbub of the previous offseason led to his dismissal. It was the one area where he differed greatly from Landry. The great Cowboys coach built his success by working within a system with team president and general manager Tex Schramm and player personnel guru Gil Brandt. Reeves never got used to that.

Going After Jones

Wellington Mara was a league guy; first, last, and always. So imagine the displeasure he had with Jerry Jones when the Cowboys owner strode onto the field during a second-quarter timeout of the Giants' increasingly disheartening 35–0 opener loss in 1995 with Nike president Phil Knight on one side and Nike client, spokesperson, and tennis champion Monica Seles on the other.

Remember, this was *in* Giants Stadium on a Monday night in front of a national audience.

Regardless of his gross lack of taste, the always publicity-hungry Jones certainly knew how to get the most bang for his stunts. Jones had arranged this one as part of his foray outside the NFL's revenue sharing business model, a setup Mara helped create in the early 1960s. Jones had signed a seven-year deal with Nike as a Texas Stadium sponsor with rights to use the stadium's name and logo in connection with Nike products. Jones would not share any revenue from that deal with the rest of the league.

Jones stood on the sideline the rest of the half, going so far as to introduce defensive lineman Chad Hennings to Knight. The league has since instituted various levels of team-specific revenues, but at the time Jones' actions were not only revolutionary but rebellious. At least in Mara's eyes.

At first the owner took Jones' stroll with a handful of salt. "I'm just honored he thought to use our stadium for it," Mara said. But after thinking about it overnight, he was in quite a different mood the following morning. "I feel sorry for Jerry," Mara said, knowing that Jones had cut a similar deal with Pepsi weeks before the Nike agreement. "He's a very successful entrepreneur who made a great deal of money for himself. Then he saw this great thing called the NFL and said, 'I want to be part of this.' But I don't think he has a concept of how to be part of a team. He doesn't realize that when you do something to enhance yourself, you hurt the rest of the team. It's like a guy who runs a great leg on a mile relay and doesn't want to give up the baton. He wants to do it all himself."

Jones fired back that the deal didn't threaten the overall revenue-sharing nature of the league, a legendary facet that still helps small-market franchises like Green Bay stay in business. But Mara wasn't buying it. "I'm sorry that a man who's highly intelligent hasn't grasped the fundamentals of the NFL that made it attractive to get into it in the first place," Mara said. "In the long run, he's hurting the valuation of his franchise."

This marked one of the few times the venerable Giants owner, a pillar of reason in often rambunctious league meetings, got it wrong. Dallas remains one of the richest franchises in the league, right there along with the Giants and Washington Redskins. Needless to say, Mara never had a real soft spot for the oil baron from Arkansas.

The Search for Reeves' Replacement

Had things turned out differently in Young's 23-day coaching search that brought in Jim Fassel in 1997, the Giants might have changed the collegiate fortunes of both LSU and Alabama. Young actually considered and came close to signing then-Michigan State coach Nick Saban to replace Reeves following the 6–10 crash of 1996. Young's assistant, Ernie Accorsi, had pushed hard for Saban. Accorsi came to know the Michigan State coach during 1991 and 1992, Accorsi's final two years as general manager in Cleveland when Saban was starting a four-year stretch as Bill Belichick's defensive coordinator.

Fassel was always Young's No. 1 choice because the former Giants quarterbacks coach (1991) and offensive coordinator (1992) under Handley had made quite a name for himself in Denver serving as Elway's position coach for two seasons. With three young quarterbacks in Brown, Danny Kanell, and Stan White, a quarterback-friendly coach would be seen as a vaulable asset. But Young liked Fassel even more for his organizational skills and work ethic.

Mara and Young also appreciated a sacrifice Fassel made early in 1992. Young had asked Fassel to move up from quarterback coach to become Handley's offensive coordinator in '92 with a modest bump in pay. Fassel agreed but had left for the Senior Bowl the day before Young put the new contract on his desk. Fassel told Young he would sign the papers as soon as he returned from Mobile, Alabama, at the end of the week.

While Fassel scouted college talent for the draft, the 49ers contacted him with a much better proposition. They wanted him for their own offensive coordinator job left vacant when Mike Holmgren accepted the Packers' head coaching spot. It would have meant more money and far more prestige given the presence of Joe Montana, Steve Young, Jerry Rice, and John Taylor on the offensive roster. "That was the hottest job in football at the time," Fassel said. "They asked me if I wanted it, and I told them I was already committed to the

Giants. They asked me if I'd signed the contract yet, and when I told them I hadn't they said, 'Well, then you're free to sign with us.'"

Fassel reiterated his intentions of keeping his promise to Young and stuck to them. He affixed his name to the Giants contract upon his return. The day Young signed him for the Giants' head coaching job five years later, Mara called his new leader into his office. "I know you could have given us your word and then signed with the 49ers back then," Mara told Fassel. "I won't say the only reason you're here is because you honored your word. But I guarantee you it would have been the reason you weren't."

Back in January of 1996, the name of this loyal coach was one of the first to go on a short list of candidates Young developed when the Giants feared philosophical differences over the organization's decision-making structure might cause Reeves to walk away from the final two years on his contract. But Young also liked Saban's defensive mind, and an impressive interview with him turned it into a two-man choice. Oakland Raiders assistant Joe Bugel and Philadelphia Eagles assistant Emmitt Thomas were also interviewed, but they were eliminated quickly. Parcells' name even came up, though only in a fleeting manner.

What followed was a sequence that had all the cloak-and-dagger aspects of an Agatha Christie novel complete with secret meetings and simultaneous contract chats. Fassel, then the Arizona Cardinals' offensive coordinator, was interviewed in the Phoenix airport on December 26, 1996. Saban was interviewed January 2 near Giants Stadium. Stops in San Francisco and Cherry Hill, New Jersey, to talk with Bugel and Thomas were also included.

Young had both men on the hook and discussed money matters with each even after Saban had publicly pulled his name from consideration to protect Michigan State's recruiting interests. "I am not a candidate for the Giants' job," Saban said through a spokesman while on a recruiting trip in North Carolina. "If it's a two-horse race, they better find another horse."

Yet the talks went on, only to go under when Saban's contract demands turned out to be a bit too exorbitant for the Giants anyway. When Fassel was supposed to be in Mobile, scouting Senior Bowl practices, he sat in a room in Atlantic City, New Jersey, discussing contract numbers with Young. The next day, January 15, 1997, the 47-year-old signed a four-year, $3.2 million deal.

Saban didn't do badly himself. He coached at Michigan State for three more years before moving on to LSU in 2000. He won a national championship there in 2003. A return to the college ranks after an unsuccessful, two-year head coaching stint with the Miami Dolphins produced national titles at Alabama in 2009, 2011, and 2012, thus bolstering his God-like status in college football.

A Man of Few—But Important—Words

Wellington Mara never said two words when one would suffice. Known for a thoughtful pause to questions followed by few well-chosen syllables, economy of the language was his game. Long, rambling speeches or lectures weren't his thing whether the owner was talking to one reporter or 76,000 fans at a packed Giants Stadium. It was to the latter where he uttered some of his most famous words. The 12–4 Giants had just finished dispatching the Vikings 41–0 in the 2000 NFC Championship Game on a field that left much to be desired as far as aesthetics and footing. The franchise had begun a three-year experiment that season with a natural grass tray system designed to replace the hard AstroTurf of the stadium's earlier years.

It failed miserably. The grass roots never did take hold. The field looked nice enough when it was new, but kickers and wide receivers slipped, and big linemen churned up big clods of grass. By the time January 14, 2001 rolled around, the field had degenerated into a brown, bumpy cow pasture, which looked suitable on the surface only by the application of green paint.

Between that and their climb back from a tenuous 7–4 record after a bad loss to Detroit, the announcers had a field day. They criticized the surface as "painted mud" thoughout the telecast. They noted how unconvincing the team looked in squeezing out three of their final five wins by four points or less.

But Mara had the last laugh in his typical succinct fashion. Grasping the Fox microphone held by Hall of Fame quarterback-turned-analyst Terry Bradshaw, he whipped the sellout crowd into a defiant roar as Bradshaw presented him with the George Halas Trophy, emblematic of the NFC title. "This is the Giant team that was referred to as the worst team ever to win home-field advantage in the National Football League playoffs," he said. "And today on this field of painted mud, we proved that we're the worst team ever to win the National Football Conference Championship. I'm happy to say that in two weeks, we're going to try to become the worst team ever to win the Super Bowl!"

That victory speech just about reached the outer limits of Mara's oratorical range. Two weeks later the owner reverted to a more concise format when he pulled television broadcaster Russ Salzberg aside in the locker room as the team packed for its Super Bowl trip to Tampa, Florida. "Hey, Russ, I just had Number 38 last night," Mara said.

"Thirty-eight what?" Salzberg asked.

"My 38th grandchild," the father of 11 answered.

Mara, a religious man and a daily communicant, was even shorter with his words the day in 1997 when he announced the signing of Christian Peter. The defensive lineman had been convicted of eight assaults in seven years and had been accused of but never indicted for the rape of a Nebraska coed. The New England Patriots had drafted him but waived him before training camp started.

The Giants picked him up with the provision that he keep his nose clean and attend counseling sessions for alcohol abuse, attention deficit disorder, and anger management. It was a highly controversial move, and Mara had made it plain that the major reason he signed Peter was because he believed the defensive tackle could help his team. Conversely he felt the Giants organization could help Peter. The idea that a much-convicted offender could change aroused the skepticism of the media.

"Do you really think a man can change?" asked Jon Gelberg of *The Asbury Park Press*.

"Yes, I do," Mara said.

"Do you have any concrete evidence that people like that can change?" Gelberg pressed.

"Read the lives of the saints," Mara said.

The answer spoke volumes. Many of the Catholic church's saints had decidedly unwholesome beginnings only to undergo various conversions to committed, holy lives. Although no one will ever canonize the defensive line-man, Peter did go on to play six trouble-free years with the Giants, Indianapolis Colts, and Bears.

General Tom Coughlin

Coughlin was sitting in his usual spot at the 2003 NFL Scouting Combine in Indianapolis —at the 40-yard dash finish line. Armed with stopwatch and notebooks, the former Jacksonville Jaguars coach sat as intently as always, eyeing closely the prospects who whizzed past and keeping small talk among his fellow coaches to his usual minimum. Coughlin's work ethic was well known in NFL circles, and nothing should have seemed abnormal about it except for one thing: He didn't have a job. The man who twice took the expansion Jaguars to the AFC Championship Game was out of football.

Accorsi approached Coughlin. "It's Saturday, and there's one Catholic Church downtown," Accorsi said. "And I'm wondering what time Mass is. I know the one person who's going to know is Tom Coughlin, and he's sitting there working as hard as ever. And I say to him, 'But Tom, you don't have a team.'

"And Tom looks at me and says, 'I will, though!'"

Coughlin's future ironically would lie with Accorsi's Giants one year later. Fassel's team had imploded into a 4–12 mess. The coach had gone to president and CEO John Mara demanding an update on his job status. The two agreed Fassel would leave at season's end, but that Fassel would coach the final two games as a lame duck. Riddled with injuries, the Giants didn't exactly rally around their coach in losses to Dallas and Carolina that closed out the era.

Starting the search for a successor right after the final game, they brought in Coughlin first. It was as much a matter of convenience as interest since his unemployment meant he'd be immediately available. League rules required the Giants to wait to interview other candidates such as St. Louis Rams defensive coordinator Lovie Smith, New England defensive coordinator Romeo Crennel, and New England offensive coordinator Charlie Weis until their teams were out of the playoffs. Also quite high on the list was Accorsi's friend, Saban, the man who made the Giants look bad during the Fassel search. The

Known for his rules and discipline, Tom Coughlin is flanked by Giants co-owners Wellington Mara (left) and Robert Tisch (right) during his introduction as Giants head coach in January of 2004. *(AP Images)*

gauging of his interest took on a secretive tone as Saban was in the process of leading LSU to a national title.

Accorsi and John Mara interviewed Coughlin at the Newark Airport Marriott. Coughlin threw the duo an immediate curve when he broke with accepted practice and asked to speak first. Mara and Accorsi found that a bit disconcerting, but in the end the two left the interview impressed. "We both had a list of questions, but he said he'd like to talk first," Accorsi said. "He rattled off for 40 minutes, but he answered a lot of the questions before we even asked them. I told John, 'He bogeyed the first hole but wound up shooting a 66.'"

Both were well aware of Coughlin's credentials. Mara knew him from when Coughlin coached wide receivers under Parcells from 1988 to 1990.

Parcells addressed Coughlin's ability to a reporter during one encounter, "Who do you think the best coach in this room is?" The reporter shrugged and said patronizingly, "You, Bill." To which Parcells replied, "Bullshit! I asked you a question! Now think about it!"

The reporter came up with another name just as obvious. "Bill Belichick." And Parcells said, "Nope. He's sitting right there."

He was pointing to Coughlin.

Accorsi's knowledge of the man came more indirectly. While Coughlin was coaching Boston College, Accorsi's son, Mike, served as a graduate assistant at Virginia. As George Welsh's UVA team prepared to meet the Eagles in the 1994 Carquest Bowl, Mike confided to his father that they could not figure out the timing on BC's passing offense for the life of them. They never did. Coughlin's squad threw the Cavaliers out of Joe Robbie Stadium 31–13.

It helped that Wellington Mara, who would be making the final decision with co-owner Bob Tisch, also recognized Coughlin as a hard-working, well-organized, and above all disciplined and honest leader. But Accorsi's appraisal of him—"If we can't win with this guy, I'm taking up tennis," he told Mara—certainly gave the owners a nudge in the right direction.

Knowing all that, Coughlin was not an anointed choice. Saban was very much in the mix, and Accorsi had agreed to wait until after LSU's victory parade to officially approach the former Browns assistant. And he said the interviews with Smith, Crennel, and Weis were far from perfunctory. Smith demonstrated enough in his breakdown of the Rams' season to convince Accorsi that he would succeed anywhere as a head coach. He would eventually do so with the Bears.

Mara and Accorsi decided they could no longer wait for Saban. Accorsi had called his house the day after the victory parade in Baton Rouge, Louisiana, but Saban wasn't home. He left a message with Saban's wife that the Giants were moving on. Accorsi presented their recommendations to Wellington Mara and Tisch the next day. "We might have had a difference in the ranking of the other three, but we both had Tom No. 1," Accorsi said. "We set criteria. I took all the great coaches from the last 30 years and analyzed them. They all had high IQs. Lombardi, he was a math and chemistry teacher. Belichick, Paul Brown…Bill Walsh. Who was smarter than Walsh? We wanted somebody who was smart and had integrity. If Tom is anything, he's honest. He'll look you straight in the eye. He doesn't play games. He was qualified on all those fronts and he knew our front-office structure."

Coughlin signed a four-year, $11 million contract on January 6, 2004. "Tom Coughlin is the right person for this job," John Mara said.

In his introductory press conference, Coughlin evoked all the fire of George S. Patton as he proclaimed the need to restore Giants pride and rid the locker room of the "cancer" of injuries. He stood ramrod straight and spoke with a strong, stern voice. Accorsi felt he hadn't just hired a good coach but that he'd hired a great one. "He was perfect for us," Accorsi said. "But he earned his position." And he would earn two Lombardi Trophies.

Unorthodox Ernie

Accorsi didn't care much for doing things strictly by the book. A fellow who did never would have picked Kerry Collins off of life's scrap heap. But he didn't just deviate from the book in his moves that brought Manning and big-time receiver Plaxico Burress into the franchise one year apart. He threw it on the ground and burned it.

The GM's most flamboyantly public move came in 2005 when he signed the 6'5", 230-pound Burress to give Manning a giant-sized target in the red zone. Burress had earned quite the reputation as a flaky malcontent in Pittsburgh, an image he would carry over to his Meadowlands career. But Accorsi only saw him as a great replacement for Ike Hilliard, whose body was deemed too battered to remain effective, and a larger, more athletic complement to the 31-year-old Amani Toomer.

Accorsi began checking out Burress' personality quirks with Steelers head coach Bill Cowher and general manager Kevin Colbert. They told him Burress was cut for financial reasons, and they gave the man three years removed from a 78-catch, 1,325-yard, seven-touchdown season glowing reviews. A meeting with Coughlin and his coaches at Giants Stadium, dinner at Manhattan's famed Smith & Wollensky steakhouse, a New Jersey Nets game that night, and an additional pitch from no less than Tiki Barber the following day had Burress all but signed, sealed, and delivered.

And then his agent, Michael Harrison, got into it. Burress disappeared, and Accorsi learned soon after that Harrison was also negotiating with the Vikings. He was using the Giants to drive the price up. The general manager wasn't just angry. He was livid, ticked off to a nuclear level. Accorsi responded in a way he had never done before or since.

He issued a press release, declaring the Giants had pulled their offer and were no longer interested in Burress. With that one very public move, he took away all of Harrison's leverage. But it didn't come without consequences. "As soon as I pulled the plug on the offer, I get word that Philadelphia is willing to throw a lot of money at him for just one year," Accorsi said. "I went to Tom and I said, 'If we have to play against him and Terrell Owens, we're in deep trouble.'"

It never came to that. A couple of days later, Harrison ran into player personnel director Jerry Reese on a scouting trip and pleaded his case. Little did he know that a competing agent, Drew Rosenhaus, was in the parking lot and was viewing the entire conversation from the car behind them. Two days after the cloak-and-dagger exchange, Burress dropped Harrison and picked up Rosenhaus, his third agent of the season and the fifth of his career. League rules required a five-day waiting period before a new agent started negotiating for his client, but never one to let legalities get in the way of a lucrative deal, Rosenhaus called Accorsi immediately.

Accorsi and Rosenhaus agreed to hold off talking. The day the waiting period ended on March 17, Rosenhaus headed for Giants Stadium, and the two hashed out a six-year, $25 million contract in 15 minutes. Manning had his tall target, and Burress would make all of Accorsi's trouble worthwhile with a late fourth-quarter touchdown catch that beat the undefeated Patriots in Super Bowl XLII.

Accorsi also threw the book out the window on his 2004 draft-day trade that brought Manning. His job probably would have gone with it had Archie's son and Peyton's little brother proved a bust. Wellington Mara was against the move. He had told Accorsi as much in the month before the draft as the GM designed a move up from the fourth spot to San Diego's top overall pick. The owner had a soft spot for Kerry Collins, a troubled quarterback who reformed himself and led the Giants to a Super Bowl in 2000. Mara didn't believe the Giants needed the scion of NFL royalty. At the same time, he made it a policy not to interfere with a front-office structure that had worked well since Mara hired Young in 1979. "You all do what you want," Mara said, "but I won't be very happy."

Accorsi loved Manning and he knew a perfect storm of circumstances was brewing in San Diego for him to land the quarterback. Accorsi had scouted the Ole Miss heir to his father's passing records himself and had deemed him a once-in-a-career talent blessed with arm strength, precociousness, and rock-solid composure. So impressed was Accorsi that he wrote in bold letters "Never Gets Rattled" on the youngster's scouting report.

Manning thus became Accorsi's Moby Dick, the white whale he'd chased his whole career. He came close 21 years before when, as the Baltimore Colts' assistant general manager, he drafted Elway over the quarterback's protests. Elway didn't want to play for the Colts and he eventually got his way. After Elway threatened to pursue a baseball career with the Yankees, Accorsi's boss, Joe Thomas, traded him to Denver. Accorsi quit over it.

In a move reminiscent of Elway, Archie Manning let it be known to the world that he had no intention of letting his son play for the woebegone Chargers. Accorsi had told Chargers G.M. A.J. Smith that he was interested in the pick, but the two couldn't come to a pre-draft deal. Instead the night before the draft, a reporter told him Smith was going to pick Manning No. 1 and then call Accorsi when seven of his 15 minutes on the clock had elapsed to propose a trade. Accorsi had little choice but to believe him.

Sure enough, Smith picked the reluctant Manning. The quarterback went to the podium and—with an awkward smile on his face—dutifully held the Chargers jersey with the No. 1 on the back. The San Diego cap, however, never touched his head.

Then the fun started. The Browns at No. 7 called as soon as the Giants went on the clock. Ben Roethlisberger was rated third overall on the Giants' draft board just below Manning and tackle Robert Gallery, who went to

Oakland at No. 2. Feeling sure the big, burly quarterback would still be there at 7, Accorsi came very close to pulling the trigger on the deal. If he really wanted a quarterback in the first round, Roethlisberger would also fit the bill wonderfully.

But something told him to wait. He put off the Browns. Six minutes, seven minutes went by, and the Browns called again. Accorsi blew them off again despite the growing knot in his stomach. Where were the Chargers? Would they ever call? As soon as he hung up on the Browns, his secretary called with the news he wanted to hear, saying, "A.J. Smith is on the phone."

Smith proposed that Accorsi pick quarterback Philip Rivers, a guy the Giants never considered drafting for themselves, and then send Rivers, the Giants' third-round pick of 2004, fifth-rounder of 2005, and veteran defensive end Osi Umenyiora over for Manning.

"Osi is a deal-breaker," Accorsi said. "We're not even going to discuss it."

"Okay," Smith said. "Would you give me next year's No. 1 instead?"

The Giants had a deal: Rivers and the third-rounder of 2004 and the first-rounder and the fifth-rounder the following year for Manning. Just seconds before the clock ran out, Accorsi had made up for the one that got away more than two decades ago. "I just believe that you can get by if you have to, but if you have a chance to pick what you think is a quarterback for the ages, you have to go after him because you're not going to get that many opportunities in your life," said Accorsi, who was great friends with John Unitas and Bert Jones in Baltimore. "It's not any big, cryptic mystery why I feel that way. I've been around great ones. I know what they mean."

Coping with Coughlin

The only thing safety Antrel Rolle had in common with Hall of Fame-bound Baltimore Ravens linebacker Ray Lewis was a college tie to the University of Miami. But Lewis most likely saved his fellow Hurricane from a life of misery when Rolle first came to the Giants as a 2010 free agent.

The safety knew all about Coughlin's military-style mentality when he signed a five-year, $37 million contract. Before the ink had even dried, he said he thought coming to New York was a mistake. And he made it public as Rolle was a player who never shied away from a notebook, a television camera, or a radio interview. After a Game 2 blowout loss in Indianapolis, he ripped Coughlin's day-before-the-game travel schedule, saying it left no time for players to get acclimated to their surroundings. He characterized the gray-haired leader as "too uptight," and marveled at the *Animal House* frat party Rex Ryan—"A coach they would die for," Rolle said—was running in Florham Park.

It all earned him a rather unpleasant trip to the principal's office, where Coughlin reminded him who exactly was in charge. Despite the rough visit, the information didn't really sink into Rolle's head until he had a conversation with Lewis, a player who had some experience overcoming personal adversity. The linebacker went to jail for 15 days in 2000 and served a year's probation for obstruction of justice in connection with the stabbing murder of two men outside an Atlanta nightclub in 1999. "He told me exactly what I needed to hear," Rolle said. "From that day on, I never, ever had an issue with coach. I've never had any concerns. I can honestly say it was great."

He asked Lewis how he should handle his dealings with the strong-willed boss. "We had an hour-long conversation just about life," Rolle said. "He was telling me how I should approach the situation, how I should be able to deal with Coach Coughlin but still get some things across. I listened to what he said, and it helped me out a lot. It boiled down to me going to someone I can consider a mentor. Someone I know is going to give it to me straight as someone who is going to tell me something I need to hear as opposed to something I wanted to hear."

Rolle's opinions might have ruffled Coughlin, but the fact was that the coach had actually improved his relationship with his players since changing his attitude in 2007. Becoming more approachable—a less-regimented coach might be characterized as player-friendly, but that would be going too far for Coughlin—was one of the conditions of his being retained after a lackluster and controversial 2006 season. The Giants snuck into the playoffs that year at 8–8 as personal attacks on Coughlin's demeanor and coaching ability intensified in the media.

He had run into some major issues even before then. Michael Strahan led a group of players in filing a grievance over his practice schedule his first year in New York. Wellington Mara supported Coughlin throughout that ordeal, essentially saying if the players are complaining, he must be doing something right. A run-in with cornerback Will Peterson over discussing injuries with the media nearly turned explosive. Barber publicly complained that Coughlin abandoned the running game too soon in a tough, 2006 loss to Jacksonville. Jeremy Shockey drew fire for opining that Coughlin was out-coached in a loss to the Seattle Seahawks earlier that season.

His rules about players wearing a collared shirt, dress slacks, colored socks, and dress shoes when leaving their hotel rooms on the road rubbed people the wrong way. Coughlin Time—a throwback to Vince Lombardi's Packers rules that required players to arrive at team meetings five minutes before the scheduled time—resulted in frequent fines.

Strahan eventually came to understand Coughlin, and Coughlin understood Strahan. During a conversation later that year, the infuriated defensive end told the coach he was losing the locker room. Coughlin took a further step after 2006, instituting a 10-man "leadership council," ostensibly a players committee, which could bring locker room issues directly to him. The council included positional leaders such as Manning, center Shaun O'Hara, Strahan, punter Jeff Feagles, and linebacker Antonio Pierce. Committee and coach met every week or so to discuss various problems that would crop up. Things had changed for the better. "Tom kind of comes down on us and lets us do the things he doesn't feel he really wants to do," Feagles said. "We've been able to do that and with that been able to kind of come together and become a really close-knit team."

Coughlin explained himself a couple of years later, saying, "There's a sincerity issue here where they know that I'm coming to them with things I think are important, information they need to know. Because what happens a lot of times is you get so busy, then you start contemplating 'When will I tell them this? When will I not tell them this?' This gives you a chance to get this information out."

Hall of Fame linebacker Harry Carson complimented Coughlin publicly on his evolution. "I was impressed Tom even went down that road because

Tom was about doing it my way or the highway," Carson said. "It showed his willingness to be flexible and to listen to guys and take on a different mind-set."

As for Strahan, he and Coughlin grew so close that the defensive end eventually wrote the foreword to his coach's book, *Earn the Right to Win*. "I hated him," Strahan wrote in the third sentence while recounting his early years with Coughlin. "Hate is a strong word, but that's the way I felt." His last paragraph reads: "When I look back on that relationship now, I tell people proudly that I love the man. I love him and if I could, I would play for him any day. And together we would win."

Carrying the Torch

The NFL had two African American general managers on January 15, 2007. On January 16 it had three. One day after America celebrated Dr. Martin Luther King's birthday, the Giants introduced Reese to succeed Accorsi. And just a few days later, former Georgetown basketball coach John Thompson impressed on Reese the gravitas of his position. "He had me on his radio show," Reese said. "Coach Thompson put it to me point-blank. 'Jerry, look, I'm holding you responsible. I'm not giving you any alternative. You *have* to do it. You *have* to succeed.' I didn't take that lightly."

Reese would help blaze a trail—as the Ravens' Ozzie Newsome and the Houston Texans' Rick Smith, the two African American general managers, did before him—for any others who would follow him. That his hiring was finalized so close to the day celebrating America's civil rights icon added not only symbolism but pressure. Major slippage from the successful legacy of George Young and Accorsi, Reese's biggest champion in the organization, would only have made things harder on future African American candidates everywhere. That much Reese recognized from Day One. "I said during my press conference that this was my time to carry the torch for the African American community," Reese said. "I told Tom Coughlin that, 'Failure was not an option. Not for me. I had to succeed for me, my family, the African American community. If I fail, it doesn't bode well for those coming after me.'"

As of 2013 he had passed the test with flying colors. Under his leadership the Giants went to two Super Bowls, though many credit Accorsi's team-building with the 2007 win against the Patriots. But Reese's draft brought in pieces such as Steve Smith, Ahmad Bradshaw, Kenny Phillips, Mario Manningham, Jason Pierre-Paul, and Hakeem Nicks—all major figures in either both or one of the Super Bowl wins. He brought Victor Cruz into the organization as an undrafted rookie and Michael Boley and Chris Canty through free agency.

His eye for talent—he started as a scout in 1994 after fellow scout Jeremiah Davis convinced him to leave a $35,000 assistant head coaching job at his alma mater, Tennessee-Martin—never left him. Accorsi took him off the road in 1999, threw him into a suit jacket and tie, and brought him inside as an assistant in the player personnel department. He was promoted to player personnel director in 2002.

But his ascension to general manager came as somewhat of a surprise. The Giants had hired minority assistants and scouts, but to call them racial groundbreakers would have been inaccurate. Reese, though, was one of the fast-rising stars and had even been interviewed for the Dolphins' GM job in 2006. "To be honest, I was kind of bummed out when I didn't get it," Reese said. "I felt great after that interview. I thought I knocked it out of the park. Really I didn't think I could have done any better, but they went in a different direction."

Reese's chance finally came when Accorsi decided to hang it up. The interview with president and CEO John Mara and treasurer Jonathan Tisch lasted less than an hour as opposed to three hours with Miami. They knew what they had in Reese, even though they also considered his former boss, Dave Gettleman, and Mara's brother, Chris. "It was so much shorter than Miami," Reese said. "With John, he'd watched me grow up in the organization. I think I gave them the confidence that communication was important to me. I said, 'I'd knock down all the walls of the organization.' He knew I was a good personnel guy, and I told him, 'The scout would never leave me.' The biggest thing was I knew we were so close. We lost that playoff game in Philly the year before without Strahan, without Toomer, without other guys, and we still had chances to win that game. So we didn't need a big overhaul. And then, I told him, 'I won't let you down.' You know, it took a lot of guts for John to step out there and say, 'Our new general manager is Jerry Reese.'"

In doing so, he passed over his brother in heeding the late Young's advice years before that a team cannot have an "unfireable" GM. Accorsi cried. So did Reese.

Doug Williams, the first black quarterback to win a Super Bowl, was the first to call. Hall of Fame linebacker-in-waiting Harry Carson said, "I'm ecstatic. I feel like a little kid. I'm glad for Jerry and I'm proud of my organization, my old team for making this statement. It's a huge statement throughout the league."

Reese carries the torch, but he also populates the roster. "We've done a good job, but we can do better," he said. "I've always felt a sense of responsibility for all the African American trailblazers that came before me. Just to have the Giants have the confidence in me to put me in that position that they would give me this chance, it just justifies all the hard work I put into it. It was a great day for me and my family."

Meeting the Wizard

The all business, all the time coach, Coughlin, got to meet his idol for the first and only time during Sweet 16 weekend of the 2009 NCAA Tournament. He wasn't a football coach either. John Wooden, the man Coughlin looked up to, did his venerated work on the basketball hardwood.

Coughlin's Giants Stadium office had as much Wooden stuff as football artifacts. Known as a legendary basketball coach during and after his years leading UCLA to national championships, Wooden's fabled list of life virtues—prepare well, live clean—sat atop a center bookshelf in easy view of visitors. Not far away was a full-color reproduction of Wooden's Pyramid of Success, which used faith, perseverance, and self-confidence as its main building blocks. His blue-covered book, *Wooden: A Lifetime of Observations and Reflections On and Off the Court,* was at Coughlin's fingertips, and its pages were dog-eared and indexed with important passages and comments in Coughlin's own hand.

Coughlin had always tried to live his life by Wooden's tenants—perhaps a bit more gruffly than the old UCLA coach might have himself—but morally just the same. "It never leaves my side," Coughlin said. "It sits right next to me. You read through this. It's like reading another one of the gospels. Very simple. It's all about being a good person and leading a good life."

But despite Super Bowl success as a Giants assistant, achievement at Boston College, and two years removed from victory in Super Bowl XLII against the undefeated Patriots, Coughlin had never found the opportunity to visit the coach who gave the world Lew Alcindor—who would become Kareem Abdul-Jabbar after graduation—Bill Walton, many others, and 10 national championships in 12 years during the 1960s and 1970s.

It wasn't until the 2009 NFL Owners Meetings at Dana Point, California, that Coughlin found himself close enough to Wooden's modest apartment in Encino, 78 miles up the road, that he took his wife's advice and went to meet the man he so looked up to from afar. "You know, people have those lists of 100 things they want to do before they die," Coughlin said. "This was a Top 10 for me."

The man who surrounds himself with military brass and the regimentation that comes with it was clearly moved in his three-hour visit with the gentle, 98-year-old legend. Surrounded by a gallery's worth of photos of Wooden's teams as the wheelchair-bound coach welcomed Coughlin to his office, what did they talk about? Shop, of course. Coughlin wanted to know how he developed his method of running practices. "His practices were legendary," Coughlin said. "They never stopped. I asked him about the running game, and he smiled and said, 'That was my game, the running game.' The pressure defense, the fast-break offense, he always prided himself on conditioning."

Wooden told him he learned about practicing as a high school coach at Central High in South Bend, Indiana. He had observed Notre Dame football coach Elmer Layden's practices and noticed their organization and intensity. He took those qualities back to the gym. His practices were sectioned off so that one drill flowed logically into the next. His players never stopped moving. Then came Coughlin's question about his motivational skills. "He talked about effort," Coughlin said. "Make the great effort, and everything else will take care of itself. He said he never talked to his players about winning. It was all about effort and preparing properly. And don't compare yourself to others. Be as good as you can be."

For Coughlin, this visit was nothing short of a religious experience. "I've always had great respect for my elders," Coughlin said. "But not just for what he's accomplished but what he stands for. That's why it was so important for me to see him. Not only does he espouse the Golden Rule, he lives it: Respect for others. Do unto others as you'd have them do unto you."

When the old coach died on June 4, 2010 at age 99, Coughlin was left with a sense of emptiness. "He wasn't just a basketball coach," Coughlin said. "He was and is a life coach, and for that we can all be thankful. He was the best living example of his teachings about teamwork, preparedness, and humility. I don't think there's a close second to him."

A Veteran Influence

None of the many speeches Coughlin offered his team during the Super Bowl championship season of 2007 were more inspirational than the ones that came out of a man who never ran a professional play, never caught a pass, and never suffered through a wind sprint.

He couldn't. Lt. Col. Greg Gadson didn't have any legs. While serving a tour in Iraq, an IED took his legs, leaving his left arm as the only fully-working extremity. But that hideous roadside bomb Gadson encountered—as he and his 2nd Battalion, 32nd Field Artillery journeyed back to Baghdad following a distant memorial service for fallen comrades—didn't take away his mind or his voice.

Promoted in 2012 to colonel and commander at Fort Belvoir, Virginia, after serving for two years as director of the Army Wounded Warrior Program, Gadson came to the Giants through former West Point class of 1989 teammate Mike Sullivan. The wide receivers coach had gone to Walter Reed Army Medical Center in Washington, D.C., to visit Gadson, who had recently endured several life-saving operations following his wounding in May 2007. When Sullivan asked him if there was anything he needed, Gadson asked if he could attend a game when the Giants played the Redskins down there.

Sullivan made it happen and told Coughlin about his friend. After hearing his story and exchanging a couple of phone calls with the officer, Coughlin asked him to address his 0–2 team the night before that September 23 game against the Redskins. The two met for the first time outside the banquet room in the team hotel that night.

The legless former linebacker spoke to the players from his wheelchair, expounding the virtues of team, unity, and fighting spirit. "You have to play for one another, for your teammates," Gadson told the players in that ballroom. "You have to fight for the guy on your left, the guy on your right. Be vigilant and fight for every yard."

From his themes of togetherness to the details of his personal story about how his Army teammates rallied to his side even as he lay unconscious in a German hospital, the words resonated. He talked about how meaningful sports were to those fighting overseas and how he wanted to get back into the fight despite his grave injuries. "Truly great teams form a bond by going through something together," he said. "Whatever you're going through right now, no success ever comes easy. Nothing is promised to anybody in this life, starting with tomorrow."

The Giants filed out of the room. Each player shook his hand and thanked him for his words and service to America. They won that game 24–17 with a dramatic goal-line stand in the final minutes. But just as important was Gadson's presence on the sideline. Coughlin brought him into the locker room again afterward and awarded him the game ball.

From that point on, Coughlin and the players treated Gadson as an honorary team captain. He was on the sidelines for several regular season games. He rolled onto the field as an honorary captain for the NFC Championship victory in Green Bay, freezing right along with the rest of them. "Everyone was concerned with me being in the weather, and they had box seats for me," Gadson said. "But I decided the right place for me to be was on the sideline by my teammates."

He was there at the Super Bowl win against the undefeated Patriots and again four years later when they beat the 49ers for the conference title and the Patriots again in the big game.

An admiring Coughlin, a man who has always surrounded himself with military heroes such as Gen. Ray Odierno and Gen. David Petraeus, gave Gadson an open invitation to address his squad. When he chose to, his words resonated with the players. So did his achievements.

Before their 2007 wild-card playoff game in Tampa, Gadson, who now walks on his own with the help of high-tech, battery-powered prosthetics called Power Knees, met them again in the hotel lobby, standing on his first set of prosthetic legs. "I knew there was a special bond because I could see it in their face when they saw me standing there," Gadson recalled. "They all either came up and shook my hand or gave me hugs. It was very personal and I really felt very special."

It truly was an inspiring sight for the Giants players. "It's hard to complain about anything when you see a guy who is a father, a husband, a fighter, lose his legs," Justin Tuck said. "Even in 2007 when he was with us, I never saw one time where it ever looked like he ever felt sorry for himself. As football players sometimes you get banged up and sometimes you feel bad for yourselves. But look at him. He doesn't have any legs, but he's learned how to drive and he's not dependent on anybody."

Booing Tiki

Between the Polo Grounds, Yankee Stadium, the Yale Bowl, Shea Stadium, and Giants Stadium, the Giants had consistently held to one franchise quirk. They had no outward, permanent monument to past greats. That changed when MetLife Stadium opened in 2010. At halftime of their October 3 win against the Bears, they dedicated the Ring of Honor for the first time.

Thirty franchise legends stood on the field in front of name placards to receive their cheers from the packed house. It was a toss-up between late owner Wellington Mara and Lawrence Taylor, absent as he faced third-degree rape charges involving an underage prostitute, as to who got the biggest ovation. Simms, Toomer, Strahan, Y.A. Tittle, and Frank Gifford also received incredible rounds of applause.

There was no doubt, however, as to who received the least amount of cheers—Tiki Barber. The franchise's record-setting running back, a figure of controversy since his 2006 retirement, had not only angered fans with some harsh comments about Coughlin and Manning in his role an NBC football analyst, but also was involved in a messy divorce. The boos showered from the stands throughout his introduction. Barber simply waved and smiled. "I don't give people grief for their opinions," Barber told the media. "You guys know, I've had plenty of mine."

Strahan, who had flown in from Los Angeles after doing his job with the Fox pregame show, defended his friend. "He's a great player for the franchise and deserves to be honored," Strahan said. "He's a Giant for life."

The other honorees were: owners Bob Tisch, Tim Mara, and Jack Mara; general manager Young; coaches Steve Owen, Jim Lee Howell, and Parcells; and players Mel Hein, Ken Strong, Tuffy Leemans, Em Tunnell, Rosie Brown, Sam Huff, Andy Robustelli, Carson, Al Blozis, Charlie Conerly, Dick Lynch, Joe Morrison, Pete Gogolak, George Martin, and Jessie Armstead.

Gifford interestingly questioned the inclusion of Howell on that list, noting that his assistants—a couple of guys named Lombardi and Landry—did virtually all the coaching on those teams of the mid-to-late 1950s. Gifford was not a fan of Howell, who once called the handsome running back "one of those Hollywood characters" because of his numerous commercials and movie roles.

Rules Rule

Reeves, Fassel, and Coughlin all had rules. Every coach in the NFL has rules. They're needed to keep order on a team and, in some cases, to keep players safe. Sometimes, though, the coaches add little twists that make their sets of commandments unique.

Reeves required that players keep their helmets either on their heads or in their hands during practice. Put the hat on the ground, and it cost that player $500. More than one player suffered that penalty during Reeves' first season in 1993, and even the ones who didn't receive fines grumbled about it. Reeves, though, had a solid, logical explanation. He wanted to keep his roster intact. "That sideline is a dangerous place," Reeves said. "A player puts his helmet down on the ground, and we run an out route to the sideline, and he gets pushed out of bounds, we got a problem. He steps on [the helmet] and breaks an ankle, and I lose a wide receiver all because one guy thought it was too heavy to carry."

Fassel demanded players show up at meetings and practices on time or risk a fine, but he often would be willing to let the player off with a threat the first time. Some players, of course, didn't quite take the hint. David Tyree, a sixth-round draft pick in 2003, decided early on to follow his own schedule. He showed up at practice late one of the first days of training camp. "I had a deal with the players," Fassel said. "If you come in late, you get fined $500. But I'm not going to take it now. You get another chance. But if you come in late again, I reserve the right to double the fine and I also pick up the $500, so now you owe me $1,500. Well, David walks in late again a couple weeks later. I take him into [equipment manager] Ed Wagner's office and I tell him he's fined $1,500. He's pissed. You could see the steam coming out, but he takes it.

"The next day he comes in and says, 'Coach, I talked to my mom, and she told me I should come in and thank you because if I continued on that road, I'd never play in the NFL again.' And I said, 'Tell your mom she's a wise woman.'"

Tyree had a couple of other stumbles after that, one of which involved an arrest for marijuana possession. But he never came late to a meeting again.

Coughlin won the prize for sheer volume of rules. They could fill a book. His list covered almost everything, even prohibiting a player leaving his room in sweats. A collared shirt, slacks, colored socks (no whites), and shoes were decreed standard lobby wear to present a businesslike appearance.

But Coughlin also took punctuality to new levels. Or should we say old levels. Coughlin Time, a throwback to Lombardi's rules with the Packers that ordered players to show up five minutes ahead of time for meetings, took those edicts to new dimensions. Every clock in the Giants training facility was set five minutes ahead. 8:55 AM read 9 AM. Players were to be in their seats, feet on the floor, and ready to go five minutes before Coughlin walked in the door for a 9 AM meeting. An arrival at 8:58—two minutes early for those keeping score—was considered late and punishable by a $500 fine that doubled for each infraction.

Most players came to respect Coughlin Time, some to the extreme. Offensive lineman Gary Ruegamer was so mindful of it that when he flipped his truck on the highway that paralleled Giants Stadium one morning, causing a closure of the roadway, he had the tow truck take him directly to the stadium. It was never confirmed what scared Ruegamer more, the accident, the $500 fine, or the thought of Coughlin chewing him out.

Players quickly realized Coughlin Time applied outside the facility, too. It traveled to other cities and time zones. Strahan learned that the hard way. Before one road game, he presented himself at the front of the team hotel several minutes before the team buses were scheduled—in real time—to depart. They were already gone, and he wound up taking a taxi.

Of course, there are always the resistant ones. Burress was fined incalculable sums for tardiness to meetings and absences at practice even if he had what he thought was a viable excuse. But they all learned Coughlin Time waited for no man.

Controversial Honors

Given the nature of the respective careers of Taylor and Parcells, it was only fitting that controversy should follow them to the doors of Canton. Separated by 14 years, the Hall of Fame selections of the legendary linebacker and the coach who made him produced two of the most spirited, divisive discussions ever heard in the voting room.

In the free-spirited Taylor's case, the lack of unanimity among what was a 36-member selection board in 1999 brought an unprecedented volley of vitriol from that year's first-ballot inductee. At least five members voted to deny the star of two Super Bowl-winning defenses his spot because of repeated troubles with drugs and the law. Their nay votes flew in the face of Hall of Fame rules that prohibit board members from considering anything but on-field achievement.

The discussion was described by several voters as one of the hottest and longest ever, and that included the debates around controversial Raiders owner

Al Davis and Colts tight end and union proponent John Mackey. They actually voted on changing the Hall of Fame bylaws to include a morals clause, though that was voted down 24–11 with one abstention.

The San Diego Union-Tribune columnist Jerry Magee cast one of the nay votes. "The Hall of Fame is a chamber for heroes," he later explained, "and Lawrence Taylor is not a hero. You can't separate athletes from society." Philosophies like that incensed Taylor as much as a quarterback dropping back to pass. He issued a written statement of thanks but eschewed a phone interview at the traditional Hall of Fame press conference the night before that Super Bowl in Miami.

On Super Bowl Sunday, he let loose. "These guys sit around—old phonies. Phonies, I call them!" Taylor ranted. "And they sit there and blast and criticize me and say he shouldn't be in the Hall of Fame because he's morally wrong while they sit around getting high on their third or fourth highball. They'll hold me to a higher standard than they hold themselves. And they'll go to South Beach, get totally trashed, and chase some little 13-year-old up and down the street, but they're all right."

Taylor, who was playing golf when he got the news, railed at the non-unanimous nature of his selection. "I was a little upset because they were saying, 'L.T. in the Hall of Fame,' but they've got to put an asterisk beside it," he said. "But the heck with it. In spite of everything, I've made it and I'm one of the best who have ever played the game. And if you sit there dissed, take your kids to the basketball court because I'm going into the Hall of Fame regardless."

Parcells produced controversy of his own, albeit without the incendiaries of Taylor's ascension. His habit of leaving jobs and then coming back—he quit the Giants in 1991 only to migrate north to New England in 1993, then retire from the New York Jets in 2000, and move to Dallas in 2003—caused voters to deny him his first time around. Fear that he would mimic Washington's Joe Gibbs, who returned to coach the Redskins after he was voted into the Hall, caused voters to pass over the finalist of 2001 and 2002, when coaches became eligible upon retirement.

The Hall of Fame changed its coach's eligibility bylaws for 2008 to include a five-year waiting period, and he became a first-time finalist under those rules in 2012. The voters, however, waited until 2013, when he hit age 71.

Even with his advanced age making it a virtual certainty that he would never again coach, Parcells' appearance on the list of 15 finalists sparked the lengthiest debate of any candidate in the longest selection meeting ever. Now swelled to 46 members, the committee squabbled for eight hours the day before Super Bowl XLVII in New Orleans, and spent a solid hour of that solely on the former Giants coach.

New York Daily News columnist Gary Myers drove home the point that Parcells not only was the 10th winningest coach in history—his regular and postseason career record with the Giants, Patriots, Jets, and Cowboys was 183–138–1 with two Super Bowl titles in three appearances—but proved a motivational master. He told the story of the 1989 playoff game against the Los Angeles Rams when Taylor would face left tackle Irv Pankey, one of the few linemen who consistently shut him down. In contrast New Orleans Saints linebacker Pat Swilling had swept past Pankey for four sacks in two games that year.

When Taylor walked into the locker room that week, there sat an airline ticket to New Orleans on his stool. Parcells, knowing full well Taylor had seen it, told Taylor, "I want you to go down to New Orleans. Now you don't have to change jerseys because he also wears No. 56. Just give Swilling your helmet and send him up here. And you go ahead and stay down there and play for the Saints this week because I need somebody that can whip Pankey."

Taylor's answer was curt and direct. "If you wanted Pat Swilling, why didn't you draft the son of a bitch?" he said.

The Giants lost that game, but Taylor went out and got two sacks and seven tackles.

Unlike Taylor, Parcells wasn't put off by the long discussion or the handful of nay votes. He was very grateful, noting the coaches before him who had paved the way. "It's just unbelievable," Parcells told the media from his home in Jupiter, Florida. "It's beyond comprehension, really."

Taylor's anger took some time to settle. But by the day of induction, it was gone. He was gracious to Carson, the teammate and defensive captain who often criticized his off-field conduct. He was thankful to owner Wellington

Mara, who supported him through his battles with drugs. And as he concluded, he was inspirational, though unrepentant for his wild ways. "Anyone can quit," Taylor said. "A Hall of Famer doesn't quit. A Hall of Famer realizes the crime is not being knocked down. The crime is not getting up again."

CHAPTER 8
BUMPS, BITES, AND BRUISES

Brawling Coaches

Dan Reeves might have had an inkling after one particular training camp brawl that 1996 was not going to go the way he expected. It's not unusual for players to get into it as defensive lineman Keith Hamilton and guard Ron Stone did on July 22 at the Giants' University at Albany training site. But when defensive line coach Earl Leggett and offensive line coach Pete Mangurian started pushing each other, well, that was a different story altogether.

Leggett, 63 and coming off shoulder surgery, was first into the scrum, followed by the 41-year-old Mangurian. The latter told Hamilton to lay off his guy, to which Leggett replied in no uncertain terms that he would take care of his own players, thank you very much. As players gathered to watch the fracas, Leggett and Mangurian started pushing each other. They only stopped when Reeves shouted, "That's enough!" Reeves rarely found need to raise his voice on the practice field, and one word from him ended many an altercation without outside intervention.

He spoke with the feisty Leggett afterward. "I just wanted to remind Earl he just had that shoulder [operated on]," Reeves said. "You didn't want to be fighting too much after that."

The whole scene brought to mind an incident from his high school days. "There were these two linebackers who went at it," Reeves said. "Our coach said, 'Okay, take the pads and helmets off.' Then he got us all around a circle and he said, 'Okay, now fight.' I never saw so much dancing around in my life."

Hazing Shocker

Hazing becomes part of virtually every rookie's training camp experience. In Giants camp the draft pick would be called upon at dinner to stand up, state his name, alma mater, and amount of his signing bonus, and belt out a tune. Pretty benign stuff as veteran antics go. But Jeremy Shockey wasn't having any of it.

The first week of training camp for Shockey, drafted in the first round out of Miami, was eventful more for what he did in the University at Albany dining room than on the field. Let's just say the bruised cheek and busted lip from his first night set a definite tone for the tight end's tumultuous career. Shockey was already six days late because of a protracted contract negotiation, so the veterans were in a mood to punish him per the traditions of the league. They told Shockey to get up and sing. Shockey put them off. "After I finish eating," he said.

That wasn't nearly good enough for Brandon Short, a solid but unspectacular third-year linebacker who put a premium on R-E-S-P-E-C-T. The two had engaged in a bit of verbal taunting in practice that afternoon, but now Short was all over Shockey. He heckled him throughout the meal. Eventually, the former Hurricane rose, went through the introductory litany including his $5.8 million signing bonus, and added, "This is for you, B. Fucking Short!"

Short went after him. The two wrestled to the floor as Fassel ordered the fracas broken up. Jesse Palmer and Collins pulled Shockey out of there while Luke Petitgout and Mike Rosenthal took care of Short. Oddly enough Fassel was angrier over the media's coverage of the event than the fight itself. "I'd rather have them feisty," Fassel said.

Players are always up for a good tussle as long as nobody truly gets hurt, so it was no surprise that defensive tackle Keith Hamilton said Shockey's only regret should be about how easy it was to separate the combatants. On a list of fights Hamilton had seen since the Giants made him their fourth-round pick in 1992, this one didn't even register. "Man, you kidding?" Hamilton said. "That was minor, like slap boxing. When I came through, things were always carrying over into the locker room. You fought on the field, you had to get ready to fight in the locker room."

Ah, the good old days.

Like the skeleton drill in training camp of 1994 when drafted defensive tackle Chris Maumalanga beat undrafted guard Scott Davis over the head with Davis' own helmet, sending him to the trainer's room for multiple stitches in his forehead. The two continued the disagreement—no doubt over the difference between Descartes and Proust—in the post-practice locker room.

Shockey was hardly chastened. His mouth got him in trouble repeatedly throughout his Giants career. Some indelicate terminology in calling then-Dallas Cowboys coach Bill Parcells "a homo" and his objectification of women in magazine articles enraged Fassel and Giants management.

The Giants sent him packing after the 2007 season. Recovering from the broken fibula he suffered in Week 15, Shockey wasn't even allowed on the sideline with the rest of his teammates as Manning led them to a Super Bowl XLII victory against the undefeated Patriots. He was told to watch from an upstairs box in University of Phoenix Stadium. But at least he could finish his meal up there in peace.

A Poke in the Eye

On July 21, 1997, venerable center Brian Williams made an ungodly sound. It was a combination screech/scream/groan that no human should be capable of forming. His eye damaged and bleeding, Williams made that noise as he lay prostrate on the lower University at Albany training camp field in the early light. Defensive tackle Bernard Holsey's thumb had invaded his facemask during a routine blocking drill and found its way right to the socket.

An offensive lineman getting poked in the eye was nothing new. Hands get tangled up in facemasks and things happen. But most of the time the victim walks away with a sore, teary eye—perhaps with a mouse underneath it. This was different.

Williams lost two years to his injury, and by extension the Giants lost the anchor of their line. Even after surgeons repaired significant damage to the iris, pupil, and cornea and inserted a plate to hold together a fractured orbital bone, Williams suffered from double vision for a long time. "You can't play center with double vision," Williams said. "And you don't want to live your life with double vision."

The doctors gave him only a 50 percent chance of ever playing again. But there he was at the opening of training camp in 1999—prepared to resume a career that had seen his rise to respected elder statesman. Despite the swelling and eye problems that afflicted him the previous two years, Williams had made himself a near-constant presence at team meetings, taking time off only to witness the birth of his third child and to tend to his mother during her battle against breast cancer.

Williams indeed returned in '99 to play 12 games that year before hanging it up. But he never forgot how close he came that morning in 1997 to having his career end and his life change forever. "You can take my knees and take my ankle," Williams said, "but don't take my eye."

Motorcycle Madness

Former Houston Oilers and San Diego Chargers running back Gary Brown had run for 1,063 yards and five touchdowns in his first year with the Giants in 1998, so naturally Jim Fassel was counting on a repeat performance the following year. That is until Brown ended up in the hospital after a hit-and-run accident on his motorcycle a month before the 1999 training camp opened. Brown had been riding his Suzuki motorcycle near midnight of June 26 in his hometown of Williamsport, Pennsylvania, when a car ran a stop sign and cut in front of him, causing the running back to wipe out.

Brown was knocked unconscious and suffered such severe cuts and bruises that he remained in the hospital for 2½ weeks. The beachball-sized hematoma across his buttocks was painful enough, but doctor's efforts to remove bits of gravel and asphalt from it when he was brought into the emergency room that night created outright agony. Painkillers and blood thinners caused the 5'11", 230-pounder out of Penn State to shrink. That would further hamper his battle against LeShon Johnson, who was coming back after non-Hodgkin's Lymphoma that cost him the previous season, and respective second and fourth-round rookies, Joe Montgomery and Sean Bennett.

When camp opened a couple of weeks after his hospital release, the Giants considered putting him on the non-football injury list. But with his hematoma now the size of a small grapefruit, Brown was allowed to wait it out. They did send him back to the hospital overnight on August 6 to have further blood drained out of the bruise, but he returned to take his first real hits on August 24. He then played minimally against the New York Jets that Saturday in what he called his "second most important preseason game" next to the first exhibition of his rookie season in Houston. "I'm sticking out like a sore thumb," Brown said, anticipating that the numerous veterans who had sweated out two-a-days would be somewhat peeved to see Brown roll in with fresh legs. "I'm getting all excited about a preseason game while the other veterans are tired of them."

Brown made it back for the start of the season, but a knee injury against the New England Patriots in Game 3 cut short his season after two starts and 177 rushing yards of production. He never played again.

Personally Speaking

A lot of players get into a lot of fights for a lot of reasons, most of them because of something that happened on the field. Sometimes even teammates get into it with each other. That happened in 2012 when running back Ahmad Bradshaw smacked Victor Cruz in the helmet after Cruz failed to block for him.

Rarely do teammates rumble outside the emotions of a game or practice. But when one player sticks his nose in another player's business—read that money issues—that's a whole different story. In late March 2002, defensive end Michael Strahan held a protracted contract holdout the year after he recorded an NFL single-season record 22½ sacks. Strahan had come out and stated that if he couldn't satisfactorily renegotiate that final year of his contract, he was done with the Giants after the season. General manager Ernie Accorsi, by the way, had already put a seven-year, $58 million deal on the table that included signing bonuses of $10 million for 2002 and $7 million for 2003, very respectable numbers back then. But Strahan had rejected the deal on the basis that the Giants could cut him after 2002 and deprive him of the second part of the bonus. Running back and good friend Tiki Barber made the mistake of publicly recognizing the value of Accorsi's proposed deal and thus injected himself into the controversy. Voicing his opinion underneath a New York Post headline that screamed "Greediest Giant," Barber blasted Strahan for not putting his team above his own personal finances.

Strahan went crazy. He called his friend and left a calm message that belied his true feelings. When Barber called back, Strahan let him have it. "Mind your damned business!" screamed the defensive end, who at 6'5", 275, stood seven inches and 70 pounds heavier than the 5'11", 205-pound running back. "And let me tell you something! If I ever see you outside or get you alone, I'm going to beat the shit out of you! You better never let me get you alone. I'm going to beat your ass!"

Once best buds, the two didn't look at each other for weeks as acrimonious negotiations continued. Strahan finally settled for a seven-year, $46 million deal. Only after an on-air reconciliation during a preseason game did they mend their fences. Barber admitted he butted in where he wasn't wanted. Strahan accepted his apology. The two continued on good terms until Barber's retirement after the 2006 season.

The Comeback Man

No Giant ever had as many comebacks from injury as Ike Hilliard. In the eight seasons after the team made him its first-round draft pick in 1997, it seemed that only Hilliard's nose escaped unbroken. Every other bone? Snap, crackle, pop.

There to take on hard-charging safeties, Hilliard went over the middle of the field without fear, which became a major reason for his litany of injuries, including a broken neck in his rookie year, various toe and leg breaks, and a dislocated shoulder and associated problems that came as a result of one particular shot in a 17–3 loss in Philadelphia on October 28, 2002.

Eagles safety Brian Dawkins, one of history's hardest-hitting defensive backs, administered it in the third quarter as Kerry Collins' overthrown pass on second-and-14 fell incomplete deep in Eagles territory. More worried about fielding the ball than meeting the charging Dawkins, Hilliard had laid out for it in typical fashion. The safety led with his head and slammed it into him late, drawing an unnecessary roughness flag but not an ejection.

Both players lay on the ground for several minutes. Hilliard got up first and walked off the field with what would later be determined as a season-ending dislocation of the right shoulder that tore both the labrum and the pectoral muscle. Dawkins suffered a sprained neck that kept him sidelined two games.

Several years later Dawkins noted that hit as the hardest one he ever delivered. "Ike, definitely," Dawkins said. "I knocked myself out on that one. [It] took me two weeks to recover from it."

In keeping with Hilliard's ultra-competitive character, he never called the hit dirty. Though Fassel questioned why Dawkins was not ejected, Hilliard saw it as simply a tough-minded play, a play that continues as a daily reminder of Dawkins' aggressiveness. "My shoulder still isn't happy based on that one," Hilliard said well after his 2008 retirement from the Tampa Bay Buccaneers, where he spent the final four seasons of a 546-catch, 6,397-yard, 35-touchdown career.

Reporters speculated that Dawkins' hit might end Hilliard's career. But they had forgotten how Hilliard returned after two games in 2000 from a helmet-to-chest leveling by Detroit's Kurt Schulz. That one sent him to the hospital with a bruised lung and bruised sternum and, as Hilliard later revealed, potentially life-threatening internal bleeding into his chest, which doctors had to work fast to close off.

Few players have possessed the sort of resilience that enabled Hilliard to continue such a long and productive career while amassing a never-ending list of injuries. He was nothing short of remarkable. Hilliard had no regrets about his daredevil style. "Maybe I didn't know what the hell I was doing out there," he said. "But you know what? I feel good actually. I made it out upright, which is the key. It's an unforgiving game. Everyone plays hurt. I took my share of bumps and bruises, but I was blessed enough to come away and feel okay."

Tough as a G-Shock Watch

Before Shockey drove the powers-that-be crazy with his on and off-field behavior, Accorsi and Fassel couldn't get enough of him. They were downright frothing for him during the run-up to the 2002 draft. It wasn't surprising, therefore, that the affable GM sent a fourth-round pick to the Tennessee Titans in order to move up one spot from the No. 15 position to grab the tight end out of Miami.

The fact that the Giants wanted Shockey became the worst-kept secret of that draft. Fassel all but let the cat out of the bag at a draft-week press conference, telling the New York media that he wanted a tight end, and the best one available was going to be Shockey.

The love affair started earlier than that, however. It essentially began when Accorsi met with Shockey in his hometown of Ada, Oklahoma, for a usual background check. Shockey ran him around town, stopping at Ada High to inspect his transcripts and even the local constabulary to look into a rumored firearms arrest during his senior year. The police had no record of it. As it turned out, Shockey and a group of friends had been arrested and tossed into jail for a few hours on possession of firearms and being under the influence, but charges were never filed. Shockey had paid $200 to have the record expunged.

After their time at the high school, Shockey took his potential future employer to Bob's Barbeque, the place where he assured Accorsi would find the best barbeque in the country. As Shockey downed a double portion— Accorsi had a single portion he claimed was so filling that he couldn't eat for three days after—the general manager impressed the kid with his knowledge of sports.

He wowed Shockey with the story of Ada native Jerry Walker, the old Orioles bonus baby of the 1950s, who became the youngest pitcher ever to start and win an All-Star Game. Walker, Accorsi said, blew his arm out at 18 when manager Paul Richards allowed him to pitch a complete-game, 16-inning shutout.

Accorsi basically told Shockey they would draft him if he was available, and the tight end remained one of his favorites even as Shockey outraged Fassel, embarrassed the organization, and tormented Eli Manning with his comments and on-field gesticulations when the ball didn't come his way. "Jeremy says things I wish he wouldn't, like the word 'out-coached,'" Accorsi told author Tom Callahan in 2007. "And he does things I wish he wouldn't, like throwing his arms up in dismay like when Manning missed him with passes. [Johnny] Unitas would have bounced the next pass off the back of his helmet, and the one after that off the front. But he's just a good-hearted kid from Ada, Oklahoma."

For all the things Shockey was—loud-mouthed, opinionated, combative—there was one thing he was not—afraid. The same swagger that enticed the Giants to pick the tight end out of Miami in the first round in 2002 was what created sometimes mixed results during his Giants career. He loved physical contact. Even more than that, he loved offering said physical contact to players he thought had understated his importance to the team.

Players like the Indianapolis Colts' David Gibson. The Wednesday before their December 22 game in Shockey's rookie season, Gibson made the mistake of saying the young tight end was "just another player" and wasn't nearly as good as Kansas City Chiefs great Tony Gonzalez.

In the long view, Gibson was right. Gonzalez was well on his way to becoming a surefire, first-ballot Hall of Famer, and Shockey's career eventually imploded. But on that gameday, Shockey would make as great an impact on Gibson as Gonzo ever did on a player.

Shockey took a screen on second-and-16 in the first quarter and progressed 25 yards down the field with it right to where Gibson awaited him at the Colts 25. As Gibson broke down to make the tackle, Shockey lowered his shoulder and—rather than elude him—headed right for him. Shockey trampled him, leaving Gibson looking curiously like an elephant hunter-turned victim on the Serengeti, and continued on for another 11 yards before a swarm dragged him down.

The Giants won that game 44–27, and Shockey's seven catches for 116 yards helped his playoff-bound team improve to 9–6. Shockey, though, was less worried about the postseason than getting back at Gibson. "I wanted to kill the dude," Shockey said. "I saw him and I ran right over him. I love proving people wrong."

But the same fire that proved Gibson's undoing got Shockey an earful from Fassel in the postseason. In the practice week before their wild-card game at Candlestick Park, San Francisco 49ers linebacker Julian Peterson had commented ill about the young man's propensity to lose his head. "He'll get frustrated and then blow a couple of plays," Peterson said.

Like Gibson, Peterson wasn't wrong. Composure and poise were about as appealing to Shockey as vegetables to a toddler. They were never functional parts of the tight end's game. Shockey was never much into self-realization either, so he took Peterson's appraisal as a tremendous insult. And insults must be paid back. Early in the second quarter, Shockey caught a pass from Collins. After knocking over safety Zack Bronson, he needed only to veer right to beat the slower Peterson for a clear path to the end zone. Instead he decided to run through him.

Or not. Peterson, far sturdier than Gibson or any other defensive back, took the hit in a huge collision, stood fast, and dragged him down at the 1. Though Shockey caught a 2-yard touchdown pass two plays later, Fassel let him have it on the sidelines. But he remained unrepentant. "Anyone who's ever done anything bad to me, anything that ever went wrong, I try to take it out on somebody—every game," Shockey said. "I take everything personally. A guy beat me up five years ago? I'll find his ass. I'll get him back."

Snap Goes the Seubert

In a 10-year Giants career that started in 2001 as an undrafted guard out of Western Illinois, Rich Seubert always kept things loose around the locker room. Whether it was Seubert pulling the old dye-in-the-socks trick on Manning or Shaun O'Hara throwing a defrosted supermarket chicken in the guard's locker to allow it to, uh, ferment, Seubert was on both sides of the pranking.

Even the media got into the act. One day at the Giants' University at Albany training camp, Seubert playfully peeled out of the cafeteria parking area in his truck, spewing gravel at reporters awaiting interviews and, purely by accident, a college-aged female public relations intern. A few of the reporters convinced her the next day to appear wearing a gauze patch over her eye. As Seubert emerged from lunch, she approached him, and the media gathered around in time to watch the guard's face drop in despair. Nearly in tears, he took the young lady aside and began a profuse apology. When she finally revealed the ruse and explained she was innocently taken in by the evil media, he turned to the real offenders, smiled, and said, "Okay. Good job. Don't worry. I'll get you...someday." By all accounts that day never came.

Seubert spent the rest of his career concentrating his efforts on making his teammates' lives miserable.

That was all fun and games. What brought Seubert true organization-wide respect involved something far more serious. If his teammates recognized anything about Seubert, it was that a lion's heart beat inside his rib cage. The undrafted free agent came back from not one—but two—potentially devastating injuries. And he has the battle scars to prove it.

The worst occurred right in front of the home crowd on October 19, 2003 against Philadelphia. With 1:22 before halftime, tight end Marcellus Rivers pushed Eagles defensive end N.D. Kalu into Seubert while the guard blocked defensive tackle Corey Simon. Kalu fell onto the back of Seubert's right leg, breaking the tibia, fibula, and ankle in a grisly moment reminiscent of Lawrence Taylor's snapping of Joe Theismann's leg on national television. "They didn't just break. They exploded," Seubert said.

Trainer Ronnie Barnes called it the worst series of breaks he had ever seen.

With more than a dozen screws and several plates, surgeons pieced together the shattered bones in the first of five operations. The work area was so big that they couldn't cover the hole completely without using skin grafts that eventually left Seubert with an ugly purple scar. The grafts, though, didn't take right away. Seubert remained in the hospital for three weeks, waiting for the covering to mend. The 300-pound guard lost 30 pounds while on his back and then spent the next six months on injured reserve.

It took a stay on the physically unable to perform list for the entire 2004 season to recover from that one, but Seubert did come back. Not only did he return, but he also eventually won back his starting spot after working his way back into games as a jumbo tight end. He played in four games in 2005 and in his only start at left guard helped Barber rush for a then-franchise record 220 yards against the Chiefs. He played in 14 games with three starts in 2006 and then permanently moved in again at left guard in 2007 to start all 16 games and the Super Bowl postseason run.

His career hit a high point in 2010 as he switched seamlessly in 16 starts between guard and center, filling in for other injured players. That earned him

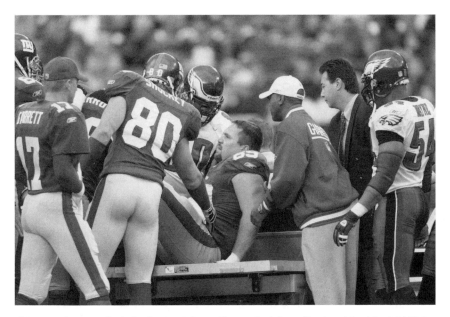

Offensive lineman Rich Seubert is taken off on a stretcher after breaking his right tibia, fibula, and ankle during an October 19, 2003 game against the Philadelphia Eagles, but Seubert would make an amazing comeback.

a verbal nod from GM Jerry Reese, who called him the team's MVP. But a torn patellar tendon and medial collateral ligament, necessitating his second major lower body operation—he also had his shoulder operated on early in his career—proved too much for him to overcome. Tom Coughlin cut him and O'Hara in July of 2011, hailing both as "two unique, highly competitive personalities who were superior in the locker room. Rich has the ability to stir it up, and Shaun has a great ability to counter Rich." Coughlin went on to call them "two of the most competitive, tough, and efficient players" he'd ever been around. "They both will be missed around here," he said.

Seubert's injuries eventually led him from cold New Jersey to San Luis Obispo, California, where the area's year-round warmth affords his battered, aching body more comfort. "My body needs a rest," Seubert said. "I was always one of those guys who knew the risks and rewards of the game. I know that 20 years from now or two weeks from now, I'm not going to be in the best shape of my life. But I wouldn't trade my career for anything in the world."

The Blows of Willie Joe

William Joseph made few plays of note from the time he arrived as a first-round draft pick in 2003 to his departure after the 2007 season. He said even less. All but mute around the Giants locker room, especially when the press was around, the 6'5", 310-pound defensive tackle did announce himself with two memorable hits, both of which knocked potential Hall of Fame quarterbacks silly.

His most stunning came October 3, 2004 at Lambeau Field. Charging through the middle in the third quarter of the 14–7 win, Joseph put Packers quarterback Brett Favre on his head. Favre wobbled to the sidelines as rarely used backup Doug Pederson came out to take over the controls. To the ecstatic cheers of the Lambeau crowd, Favre charged off the sideline two plays later on fourth-and-5, pointed at Pederson, and told him to get the heck out of the game. He then floated a 28-yard touchdown pass to Javon Walker for the Packers' only score that day. "I wasn't surprised he came back in and threw a touchdown pass like that," Strahan said.

The concussed Favre was, however. He didn't remember throwing the pass or that the Green Bay medical staff had declined to give him clearance to return to the game.

Kurt Warner, the St. Louis Rams quarterback who orchestrated "The Greatest Show On Turf" during the late 1990s and early 2000s, was Joseph's teammate that day. But the year before, Joseph lowered the boom on the then-Ram in the first quarter of a 23–13 Giants Stadium win on September 7 and ruined his entire afternoon. Joseph smashed the great passer as Warner stepped to the right in the end zone to elude the rush of defensive lineman Kenny Holmes, causing a fumble. Holmes jumped on it for a touchdown.

Warner finished the day with 342 passing yards but was never really the same after that hit. The rest of the defense slammed him a dozen times and caused him to cough up six fumbles. Warner suffered nausea and a bad headache after a 34-of-54 outing and spent the night in the hospital as doctors took a CT scan.

Rams coach Mike Martz traced his issues back to the hit administered by the man nicknamed "Willie Joe." "I didn't know about it until the third quarter," Martz said. "He just wasn't himself. He looked confused when you gave him a play, and I shouldn't have played him. I regret playing him."

Joseph's highlight reel basically ended after those two hits. A season-ending injury in 2007 led to his departure from the Giants and a two-year career with the Oakland Raiders. In typical fashion he left without comment. Nor was he particularly garrulous on August 31, 2012 when he pleaded guilty to one count of theft of government money and one count of aggravated identity theft for his part in an identity theft tax refund fraud scheme. He was sentenced to two years in prison and three years of supervised release. Uncle Sam had leveled Willie Joe a major hit of his own.

Kiwi Lets Go

Had Mathias Kiwanuka turned into less of a player, his 2006 game in Tennessee would have contained his career-defining moment. And it wouldn't have been a good one.

Bad enough the Giants had made all sorts of mistakes against the Titans. Manning had thrown two interceptions to Adam "Pacman" Jones, and the Titans were in the process of coming back from a 21-point, fourth-quarter deficit. The Giants play calling had been questionable at best. And yet they still led 21–14 with 2:44 remaining.

All the rookie first-round pick had to do was to complete his one successful rush on mobile quarterback Vince Young on fourth-and-10 from the Tennessee 24, walk off the field, and let Manning kneel out the rest of the time. It all started perfectly. Kiwanuka, a defensive end, came right through the Titans' right side. He buried his helmet right in Young's chest as he pushed the quarterback five yards back. And then he inexplicably let go.

One of the biggest catastrophes in Giants history followed, which is saying a lot about a franchise that turned the words "Joe Pisarcik" into a league-wide punch line back in 1978. One of the league's new breed of running quarterbacks, Young almost couldn't believe his good fortune. He took off and didn't stop until he was forced out of bounds 19 yards and a first down later.

The 4–7 Titans had new life, and Young made use of it. Roydell Williams caught his pass for 18 yards, and then Young scrambled another 16 yards to the Giants 21. A 7-yard throw to the 14 set up his tying touchdown pass to Brandon Jones, who had broken free from cornerback Frank Walker's coverage.

Manning's second interception to Jones followed, a horrible mistake considering the quarterback could have run the ball, killed the remainder of regulation, and taken his chances in overtime. Instead, Young hit two passes, and Rob Bironas put through a 49-yard field goal with six seconds left to win it.

In a horrific collapse, the Giants had given up 24 points in just under 13 minutes.

It was an epic fail by the Boston College product whom Accorsi couldn't resist in the first round. Despite a well-stocked pass rush featuring Strahan, Justin Tuck, and Osi Umenyiora, Accorsi found the 6'5", 267-pound Kiwanuka irresistible. "Pass rushers are like pitchers," Accorsi proclaimed on draft day. "You can never have too many of them."

Accorsi's words turned prophetic when Umenyiora went down for five games with a hip flexor injury. Kiwanuka took over as starter and did a commendable job. That commenced Kiwanuka's career in earnest, one that would see him become the most versatile of defenders. He jumped between defensive end and linebacker over the next five seasons, reaching the point where he would start games standing at strong-side linebacker and then put his hand on the ground in a defensive end alignment on passing downs.

But on November 26, 2006, he was an embarrassed, shaken rookie who had reacted poorly in the wake of a roughing-the-passer penalty a few weeks earlier. "I had my head down, buried in his chest. I thought he was throwing the ball," Kiwanuka said. "I thought he went into his passing motion. If I drive him in at that point, I thought it was going to be a 15-yard penalty. Obviously, I made a mistake that cost us a game."

Coughlin went wild on the sideline. Aside from what was believed to be a tenuous hold on his job, the head man had just listened to defensive coordinator Tim Lewis shout through his headphones, "We've got him! He's down! The game's over!" only to look up and see Young rushing up to midfield.

From the opposite sideline, even Titans linebacker Keith Bulluck sympathized with the rookie. The league had just put new emphasis on the rules regarding quarterback safety, and taking one down hard carried definite risks for a defender. "That's where a lot of silly rules in the NFL come into play," Bulluck said. "As a defensive player, I'd take the penalty over letting a quarterback go and scramble. I guess he felt he had him in the grasp, and he felt Vince struggle, make a throwing motion, and he let him go."

Virtually every team in the league showed that play in their defensive meetings the next week with the following directive: Don't throw the quarterback to the ground, but squeeze him, hold him, do whatever is necessary to keep him in one place until the whistle blows.

Kiwanuka took the message to heart. "I can tell you," he said, "if I'm put in the same situation again, I won't make that mistake again."

Coughlin's Biggest Hit

Everyone knows Coughlin's reputation as a coach who is tough on his players. Turns out he's one tough hombre, too.

D.J. Ware, a 6'0", 225-pound backup running back, crashed into the coach after New York Jets linebacker Aaron Maybin pushed him out of bounds on the Giants 42 during the fourth quarter of the Giants' 29–14 must-win victory in December 2011. Coughlin didn't go down, but his semi-split caused a considerable amount of pain. Equipment director Joe Skiba and others helped him to the bench. He stayed in the game, spending only two plays on the bench while the trainers looked him over. Unable to see the field, he got up and resumed his usual position on the sideline with no further incident.

Coughlin found out later that the hamstring in his right leg had torn clean off the bone.

He found little sympathy among the players who heard him preach all season, "No toughness, no championship." Aside from walking gingerly for the next few weeks, he didn't let the injury get in the way of his coaching. He remained on the sidelines instead of taking a safer position in the upstairs coaching box.

The Giants did receive one benefit from the injury. Maybin was flagged for a 15-yard unnecessary roughness call on the hit out of bounds. "As John Mara said, 'Too bad you got hurt, but we got the 15 yards,'" Coughlin said.

CHAPTER 9

DRAFT BUSTS, FREE AGENT MISSES, AND CAST-OFFS

Another Bulldog Back

Herschel Walker proved in 1995 that physical specimens don't necessarily translate to on-field success. Walker, formerly an all-world running back at Georgia and for three years after that with the New Jersey Generals of the USFL, came for his only season in the Meadowlands as a 33-year-old free agent. He had had good success with the Dallas Cowboys starting in 1986 and later with the Philadelphia Eagles, and the Giants believed he still had plenty left in the tank when they signed him to complement running back Rodney Hampton and pump up a sagging kick return game.

Walker certainly looked the part. Rock solid, he wowed the coaches and the Fairleigh Dickinson-Madison crowd during the 40-yard dashes on the first day of training camp. An incredibly gifted athlete, Walker eschewed weightlifting, doing thousands of push-ups and sit-ups instead. His resume included stints as a world-class sprinter and Olympic bobsledder.

The Giants had major plans for him, too. They were going to use him in the backfield in various manners—paired with Hampton in a two-back set behind Dave Brown and as a one-back, wing-back. Whether pounding up the middle or slipping out for passes, the Heisman Trophy winner's presence was going to confuse the daylights out of defenses.

Hampton's condition made Walker even more attractive. The prevailing opinion among the staff was that Hampton was an old 26. Ever since he came out of Georgia as an underclassman, his knees were a problem. More recently he had taken two months to get over a bruised kidney suffered during a physically debilitating, 1,075-yard, six-touchdown season in 1994. The tread was wearing thin to the point where the raw speed Hampton—a Georgia Bulldog five years after Walker left—had shown since his rookie season of 1990 was supposedly long gone.

And so Walker wouldn't start, but he'd become Hampton's perfect complement—at least in theory. On kickoffs he would make everyone forget the Giants' former return whiz, David Meggett, who went to the New England Patriots in free agency after agent Tony Agnone reneged on a promise to give general manager George Young the final chance to re-sign him.

Things didn't quite work out that way for Walker. He never lived up to his three-year, $4.8 million contract mainly because of how strong Hampton came back. Almost from the start of the regular season, Walker became an afterthought. Even after Hampton suffered a broken thumb in early October and returned a week later at the cost of his usual sure-handedness, the featured back overshadowed the aging veteran.

Walker, whose limited blocking skills also made him ineffective as a third-down back, finished the season with 31 rushes for 126 yards, 31 catches for 234 yards and a touchdown, and 41 kickoff returns for an unspectacular 21.5-yard average.

Hampton, meanwhile, put together the last of his five straight 1,000-yard seasons, finishing with 1,182 yards on 306 attempts and 10 rushing touchdowns. The Giants released Walker at season's end. He spent the last two years of his career returning kickoffs for the Cowboys.

In Reeves' Doghouse

Running back Tyrone Wheatley defined the word "controversial" from the moment he started his four-year Giants career as a first-round draft pick in 1995. Dan Reeves wanted Colorado's Rashaan Salaam, but Young was intent on picking Wheatley, who had had a sturdy career at Michigan. So the Giants' supposed featured back of the future started a step back in Reeves' mind, a fact borne out when the former Denver Broncos coach led off his draft-day press conference proclaiming the Giants as "the most argumentative" organization with which he'd ever been associated.

If Wheatley had even the slightest grasp on reality, his troubles might have started and ended right there. He might have gone on to prove Reeves wrong, earn his love and respect, and carve out a wonderful career. That wasn't Wheatley, though. He never helped his own cause. He was considered a tad strange by NFL standards. In an era well before Michael Vick brought the evils of dogfighting into the public consciousness, Wheatley owned three pit bulls and kept pictures of them in his locker. He fielded several neighborhood complaints about the dangerous environment the dogs created by tunneling under his fence and wandering through the community at large. Though he never openly admitted to fighting them, it was suspected.

A first-round draft pick in 1995, Tyrone Wheatley lacked the discipline to fulfill his potential for the Giants.

In later years he said he deplored the practice of pit bull fighting and had never put the dogs in harm's way. He said he never raised his dogs to be violent. Yet letters to commissioner Roger Goodell from the Humane Society of the United States and People for the Ethical Treatment of Animals (PETA) regarding the 2007 investigation into Vick's dogfighting activities linked Wheatley along with Nate Newton and LeShon Johnson to the illegal sport. The writers used a 2001 interview in *Sports Illustrated* in which Wheatley likened his own personality to that of a fighting dog. *SI* quoted him calling the sport "motivational" and "inspirational." Wheatley later clarified his statement, but he often talked about his dogs and the world of dogfighting in the Giants locker room.

What gnawed at Reeves—and later Jim Fassel—was Wheatley's football attitude. As a rookie he bucked the veterans' traditional hazing, refusing to sing at training camp and exhibiting a lax attitude in other rookie duties. He immediately got on Reeves' bad side his first day of training camp—after reporting 17 days late—by pulling a gluteal muscle during his conditioning run. (Reeves certainly would agree he was a pain the butt.) Always struggling to make the 233-pound weight the Giants demanded of him, Wheatley eventually complained about a double standard. "Other guys bust weight every week and they get off with nothing," Wheatley said. "But let me bring the wrong doughnuts for breakfast on Saturday and oh, boy."

The rocky relationship exploded on December 9, 1996, an otherwise dreary Monday following a 17–7 win in Miami during Reeves' final 6–10 campaign. Wheatley had carried 13 times for 59 yards but also had overslept on Saturday, missed the 8 AM walkthrough, and barely made the 10:30 AM charter to Miami.

A simple question set Reeves off. A reporter asked, "So, Dan, how's Tyrone doing?"

"If Tyrone starts becoming disciplined and you can count on him for the little things, then you can count on him for the big things," Reeves said. "Being on time, being where you're supposed to be, doing what you're supposed to be doing, he's getting better, but he's still got a ways to go."

Wheatley had drawn $10,000 in fines that year, a number that included missed meetings, failure to make weight, and a $5,000 league levy for kicking a Detroit Lions player. And that paled in comparison to his rookie season the year before when he was the team's most fined player. Wheatley, though, was unrepentant. He had his own world view, and it never quite jived with the team-first, all-in attitude of the NFL. "This is almost like the military," Wheatley said. "Only thing about it, I'm not killing anybody. And it's got nothing to do with money. They're paying me $1 million to play ball. We can go back to the days of guys being high, guys coming in drunk, failing drug tests. When they come and show up on Sunday and play ball, they play ball."

The disciplined Reeves was gone after that season, but even a switch to the more laid-back Fassel couldn't save Wheatley. Tired of the back's lax work ethic, Fassel cut him loose after five games of the 1998 season. He never rushed for more than the 583 yards and four touchdowns he recorded in Fassel's first season of 1997. A change of scenery with the Oakland Raiders, though, did him some good as he rushed for 936 and 1,046 yards, respectively, during the first two of his six seasons in the Silver and Black.

The Blind Side

Believe it or not, Cedric Jones is as much responsible for turning Michael Strahan into a Hall of Fame-quality player as anyone in the Giants organization. Yup, we're talking about Jones, the Oklahoma defensive end and school-record holder for career sacks, whom the Giants drafted fifth overall in 1996. This is the same guy ESPN once ranked among the 100 worst picks in the entire history of the league.

Jones turned out to be something less than his scouting report appraisals as "the most complete defensive player in the draft." Unbeknownst to the Giants, a team that had more than its share of busted picks over the years, Jones was blind in his right eye. That meant he couldn't see the ball off to the right unless he turned his head all the way around, which is a less than desirable way to start a play when you're facing a 300-pound tackle looking to block you into next week. That shortcoming restricted him to the right side of the defensive line—typically the weak side. And that's where Strahan happened to play the first three years of his career. Drafting Jones created a positional logjam—especially after the Giants found out about his condition.

So what does a coach do when confronted with overcrowding? Shuffle the pieces.

That's exactly what Dan Reeves did a week into camp. He put Strahan on the left side, where he would constantly confront a double team from the tight end and tackle and be forced to play the run and rush the passer with equal proficiency. Strahan was none too happy. "Of course I was upset," said Strahan when Reeves and defensive coordinator Mike Nolan first approached their 1995 sack leader about the switch. "That first day I wasn't going to do it. Then I went back to my room and talked to some people and I said, 'This is what I've got to do if I want to play.'"

Sometimes the worst-tasting medicine is the best. Strahan eventually asked Reeves to leave him planted there so he could better learn the nuances of the spot without worrying about right end. Reeves gave him his wish, and Strahan became a premier run stopper *and* pass rusher, eventually setting the single-season sack record with 22½ in 2001.

As for Jones, he lasted five seasons and collected all of 15 career sacks. He found himself in Reeves' doghouse almost immediately when he reported to camp a week late—with a pulled hamstring. That continued a frustrating trend for Giants first-round draft choices. The Giants' 1994 first rounder, wide receiver Thomas Lewis, had missed 11 days with a hamstring injury, following a six-day contract holdout. The 1995 first rounder, running back Tyrone Wheatley, arrived 17 days late and then pulled a gluteal muscle during his conditioning test.

The Dumbest Smart Guy

To envision Rob Zatechka as a practicing anesthesiologist in Omaha, Nebraska, isn't hard at all. In addition to his exploits as a University of Nebraska guard that were impressive enough to entice the Giants to draft him in the fourth round in 1995, he won the Draddy Award in 1994 as the top scholar-athlete in college football.

The 6'4", 320-pound Zatechka had successfully double-majored in the biological sciences, earned a 4.0 cumulative grade point average, and become a Rhodes Scholar finalist. Those things don't happen to dummies. Zatechka was very smart. And strong. Regarded as one of the most powerful players in the NFL, Zatechka was a weight room monster capable of bench-pressing 500 pounds. The only thing he couldn't do, apparently, was play football—at least on the NFL leavel.

Zatechka started just nine games—all because of injuries to starters—in his three seasons. Reeves' and Fassel's assistants constantly implored him to recognize defensive schemes faster, react quicker, and move more aggressively. But Zatechka only could plod along. He was no football valedictorian. "Dumbest smart guy I ever met," Fassel's offensive line coach John Matzko once lamented.

Zatechka's career wasn't a total waste, however. He left youngsters one piece of advice during his time in football. "Do everything," he said. "Anybody can get straight As if they just sit in their room and study. Go out and do everything. Make yourself well-rounded."

Zatechka took his own advice. He used his football salary and the thousands he received from the many scholarship awards he won at Nebraska to put himself through medical school at the University of Nebraska. He completed med school in 2000 before serving his residency at the same facility.

Keeping Up with Jones

Dhani Jones was a different kind of breed. Starting with his sixth-round selection in 2000, the 6'1", 236-pound linebacker out of Michigan earned a reputation as a solid on-field defender and a rather ethereal personality off of it. In fact he might have been the oddest fellow the Giants ever employed. It wasn't flakiness. Well-bred and well-read, Jones was a Jack Kerouac type: restless, easily bored, always searching for the next new experience.

Born to an anesthesiologist mother and a retired Navy commander father, he had a sharp, inquisitive mind and loved to use it to engage in extended debates with whomever might be standing in front of him. Strahan recalled that teammates limited Jones to two inquiries during team meetings because if they didn't, "he'd ask a question every two seconds."

His musical tastes covered a wide range, though he was especially partial to classical and jazz. To relax he'd hire a Juilliard student to play the Steinway piano that served as his living room's centerpiece. He once guest conducted the Philadelphia Pops orchestra. He played the sax and classical piano with great proficiency. Many people do that. Few actually take their saxes into the New York City subway and play for spare change—especially if they're earning a professional football player's dough. He didn't do it for the dimes and quarters. He just liked the acoustics of the tunnels.

Jones traveled the world, including Scotland, Cambodia, the Basque region of Spain, and several African nations. He became the quintessential world's guest, eventually landing his own show on the Travel Channel called *Dhani Tackles the Globe.*

He painted, wrote poetry, and studied religion. He rode to practices on a bike—not some fancy motorcycle but a fixed-gear pedal bike with one gear and no switching. And when he stepped onto the team charter for away games, he generally did so in a silk bow tie, looking more like a Harvard professor than a starting linebacker.

Oh, yes, the linebacker part of it. He spent the 2000 Super Bowl season on injured reserve with an injured knee and served as a backup linebacker and special teams player in 2001. A starting linebacker his last two seasons, he finished up his Giants career with 162 tackles, three sacks, two interceptions, and a fumble recovery.

Jones went into unrestricted free agency and signed with the Eagles, where he became the weak-side starter on their 2004 Super Bowl XXXIX team that lost to the Patriots. After three years there, he migrated to the Cincinnati Bengals, playing there four years until his retirement after the 2010 season.

His offseason preparation was unorthodox, to say the least. "For some players, the offseason means rest and relaxation," Jones wrote in 2011. "A more dedicated player might hire a personal trainer, start a new workout regimen, or change his diet. For me the offseason means playing rugby in London, cricket in Jamaica, and jai alai in the Basque country of Spain. I've had dozens of fights: Muay Thai boxing in Bangkok, Lutte wrestling in Senegal, and Schwingen in Switzerland. I've raced bicycles up the mind-numbingly steep Italian Alps and dragon boats through the canals and quays in Singapore. I've practiced Sambo in Russia and the ancient art of Pradal Serey in Cambodia. I've even climbed most of the way up Mount Everest."

He regarded his full-time job as contradictory. "Football is a sport of paradox," he told *Sports Illustrated* in 2004. "It requires reaction, not reflection. Yet you must use your mind to calculate, to anticipate—to think and not think at the same time."

The Secret Weapon

Fassel was already anxious about Sean Bennett's sprained knee a couple days after he went down while blocking for Tiki Barber on the first play of the 2000 preseason opener. His admonition to the media not to look to outside sources for injury information made the newspapers and radio stations all the more curious about a right knee that cost him seven games as a fourth-round rookie the year before.

Why was the running back from Northwestern such a curiosity? Because he had a unique versatility. At 6'1", 230, Bennett had blazing speed, suiting him well for tailback. But he also had hands that would have made him a good H-back, and a ferocity and tight-end strength that allowed him to bowl over defensive backs. Need to block on third down? He did that, too, willingly and enthusiastically.

So what that Ernie Accorsi had reached all the way to the back of the draft to turn the unknown into a surprise mid-round pick? So what that the kid had wound up as a little-used fullback in the Big Ten in 1998 because Evansville dropped its Division I-AA program after he set seven rushing records there?

He was the goods. And, boy, did Fassel and offensive coordinator Sean Payton have plans for him. They saw Bennett as a secret weapon. They dreamed about downfield mismatches and long plays like the screen pass he turned into a 53-yard touchdown against the Minnesota Vikings in his rookie preseason opener on only his second professional touch. That landed Bennett the starting job in that regular season's opener. Their imaginations soaring, Fassel and Payton had devoted a hefty section of the 2000 playbook to strategies featuring Bennett.

It all went down the drain when Bennett realized the explosiveness that enchanted the staff was gone despite two weeks of rehab. He sought out the doctors. The day before the Giants broke camp in Albany, New York, Bennett went for an MRI. The results devastated Fassel. The pictures showed the MCL was damaged beyond what anyone expected. Bennett was headed for season-ending surgery. A second opinion confirmed the findings.

Bennett missed the whole season. A hamstring injury incurred during rehab the next offseason kept him out of 2001. By the time he returned in 2002, he had become a mere afterthought.

Power Punter

Having bid adieu to Brad Maynard during the offseason, the Giants found themselves in need of a punter in the spring of 2001. The St. Louis Rams' former seventh-round pick of 1999, Rodney Williams, certainly fit the bill—and more—at least at the start of training camp. Blessed with a tremendous leg, Williams wowed the University at Albany crowds with punts that traveled 80 yards in the air. Unfortunately, Williams lacked a certain consistency factor, and for every ooh and aah, there was a groan as he shanked the next one 28 yards.

The highlight of Williams' single season with the Giants came just days after his involvement in what could have been a disastrous car accident. The Tuesday before the Giants beat the New Orleans Saints 21–13 on September 30, a taxi bumped Williams' SUV as he approached the New Jersey Turnpike and sent his Land Rover into a roll. Metal twisting, sparks flying, the car flipped three times. But Williams knew as he climbed out the window that he and his powerful leg had come through the impact unscathed. Credit the seat belt, a safety implement Williams wore only reluctantly.

Actually, it was a certain conversation that led him to buckle up. He had spoken the weekend before to the mother of the Kansas City Chiefs' late, Hall of Fame linebacker Derrick Thomas, who died the year before from a blood clot stemming from a similar accident that left him paralyzed. Thomas hadn't been wearing a seat belt. The message from Thomas' mother apparently got through. "I don't even want to think about what would've happened if I didn't have my seat belt on," Williams said.

Having avoided disaster, Williams booted eight punts for a 46.5-yard average, depriving Jim Haslett's Saints of acres of field position in the predominantly defensive battle. He boomed a 63-yarder and a 58-yarder that dropped and then died at the New Orleans 6.

Williams had banged a franchise-record 90-yarder against Denver in the September 10 opener, breaking Len Younce's 1943 mark by 16 yards. It was the main reason for Williams' season-high, 55.1-yard average over eight punts that game.

He never achieved the kind of consistency that lets punters stick around for long, though. He was down in the mid-30s and low 40s in nine games. Frustrated with his erratic distances and lack of hang time, and obviously dismayed at Williams' admission that he was struggling with a conversion to directional kicking, the Giants released him and picked up Matt Allen after a late training camp tryout. Allen was far from a proven commodity, having been released once by the Seattle Seahawks and twice by the Atlanta Falcons following his career at Troy State.

Williams' time with the Giants marked his only stint on an active NFL roster. Training camp and practice squad appearances with the Rams and Washington Redskins preceded his short career, and similar stints with the Seahawks and Chiefs followed before he headed northward in 2006 for one game with the CFL's Edmonton Eskimos.

Keep Your Motor Runnin'

Frank Ferrara was far from the most talented player on the field during his short but eventful stay with the Giants. But nobody ever questioned his energy. "He's got a motor unlike anyone I've ever seen," Strahan said. "It just goes to show that perseverance and hustle, you can't beat those things. That's what Frankie's all about."

But Ferrara kept that motor revved 24/7—even when the coaches begged him to throw it into neutral. Jim Fassel tossed the Staten Island-bred defensive end out of practice on a semi-regular basis. The 6'3", 280-pound Rhode Island product had real issues obeying the "hands off the quarterback" rule. A player with a ball in his hands and a red shirt on his back could supercharge Ferrara as well as any matador's cape could an angry bull.

"Ferrara! Get out!" Fassel often yelled after his reserve defender dropped yet another of Kerry Collins' backups in 2001 and 2002, his only years on the active roster after two seasons on the practice squad. Ferrara would then head to the locker room. He saw limited action in games but did manage one highlight. It was his first of three career sacks, and it came against none other than the Cowboys Hall of Fame tackle Larry Allen on November 4, 2001.

Ferrara hadn't even sniffed the active list on gameday before that 27–24 win in overtime. He didn't expect to see action either and was surprised when he entered the goal-line defense in the first half for one play. But when starter Keith Hamilton's injury replacement, Ross Kolodziej, went down in the second half, the Giants had little choice but to insert the high-motor Ferrara. Quarterback Ryan Leaf moved the Cowboys into Giants territory after Ron Dayne fumbled at the Dallas 3, but Ferrara beat the 326-pound Allen for a sack that pushed Leaf past midfield.

Ferrara's father was a James Gandolfini body double on the hit HBO series *The Sopranos*, and Ferrara, himself, had done some part-time stunt work when not playing football. Typical of that penchant for entertainment, the newbie went into a dance-crazy frenzy after his big play. "I thought he got rid of the ball," Ferrara said. "I didn't realize I'd sacked him, but when I did, I lost all control." His teammates were less than thrilled with the display. "The guys were yelling, 'This game's not over yet! You'd better wipe that play away right now!'"

Never expecting to see the field again after that first-half shot on the goal line, he had treated himself to a halftime hotdog. "I'm chasing Ryan Leaf and I'm burping sauerkraut," Ferrara said.

The Lambuth Special

Had Ron Dixon lived up to his true potential after Accorsi picked him in the third round of the 2000 draft, he could have become a sleeper. Instead the fast wide receiver from a tiny Tennessee university called Lambuth became one in the most literal of uses. Dixon just couldn't wake up early enough to gain the consistency the coaches demanded.

Fassel fined him repeatedly for missing meetings, missing buses, and missing walkthroughs. He so exasperated a head coach who would rather have cut off his arm than suspend a player that Fassel actually dished out that punishment to Dixon twice. Fassel did so once in 2000, suspending Dixon for arriving late to a walkthrough after he'd already been fined that season for missing a meeting and again in December of 2002 for missing two treatment sessions and a doctor's appointment for a sprained knee that kept him sidelined the rest of that season. Fassel took $22,000 out of his pocket for that one.

He was the only player Fassel ever suspended.

But when Dixon did deign to rise and shine—or at least pick up his phone and call with his whereabouts—he lit up the stadium. Fast and lanky at 6'0", 190, Dixon could outrun anyone before knee problems ended his three-year career. He showcased that speed during the 2000 postseason with a 97-yard touchdown return of David Akers' opening kickoff in the divisional win against the Eagles. Two games later he scored on another 97-yarder to produce the Giants' only points in a 34–7 Super Bowl XXXV blowout loss to the Baltimore Ravens.

Despite becoming the only player to score twice on postseason kickoff returns, Dixon was most famous for a play where he never touched the end zone—76 Lambuth Special. The play was a last-ditch, hook-and-ladder idea that originally called for Ike Hilliard to catch a short pass from Collins and lateral it to Barber, who would then lateral to the trailing Dixon for a touchdown. The play was primarily a chalkboard concept. The Giants repped it in training camp a couple of times but never during the season.

Fassel finally pulled it out in the final seconds of a 24–21 loss on December 30, 2001 in Philadelphia's Veterans Stadium. It didn't quite unfold the way they drew it up in the classroom, but it nearly kept their fading playoff hopes

Ron Dixon outraces kicker Matt Stover while returning a kickoff 97 yards for a touchdown to produce his career highlight and the Giants' only points in a 34–7 Super Bowl XXXV loss to the Baltimore Ravens.

alive. With the ball at the Giants 20, Hilliard was unable to get off the line cleanly, so Collins tossed it to Barber over the middle 14 yards away. Crossing over from the right side, Dixon grabbed Barber's flip at the Giants 40 and took it down the left sideline. But the receiver had to slow up as the defensive backs angled toward him, and safety Damon Moore knocked him out of bounds at the Eagles 6 as the clock hit 0:00. "It would have been a special way to win that game," Collins said afterward.

What would have gone down as a legendary play in a fantastic win went into the books as simply a 74-yard non-scoring pass in the 15th game of a 7–9 season. One year after a Super Bowl appearance, they were out of the playoffs because of two losses to Philadelphia and one to St. Louis, which all came in the final seconds by a total of five points.

Junkin's Snap

For 19 years, Trey Junkin earned a quiet reputation as a dead-on snapper of punt and field goal attempts. In other words, fans wouldn't have known him if they'd run him over with a truck. Just like every other long snapper who ever played, he reveled in his anonymity. But it took just four days and one snap in the 2002 playoffs to turn Junkin's name into the infamous answer to a trivia question: Whose errant snap cost the Giants a wildcard win in San Francisco?

It was hard to blame Junkin. He'd been snapping footballs since he was nine and he was a grizzled 41 when the Giants called him out of retirement four days before their wild-card matchup against the 49ers in Candlestick Park. Had any other team called, he probably would have hung up. But the Giants, he figured, represented a final chance to get the Super Bowl ring that eluded him his entire career.

That dream stayed alive through more than half the game. Had the Giants held on to that 38–14 third-quarter lead, nobody ever would have heard of Junkin, and who knows? Maybe he would have gone back into retirement with that long-sought piece of jewelry. But San Francisco did storm back in alarming style, and by the time Junkin cradled the ball in his hands at the Niners 23 with six seconds to go, the Niners led 39–38.

All Junkin had to do was put it on the hands of the holder, Allen, and let Matt Bryant swing his leg for an eminently makeable 41-field goal, and the Giants would be off to Green Bay for the divisional round. "Just make it a nice, easy snap," one of his new teammates said as he trod out on the soggy field for the third-down try.

It wasn't. The snap went low and left; the ball skipped. Allen could have smothered it and called timeout to fight again on fourth down. He could have heaved it out of bounds immediately to stop the clock. Instead, he lost his composure and unloaded a wobbler to eligible guard Rich Seubert, with whom 49ers defender Chike Okeafor had clearly interfered. No flag came out.

The 49ers had completed one of the greatest, most stunning comebacks of all time, and Junkin went from solid, steady unknown to vilified goat in a blink of an eye.

The irony of it was that Junkin should have had a chance to redeem himself. Commissioner Paul Tagliabue deemed that non-call on Okeafor's interference with Seubert the worst officiating mistake of his tenure. The flag should have gone down, and the Giants should have had an untimed down from even closer to kick the field goal. "It's still kind of amazing," Fassel said years later. "The referee announced over the PA system that 'No. 69 [Seubert] is eligible.' So there were 90,000 people who knew Seubert was eligible. The only one who didn't know it was the back judge. We should have had a re-kick."

That never came, though, and Junkin re-retired in the post-game locker room. "I cost 58 guys a chance to go to the Super Bowl," Junkin said at his locker. "Quite honestly, I screwed up. And there it is. That's it. I'm retired."

A Hero At Last

Matt Bryant finally became a hero in the 2012 playoffs when he kicked a field goal for the Falcons in a 30–28 divisional playoff victory against the Seahawks. It represented the first playoff win for Matt Ryan, coach Mike Smith, and Tony Gonzalez. Coming with just eight seconds left in what would have been a monumental collapse, his kick brought back memories of the less fortunate circumstances of his two-year Giants career from 2002 to 2003.

Bryant had made Fassel's team with little fanfare and less reputation. Already at it for four years with teams in NFL Europe and the Arena League, Bryant was signed two days before the opener against San Francisco because of an injury to Owen Pochman. The balding, funny-looking kicker from Baylor, who hailed from a tiny Texas town called Bridge City, offered great perspective about his signing. "It's been a long and winding road," said Bryant, who had also worked in a pawn shop while pursuing his gridiron calling. "They say it takes a kicker two to three years to really catch on. I'm already on my fourth."

Strahan took to calling him "Sling Blade" because of his slow drawl and stooped, almost bow-legged gait. But that was about as good as it got during an up-and-down career in blue. His most disappointing moment wasn't even his fault, but they were six seconds at San Francisco's Candlestick Park that played over and over in his mind. He never got a chance to attempt the

41-yard field goal that would have staved off the second-worst collapse in playoff history because of Junkin's errant snap. He knew he could have been a hero. "That one was pretty bad," Bryant said. "It seems like so long ago and yet it keeps getting played."

Bryant had kicked the Giants into the playoffs the week before with a 39-yard field goal 5:10 into overtime against the Eagles, but that came after he missed one field goal and clanked an extra point through off an upright. Barber, who fumbled three times during a career-high 203-yard rushing performance, had told Bryant he "owed him one" and sat crying with joy as Bryant put the winner through.

His teammates couldn't blame him for the San Francisco fiasco, but his career never really kicked into high gear until after his Giants release. While playing for New York, Bryant was an unremarkable 37-of-46 on field goals and 47-of-49 on extra points. It was an eye-opening experience for me," Bryant recalled of his Giants years. "Granted, it was my first shot in the NFL, so I was very appreciative of getting my foot in the door. But it was no bed of roses." His 33-yard miss off a perfect hold cost the Giants a 16–14 loss against the first-year expansion Texans in 2002 and earned him Barber's direct ire. "We couldn't hit a freakin' field goal," Barber spat.

Coughlin cut him the first day of the 2004 training camp to clear a roster spot for a draft pick. Bryant would find redemption with the Falcons almost a decade later. The high-pressure kick, coming after a timeout designed to freeze Bryant, automatically became his career highlight. It moved Smith to remark, "I feel like we have two Matty Ices. We got Matty Ice Ryan and Matty Ice Bryant."

J-Load

Jared Lorenzen was a 6'4", 285-pound, left-handed quarterback who had just about as many nicknames as he had pounds. The good-natured kid from Covington, Kentucky, took those names—the Hefty Lefty, J-Load, The Round Mound of Touchdown, The Pillsbury Throw Boy, Lord of the Ring Dings, BBQ (Big Beautiful Quarterback)—in stride.

Lorenzen had his oversized physique since birth. He announced himself on February 14, 1981 at 13 pounds, three ounces, a Kentucky record at the time. And he never quite stopped growing. Lucky for him, though, he kept getting stronger as he packed on the pounds. His arm seemed to be made of the same stuff the military uses to hurl long-range projectiles. On the few occasions he did get the ball as a backup between 2005—when he unseated Jesse "The Bachelor" Palmer—and 2007—his final season when he earned a Super Bowl ring as an inactive third-stringer—he showed he could push a pile of defensive linemen and linebackers on a couple of short-yardage keepers.

The weight didn't stop him from becoming a record-setting passer at Kentucky with 10,354 career yards and 78 touchdowns. The Giants signed him as an undrafted free agent in 2004, but family issues kept him out of football that year. The Giants welcomed him back in '05 on the condition that he lose some weight. He had tipped the scales at Kentucky at 300-plus pounds. The Giants wanted him at 275 tops. Lorenzen made no promises. "I don't know if it'll happen this year," he said. "But eventually it will."

He tried. They set him up with a nutritionist to turn around some bad eating habits. He started consuming a lot of broccoli. For a kid who grew up on fast food, that was kind of like taking medicine every day. "I can't eat late at night anymore, fast food restaurants, all the stuff I lived off of," Lorenzen said in 2005. "But I feel better. I don't have as many back problems. I can run around a little bit better. It's a long-term thing."

Lorenzen never saw much action outside preseason games. A start against the New York Jets in the '06 preseason produced a 7-of-12, 60-yard performance with Lorenzen barely missing rookie tight end Darcy Johnson at the goal line. Against the Baltimore Ravens two weeks earlier, he led the team on a game-winning, fourth-quarter field goal drive.

He won the primary backup spot that year ahead of Tim Hasselbeck, but he saw only one regular season snap when Manning came out to shake off a bruise. He had nine snaps in 2007, going 4-for-8 for 28 yards before he fell back to third-string.

Lorenzen migrated to the Ultimate Indoor Football League, where he played the 2009 season with the Northern Kentucky River Monsters. He eventually became quarterback coach at his old high school, Highlands High in Fort Thomas, Kentucky. At well over 300 pounds, he returned as the River Monsters' quarterback in 2011 and won the league's MVP award. He's now commissioner of the UIFL. Perhaps he earned another nickname: Large and In Charge.

CHAPTER 10
FAREWELLS

Ending It

As the final seconds of the Giants' 1993 NFC semifinal playoff loss to the 49ers ticked down, Lawrence Taylor approached referee Bernie Kukar and asked him for his yellow penalty flag. The clock then hit zero, ending the 44–3 drubbing. The great L.T. complimented running back Ricky Watters on his five-touchdown day and walked off Candlestick Park's field into the rest of his life. "I'm calling it quits," Taylor said, wearing sunglasses to hide any emotions the Giants' greatest linebacker ever might show. "I've had a great career. I've been to the playoffs and the Super Bowl, and I've done things that haven't been done before. I think I've earned the respect of the players around me."

Getting the flag for his personal collection was simply his last act. "I figured he's thrown it against me enough," Taylor said, "so I wanted it."

Taylor's departure was hardly premature, though most would rightfully say L.T. playing at half speed was as good as most linebackers at full speed. Coming off a torn Achilles tendon that shortened his 1992 season and a hamstring injury that limited him to six sacks—the second lowest total of his career—in 1993, it was time for the soon-to-be 35-year-old. He had spoken to Dan Reeves about it several times over the last weeks of the season, but the discussions went no further for fear of creating a distraction.

He even kept it from his good friend, Phil Simms. "We've gone through a lot of ups and downs," Simms said. "[Taylor] never told me, but we all suspected it."

The magnitude of the playoff loss had nothing to do with Taylor's decision. Whenever the Giants season ended, he was going to retire. As far as Taylor was concerned, he was walking away on top. "You guys know what I can do and can't do," Taylor told the assembled media. "I'm as good as 90 percent of the players in this league. I've put in my time. This is the time I want to leave the game."

The five-year clock on Taylor's Hall of Fame eligibility started at that moment, climaxing in Canton opening its doors to him on the first ballot in 1999, though not without some rigorous debate. His off-field behavior caused huge disagreement among the voting board, but there could be no argument about his playing ability. He retired with 132.5 sacks in a 13-year career, including 9.5 as a rookie, one year before sacks became an official stat. He earned two Super Bowl rings, was voted to the Pro Bowl 10 consecutive times, and compiled a highlight reel that ran about as long as a Cecil B. DeMille epic.

Anxious to turn the page on the remnants of the Bill Parcells era and put his own stamp on the team, Reeves was nevertheless thankful he had a chance to work with one of that era's biggest stars, one whose play was largely responsible for the Giants' win against his Denver Broncos in the 1986 season's Super Bowl. "I just wish I had 12 more years of coaching Lawrence because it's been fun," Reeves said. "I'm just glad the good Lord gave me a year to work with him. All I ever had was bad memories of him from the Super Bowl. I'm glad I have some good memories of him now."

Cutting Phil

Fresh off a 1993 season in which he piloted his squad to the NFC divisional playoff round, the 39-year-old quarterback thought that year's NFL Coach of the Year had summoned him to his office for a friendly, mid-June visit. "I thought he wanted me to autograph some balls for charity or something," Phil Simms said.

Instead, Reeves simply told the 15-year-veteran his services were no longer required. The Giants were going in a new direction. Sensing Simms' troublesome right shoulder made him too much of a question mark to commit $2.5 million of a $34.5 million salary cap to him, Reeves had decided it was time to move on as did general manager George Young. This was the beginning of the new era of free agency and salary caps, and sentimentality over former stars was quickly going the way of the dodo bird. The only concession to past deeds Reeves and Young made was giving Simms the option to retire. The quarterback opted for his release instead, thinking the injury that plagued him throughout the spring would heal well enough to entice some other team to take a chance on him.

While the coach and general manager were acclimating themselves to the newer, colder ways of the NFL, owner Wellington Mara still clung to the old.

Quarterback Phil Simms, a 15-year veteran and Giants franchise pillar, throws a pass against the Miami Dolphins in 1993, his last season. *(AP Images)*

He was totally against the move and he left no uncertainty about his position at the June 14 press conference. Departing from his usual separation of powers policy and inserting his nose squarely into the matter, Mara barged up to the front of the room with a prepared statement. "This is a day of overwhelming sadness for me," said Mara with eyes red and watery from the emotions of the day. Then he laid the whole affair at Young's doorstep, saying he disagreed with the decision but would stand with it.

Mara could have vetoed the move, but "I just thought we've given [Young] this job. It's his responsibility," Mara said years later. "I don't think I should impose my judgment on his. I had a very strong personal distaste for that deal. I felt Simms had done so much for the team and I had great confidence in him that he could do it again."

It was not the first time Mara had ever taken up the cause for his favorite quarterback. A rumor in August of 1992 indicated the Giants were on the verge of trading Simms to the San Diego Chargers. Mara stormed into the press room and left no doubt about its veracity. "I just heard a report that Phil Simms is on his way to San Diego," Mara said. "Let me say this as unequivocally as I can: Phil Simms is not being traded this year, last year, or in the 20th century to San Diego or anywhere else. Period. Okay?"

Mara didn't entertain questions either day. But clearly in 1994, he was distraught over the closing of a glorious era that saw the Giants win two Super Bowls and the beginning of another under Dave Brown and Kent Graham.

Simms, the first big-name cut of the salary cap era, never did find that next quarterback job, though there were some overtures by the Cleveland Browns. He signed with ESPN a few weeks later and started a broadcast career that has made him one of the most prominent football analysts. But on that day, he was not happy. "When the decision was made, I said, 'Oh, my God,'" Simms said. "Afterward when I was driving home I was still kind of shocked, and it was like I didn't know what happened. I can honestly say I was not prepared for it. I was shocked. I did not know this was coming."

Young's Historic Legacy

Of all the many characters the Giants have employed over the years, general manager George Young stood out as one of their most idiosyncratic. When he died at age 71 on December 8, 2001 of Creutzfeldt-Jakob disease, a rare brain malady resembling mad cow disease, he left behind a legacy and style that is still remembered around the executive offices.

Young couched a lot of what he said in historical terms—just as anyone would who taught that subject at Calvert Hall High and City College High in Baltimore. The agreement that brought him to the Giants on commissioner Pete Rozelle's advice, thus settling the franchise-threatening dispute between co-owners Wellington Mara and his nephew, Tim Mara, by giving Young control of the day-to-day personnel operations, was termed "the Accord of 1979." Young frequently quoted Prussian military strategist Carl von Clausewitz. An avid reader of history, he refused to consider any book shorter than 300 pages because he said, "You can't do a subject justice with anything less." He loved reading about the Civil War but never visited the battlefields. "I only taught history. I don't get sentimental over it," he said in his high-pitched voice upon rejecting one particular invite to Manassas, Virginia, the site of the Battle of Bull Run, on one road trip to Washington, D.C. And he had the peculiarity of not caring for Chinese restaurants: "I'll buy you anything you want," he said. "But I don't want to share my food. I want my own plate."

An imposing man who easily topped 300 pounds—he eventually lost 100 of those in his later years when a doctor warned him to either shed pounds or die—he was generally irascible, always educational. He demanded reporters do their homework about the workings of contracts before they called him, and more than one had to withstand an initial bellowing before Young issued some truly useful information. Perceived troublemakers were called "brown stickers." Sons of owners were called "silver spooners."

Always secretive about the contract negotiations he always seemed mired in, he would treat his boss' money like his own, saying, "an owner has the right to make a profit." He viewed player holdouts for exactly what they were. "A holdout is a four-letter word!" he'd bark. "P-L-O-Y!" Heaven forbid one of his holdouts tried to put his dispute on ground higher than dollars and cents. "Anytime they say it's not about the money, it's *always* about the money," Young would growl. Football was "not a game for well-adjusted people."

He called the stretch in every draft where big linemen get taken in quick succession, "the Dance of the Elephants." The various predictive draft publications didn't annoy him, but he refused to give them much attention either. "I don't believe in the Hindu stuff," he'd say. "I don't read tea leaves."

When asked a few years before he stepped down after the 1997 season if he was beginning to feel burned out from the constant haggling with agents, he famously answered, "Burnout is a rich man's disease." He had little patience for labels of honor even in retirement. "We brought in Jim Fassel as a 'quarterback guru,'" said Young's successor Ernie Accorsi. "So we're not throwing the ball well this one year, and he calls me and says, 'When is the guru going to start guru-ing?'"

Political correctness was never part of Young's world. He was a GM, not a mayor. When relating the Italian heritage of his assistant GM, Ernie Accorsi, to others, "[Young] used to say, 'Ernie's more Mediterranean than I am,'" Accorsi said. "I'd say, 'George, you'd better be careful. This is an Italian city, and they know what you're talking about.'"

He loved the idea of non-guaranteed contracts, saying, "There's nothing like the hot breath of competition on the back of a man's neck to drive him to better things." George Young was old school. But his approach worked. He won the NFL Executive of the Year award five times in his 19-year tenure with the Giants. He engineered two Super Bowl championship squads. He brought in Simms and L.T.

At his December 12 funeral mass at Baltimore's Cathedral of Mary Our Queen, 600 mourners gathered to bid Young farewell.

Well's Farewell

On the morning of October 28, 2005, a throng of NFL greats, league executives, ranking clergy, and Giants fans gathered at St. Patrick's Cathedral to cheer the humble Wellington Mara one last time. His eldest child, John, knew exactly how his father would have regarded the proceedings as he began a touching, 15-minute eulogy before the 2,200 that crammed the Manhattan church. "As we made our way over from the funeral home this morning, I couldn't help but think he'd be so embarrassed by all this; the police escort, the stopping of traffic, the bagpipes," John Mara said. "He'd have just shook his head and tried to hide."

Mara had died at his home that Tuesday, October 25, at age 89. His once sturdy body had been worn away by cancer. Now it was Friday, and the worlds of professional football and Roman Catholicism had mobilized in the interim to form an honor guard of immense proportions.

Pomp and circumstances all come as part of the job of being a venerated owner, a man, who with his father, Tim, and brother, Jack, was there on the Giants' ground floor as a nine-year-old in 1925 and quickly rose to the status of an innovative, level-headed, and tough commander of a marquee franchise. When people want to show their appreciation to a man like that, well, it's kind of like trying to stop the tide from flowing

Mara learned that the hard way a couple of years before his death. His wife, Ann, had conspired in 2003 with Frank Gifford, CEO Bob Tisch, and others in the organization to throw a once-in-a-lifetime surprise get-together for him at Tavern on the Green. When that night rolled around, the 87-year-old Mara had a cold and decided he wasn't going anywhere. Ann concocted a story about Gifford's wife, Kathie Lee, being honored, so sniffles and all, Mara went.

He didn't go happily, though. The season opener was scheduled for the following day, and Mara wanted to be fit for the game. "He hasn't spoken to me since we left," Ann told Gifford as the honored couple arrived at 6:40 PM. Mara immediately spotted L.T., then Sam Huff, Andy Robustelli, and Y.A. Tittle. Suddenly it sunk in that this night was about him, not Kathie Lee Gifford. He smiled broadly and joked to the star-studded crowd, "I hope they know I'm leaving early."

The 2005 funeral procession began as the mahogany coffin journeyed up the aisle. Two priests filed out from behind the altar to meet it. Thirty-eights priests and five bishops preceded celebrated Cardinal Edward M. Egan. There are religious figures who haven't been given such illustrious sendoffs. But Mara had a devoted involvement with the church and its charities, a part of his life he kept separate from the football. "I never knew until I played a few years that he believed in the same things I did," said tough and equally devout tight end Mark Bavaro. "He never wore his religion on his sleeve. I always saw him at church before games. When you see the owner there, that's all that matters."

Gifford offered his own eulogy, which was of the appropriate duration to appease Mara: "I have a feeling Wellington's looking down from his celestial skybox saying, 'Keep it short, Frank.'" Gifford spoke of their respective Hall-of-Fame ceremonies where each served as the other's presenter. "As he looked out over the audience, Wellington turned to me and said, 'This is a man that any father would be proud to have as a son,'" Gifford said. "I will never forget that. A few years later, I had a chance to stand in the same place as his presenter and I said, 'This is a man who any son would be proud to have as a father.'"

But it was John who showed, perhaps for the first time, that he had his father's quality as a communicator. He took the parishioners through his childhood. "We had to go to confession before Christmas," John Mara said. "And Dad would always put a note on the refrigerator that said, 'No confession, no Santa.'

"I remember one game years ago when a particular player was having a tough day, and some of us became a little exasperated with him. At one point I yelled out, 'What is he doing out there?' My father put his hand on my shoulder rather firmly and said, 'What he's doing is the best that he can.'"

Mara also recounted the last days. "There were so many lessons my father taught us over the years, maybe none more important than in the last few weeks of his life," John said, his voice breaking. "He never gave up his will to live. He tried so hard to get out of bed and walk. He never complained. The last day before he got out of the hospital when he came to the realization that the doctors couldn't help him anymore, he summoned me to his bedside. He could barely talk. I held his hand. He looked at me, smiled, and said, 'I'll be there when you get there.' It was his way of telling us he'd be okay. He was going to a better place."

John ended with a quote from *Hamlet* taken from a framed column on his father's desk composed by the great *The New York Times* writer Arthur

Daley upon the death of his brother, Jack Mara: "Now cracks a noble heart. Goodnight, sweet prince, and flights of angels sing thee to thy rest."

The one-hour, 45-minute Mass ended as the coffin was escorted out to the strains of "On Eagle's Wings." Players had come from all over the country, including kicker Brad Daluiso from San Diego and Tittle from Texas. Local greats like Simms, Jessie Armstead, Phil McConkey, and Harry Carson and the current squad led by Tiki Barber lined the cathedral steps as the coffin was loaded into a hearse for its trip to Gate of Heaven Cemetery in suburban Valhalla.

Carrying On After Wellington

Life went on after Wellington Mara was buried. There was a game to be played, and even the death of one of the NFL's most beloved owners wouldn't keep the schedule waiting. But if anyone thought moving on was a snap, think again. Football players are creatures of habit and are easily thrown off their game by changes in schedule, switched kickoff times, and fast-moving weather. So imagine what was going through their minds as they took the field against the Washington Redskins on October 30, 2005, five days after star running back Barber and tight end Jeremy Shockey had paid a bed-side visit to the dying owner and two days after an emotion-packed funeral Mass at St. Patrick's Cathedral. "It's hard to figure out what you're going to do or how you're going to react in a situation like we experienced this week," Barber said. "We did what Mr. Mara would have wanted us to do, which was carry on."

Barber said those words after the Giants dispatched the Redskins 36–0, a bravura performance at Giants Stadium that saw the running back have one of his greatest days with 206 rushing yards and a third-quarter touchdown. He and his teammates had no way of knowing then, but they would soon have to overcome another emotional challenge. Diagnosed the year before with a malignant brain tumor, co-owner Bob Tisch died at age 79 two weeks later. After the passing of Tisch, the Giants emerged victorious again amid the grief, beating the Philadelphia Eagles at the Meadowlands 27–17.

But October 30 was all about Wellington Mara, and the Giants left no doubt about their focus and effort. Barber's total represented a career high at the time, which he eclipsed that December with 220 against the Kansas City Chiefs and again with 234 in his final regular season game against the Redskins in 2006.

On this day, though, all the Giants were outstanding. The offense put up 262 yards rushing for an owner who believed strongly in the efficacy of a good ground attack. Barber didn't exactly build his total gradually. On the very first play from scrimmage, Barber took the handoff from Eli Manning around left end and sprinted down the sideline for 57 yards, setting up a first-possession field goal.

Early in the second quarter, Barber again hit the Washington defense in the solar plexus, going for 59 yards and falling just short of the goal line as he was dragged down from behind. Brandon Jacobs finished up the drive two plays later, and the Giants eventually went into halftime up 19–0.

Barber finished his day with a 4-yard touchdown run. Standing in the end zone was Mara's grandson, Tim McDonnell, who—since he was old enough to hold a helmet—spent summers and off-days helping with equipment, fielding punts, and doing odd jobs. Like the other Giants, Barber had come to know and like McDonnell. Barber flipped him the ball. "This one was for the Duke," Barber said, using Mara's nickname.

The scene in the locker room was equally emotional. John Mara, now the team's president and CEO, took his father's traditional place at the locker room door where Wellington would welcome his players back, win or lose. He shook every player's hand. Manning gave the son a game ball, which John Mara accepted teary-eyed. He knew his father would have approved of the way the Giants handled themselves. "If he said it once, he said it a hundred times, 'Run the ball, run the ball, run the ball,'" John said. "That was always his mantra when he came to the stadium. He would have had a big smile on his face."

Team vice president Steve Tisch and treasurer Jonathan Tisch received game balls from Barber and Manning after the Eagles game. But Barber still had one more task left. He spoke at the December 9 memorial service for

Tisch before a packed Avery Fisher Hall at Lincoln Center. After Broadway star and Tisch family friend, Brian Stokes Mitchell, finished his rendition of "The Impossible Dream," opera star Beverly Sills recounted her memories of growing up with Tisch in Brooklyn, a time when she was known as Bubbles, and he was known as Bobby. Barber then ad-libbed a heartfelt speech about his friendship with the late unassuming billionaire. He credited his friend for making "a 29- or 30-year-old black guy from Virginia feel Jewish."

The Giants lost just two more games in the aftermath of the deaths, finishing the season at 11–5 before bowing out 23–0 to the Carolina Panthers in the playoffs. But the fact that they stayed focused during an emotionally turbulent time represented a season's worth of success in itself. "As convoluted as it sounds," Barber said, "it gives us an emotional lift instead of an emotional downer. It gives us inspiration and celebration of what they meant as men to this league and to this game, especially to our team."

Barber Goes Bye-Bye

Hall of Fame coach Bill Parcells often said once a player contemplates retirement, he already has. You couldn't tell that was the case with Barber as he piled up 1,662 yards rushing in 2006. Yet he had announced in mid-October his intention to hang up the cleats at season's end. Tired of taking the weekly physical beatings of practice and games, the drudgery of offseason workout routines that grew more grueling to ward off the degeneration of his body, critical of Tom Coughlin's methods and strategy, and long prepared through internships and offseason gigs to head into the broadcasting business, Barber staged one of the longest good-byes of any player past or present.

The thought actually crept into his mind the year before, but at 30 and ringless, he decided to stick around for one more year to take a shot at a Super Bowl. The Giants instead struggled to an 8–8 record and a first-round playoff exit.

Barber's early retirement proclamation was considered a team-wide distraction, though it never affected him personally. He had eight 100-yard rushing efforts, capping off his regular-season career with a personal-best 234 and three touchdowns against the Redskins at FedEx Field. All the while, fans expressed their ambivalence toward Barber, alternately cheering him and cat-calling him as selfish for leaving the future depth chart bare except for an inexperienced Brandon Jacobs. Even president and CEO John Mara made a last-ditch play to keep him around.

But with his abilities and marbles intact, Barber was determined to end his career on top. He had 137 yards, including a 41-yard gallop that set up a tying field goal in the second quarter, during the 23–20 wild-card loss in Philadelphia and left the field after hugs from rival safety Brian Dawkins and middle linebacker Jeremiah Trotter. "Football is something I've relished for years, going back to when I was 10 years old," Barber said after that game. "And now it's done. There's a sadness that comes with that. There's also a loss I feel. But I'm also excited about life. That tempers the sadness some people might be looking for."

Four days after he scored a Pro Bowl touchdown, NBC introduced him as a correspondent for *The Today Show* and an analyst for *Football Night in America*. Barber, however, lost those gigs amidst on-air gaffes and issues with his personal life. He attempted an NFL comeback in 2011, but no team signed him, proving how tough it can be to say good-bye for good.

The GM's Final Transaction

Throughout a 35-plus-year career, which included stints as a public relations man for the Baltimore Colts, general manager for the Browns, and Giants GM, Ernie Accorsi forged a reputation as a raconteur, historian, and epicurean as well as a keen evaluator of talent. On the day before Accorsi resigned in January of 2007, John Mara forwarded to Accorsi a consent form he had been faxed. It was the same official form NFL teams use when seeking permission to pursue club employees for an open position. The joke served as a fitting epitaph.

It came from one of his less successful draft picks, a skinny punter named Bruce Allen, whom Accorsi had selected for the Colts in 1978, and the kid lasted all of a week. But he rebounded from that disappointment well enough

After more than 30 years in the NFL, Giants general manager and shrewd talent evaluator Ernie Accorsi resigned from his post in January of 2007.

to find a job as a scout and eventually become the general manager of several teams, including with the Tampa Bay Buccaneers at that time.

CONSENT FORM

Club Requesting Consent: Tampa Bay Buccaneers

Employer Club: New York Giants

Employee's Name: Ernie Accorsi

Employee's Current Position: General Manager (motto: "God doesn't want me to be happy.")

Position to be Interviewed For: TBA.

We are looking for a talent evaluator (especially punters), friend, storyteller, NFL historian, Major League Baseball historian, negotiator, advisor, medical translator, scout translator, head coach's confidante, golfer, writer, PR advisor and, most importantly, we want somebody who is loyal to his organization.

Signed: Bruce Allen, General Manager, Tampa Bay Buccaneers.

Permission is Granted:

Permission is Denied: X

Under the X, John Mara wrote: "Sorry, but we do not have anybody here with these qualifications."

A Terrible Way To Bid Adieu

The final game at Giants Stadium on December 27, 2009 was supposed to be a celebration of the past, a time to resurrect the ghosts of the good seasons that produced Super Bowl glory in the fifth stadium in the franchise's history. It was to be a time to look forward to even better days in the $1.7 billion building they would move into across the parking lot the following season.

With a well-played game, the 8–6 squad could also move one step closer to a playoff berth. They couldn't have made up a better setting for a storybook curtain-closer. But that's the problem with those things. Reality often ruins the fairy tales, and things don't always end happily ever after.

Whatever fond memories were supposed to be conjured up against the Panthers that day got plowed into the muck of a 41–9 shellacking. It wasn't just the score either. Panthers running back Jonathan Stewart set a record for rushing yards against a Giants Stadium-era defense with 206.

So much for fairy tales. "It's as low as I've been in a Giants uniform," defensive end Justin Tuck said. "The thing that's hard is they're showing all those highlights of L.T. and Simms and everybody that played there. And you have yourself on a team that was booed off the last game at Giants Stadium. I don't think you're going to get anybody that wants that to happen." Brandon Jacobs was equally despondent. "We disrespected this ground so much," the running back said. "We don't deserve to play in the new spot."

Apparently they didn't deserve to play their season finale anywhere. Now down to an outside chance at the postseason, needing at the least a win against the Vikings in Minnesota, they collapsed 44–7 in an equally embarrassing effort.

One might say they crawled in—rather than burst through the door—of the new stadium. But at least they didn't let down the September 12, 2010 opening day crowd, every one of them now in possession of a personal seat license ranging from $1,000 to $20,000 that allowed them to buy tickets as expensive as $700 per game. The Giants beat the Panthers 31–18 but not before they heard those familiar boos of the previous season's farewell as they went three-and-out on the first two possessions.

CHAPTER 11
INTO THE FUTURE

A Cold Super Bowl

The 8–8 non-playoff record of 2009 that ended a 34-year stay at Giants Stadium did not prove completely fruitless, at least in a league-wide sense. Four months after the Giants finished that season, the NFL awarded history's first outdoor Super Bowl in a cold-weather city to what was then called "the New Meadowlands Stadium."

It didn't come without some convincing. It took four secret ballots among the co-inhabitant Giants' and Jets' fellow owners to turn what started as a long shot proposal into reality. Even as the idea grew in popularity over the weeks leading into the final vote on May 24, 2010, John Mara never truly counted on it happening until all the ballots were counted. "I felt like we were eventually going to win it," Mara said. "But until they tell you that, you never know."

The weather and the prospects of having fans who pay upwards of $1,200 per ticket freeze in the uncovered stadium was the league's main concern. In fact it was the only concern as everything else about the new, state-of-the-art, $1.7 billion structure met the owners' guidelines. And even that one sticking point could have been avoided had the two teams decided to follow common practice and include a retractable roof with the original building plans. That would have cost another $250 million. Given that the vast majority of funds for the new building came from the private sector, using few taxpayer dollars, the roof concept was abandoned.

But the combined forces of Mara/Tisch and Jets owner Woody Johnson had no qualms about disregarding the NFL's minimum 50-degree average temperature requirement for outdoor venues and submitting their bid in December of 2009. The league accepted the bid as a conditional, one-time-only shot to celebrate the new stadium and the history of football in the New York area. "Some of the greatest games in NFL history have been played in cold weather, including our championship game in Green Bay two years ago," Mara said. "So why not the Super Bowl? There is no better place in New York and New Jersey to showcase the premier sporting event in the world."

Former Giants coach Dan Reeves played in Ice Bowl I in Green Bay in 1967 as a Dallas Cowboys halfback and remembered it fondly. "People still talk about what a great game that was," Reeves said. "The weather is something people talk about a lot. It was difficult to play in it, don't get me wrong. But football is an outdoor sport, and I loved to play outdoors. That's the way the game is supposed to be played, and I'd like to see that."

Eventually, the owners agreed with both men. They approved the proposal for the 2014 game just as workers applied the finishing touches to the 82,500-seat stadium.

Always a Coach

As the Giants move forward from the past two decades, they will do it with Tom Coughlin—at least in the short term. But with a coaching lifer like Coughlin, who knows?

At 66 the man who put two Lombardi Trophies in the Timex Performance Center's lobby showcase had no plans of retiring. Even though no coach ever really writes his own ticket, it is quite likely that Coughlin, not management, will make the ultimate decision about when to heed the call of his Jacksonville, Florida, beach house. "The energy's still flowing good," Coughlin said shortly after his squad fell short of the playoffs in its 2012 defense of the Super Bowl XLVI title. "You know what? I'm a football coach. I don't think the way a lot of people think. And certainly I don't think about *here's the next phase of it*. Maybe at some point I'll get the message. But it certainly isn't right now."

Coughlin's sole, forced experience with leisure in 2003 may have been an educational time, but it certainly wasn't a happy time. The Jaguars hadn't fired him because of any coaching deficiencies but because of the contracts he put together while building the Jags into an AFC Central power had put the team in salary cap jail. The team's inability to replace key departures with comparable free-agent talent led to a dip in the on-field results.

So out Coughlin went. He treated the firing as more of a sabbatical than a vacation. Coughlin crisscrossed the country to study several teams. He viewed practices and perused college talent to keep himself up to date for the time he got the next job. It was the coach putting into practice the type-A personality the Giants had come to know during his stint as Bill Parcells' wide receivers coach from 1988 to 1990.

Former offensive line coach Fred Hoaglin saw that quality firsthand. Hoaglin was a laid-back kind of guy, a congenial fellow who enjoyed a good cigar and friendly conversation. One might have been hard-pressed to find polar opposites like that co-existing in the same car. Yet Hoaglin and Coughlin often carpooled together.

On one day when it was Coughlin's turn to drive, a major accident on I-80 snarled traffic so badly that nobody moved for an hour. Hoaglin, in keeping with his personality, got out of the car, lit up, and chatted amicably with other motorists, all of whom had shut down their engines. When the traffic started moving again, Hoaglin returned to the passenger seat and found that Coughlin had never turned the motor off. In fact his hands had never left the wheel!

When reminded of the story, Coughlin had just one addition. "I never took the car out of drive the whole time," he said.

Even president and CEO John Mara was hard-pressed to see a day when Coughlin would voluntarily step down. Terrell Thomas, the hard-hitting cornerback staging a comeback from a third right ACL tear, had hinted shortly after the 2012 season that 2013 could be his coach's final season. Mara scoffed at the thought. "I don't see him going to Florida to play shuffleboard anytime soon," Mara said. "He's still got a lot of fire left in him and he's still a great coach."

As for Coughlin he still had some weekly messages to deliver, inspirational speeches to make, mentally intense practices to run, and rules of discipline and comportment to enforce. "I've got goals. I've got things I want to get done," Coughlin said. "I've got all these things I would still very much like to accomplish and be part of this great New York Giants organization."

A third Super Bowl title would certainly secure a spot in Canton for him. As far as Mara is concerned, it's a matter of time. "Hopefully, he's going to be around for many more years," Mara said.

The Last Word

When John Mara was fielding the barbs about the Giants' irrelevance as a schoolboy, collegian, and young attorney back in the 1960s and

1970s, he often went to bed dreaming about taking part in the big turnaround.

He missed the first part of it; the point where commissioner Pete Rozelle all but insisted the Giants hire George Young as general manager to quell a franchise-threatening feud between Wellington Mara and co-owner/nephew Tim Mara. But he eventually got his wish. Together with Steve Tisch, Mara has sat at the head of the marquee franchise since Wellington's death in 2005 and has tasted two Super Bowl victories. "Yeah, it's been fun," Mara said. "The years where we don't win aren't fun, but for the most part it has been. We've gotten back to a point where our organization is universally respected, and that's something we were always aiming for."

A 20-year record of 172–147–1 with nine postseason berths, three Super Bowl appearances, and two Lombardi Trophies offered plenty of fun for Mara. But at the end of the 2012 season, he was just as intent on looking toward the future as savoring the past. He spoke of more Super Bowls, an improved stadium, and changing rosters. What he didn't see was any change in the organizational continuity that led the Giants from laughingstock of the mid-1960s and 1970s to their current prosperity. Sure, some people will move on. Personnel comes and goes, but the system will remain. "You won't see a significant change in the way we've operated," Mara said. "We've managed to keep our core people intact, and that's very important. We won't deviate from the head coach/general manager structure that's proved so successful for us. We're going to continue that way. Our scouts are the backbone of our organization. Certainly, free agency is important also, but our success in the draft will determine the real future of our franchise."

Key draft products such as defenders Mathias Kiwanuka (first round in the 2006 Draft), Jason Pierre-Paul (first in 2010), Justin Tuck (third in 2005), and Prince Amukamara (first in 2011) will be kept around for the foreseeable future. So, too, will wide receiver Hakeem Nicks (first in 2009), guard Chris Snee (second in 2004), and, of course, two-time Super Bowl MVP Eli Manning (first in 2004 in a draft day trade).

And MetLife Stadium will continue to evolve with yearly improvements. "Were seeing a lot of different faces in there now," Mara said. "We'll keep making improvements every year and try to constantly monitor the gameday population. With the explosion of the secondary-sales ticket market, we're trying to determine what changes our fans would like to see."

The first outdoor Super Bowl in a cold weather city in 2014 will be a key event. A success there could open the way for other open-air buildings in wintry venues such as Chicago, New England, Washington, Seattle, Green Bay, Cleveland, and Philadelphia to earn Super Bowls. Mara has seen it all come together. In the next 20 years, he expects it to stay together under his and the Tisch family's leadership. "I always hoped to play a role in getting back to that point where we were relevant again," Mara said. "Back then we were so far away from being there, just to get to .500 was a dream and would have been a reason to celebrate. I always dreamed of getting back to the late '50s and early '60s where we went to the championship game six times. Even though we lost five of them, we had an organization that was respected. We had lost that a little bit. So I always dreamed of getting back to the top of the mountain. We got back. Now we have to continue to maintain and build our organization. You can't ever sit back. And things won't always work out. But if you've got a solid organization like we have, you'll always have a chance to compete for a title."

For Mara two Super Bowl titles just aren't enough. "I'd like to think we'll compete for more Super Bowls, maintain the type of winning tradition we've been able to establish here recently," Mara said. "That's what you wake up for every day."

ACKNOWLEDGMENTS

A book of this kind represents as much a collaborative effort as an individual endeavor. Without accessibility to the athletes, the wise and often tough questioning by reporters, and the skilled writing of my incredible media colleagues, none of what you have read between these covers would have been possible.

Since 1989 it has been my privilege to stand among the players, coaches, and management of the classiest franchise in the NFL and question, grill, or chat up the people who make up the New York Giants. Covering the ups and downs of the league's marquee team has its own innate rewards for a reporter and indeed produced a treasure trove of stories from the heroic to the offbeat. Much of this book springs from my own story files and personal reminiscences, but many of the stories come from the work of others.

It is to those whom I owe much; good reporters such as Ralph Vacchiano of the *Daily News*, Patti Traina of Inside Football, Paul Schwartz and Steve Serby of the *New York Post*, Tom Rock of *Newsday*, Judy Battista of *The New York Times*, Mike Garafolo of *The Star-Ledger* and *USA Today*, Tom Canavan of the Associated Press, Alex Raskin of CBSSportsline.com, Vinny DiTrani and Tara Sullivan of *The Record*, Dom Amore and John Altavilla of the *Hartford Courant*, Kim Jones of the NFL Network, Jane McManus of ESPN, Russ Salzberg of FOX News, Paul Dottino of WFAN, and so many others who either held a notepad or a microphone and asked just the right questions or wrote just the right story. These folks are not just my opponents in a competitive business. I count them all as friends.

There could be no book without the subjects. To the players of the last 20 years, all of them, whether they lasted one game or 16 years, thank you for sharing your thoughts. I stand in particular debt to head coaches Jim Fassel and Tom Coughlin, general managers Ernie Accorsi and Jerry Reese, and players Kent Graham, Rodney Hampton, and Rich Seubert for spending extra time to give me their personal insights into this era of Giants football.

Thanks also to the Giants public relations department of Pat Hanlon, Peter Jean-Baptiste, DeAndre Phillips, and Phyllis Hayes for helping me track down the ex-Giants.

President and CEO John Mara not only wrote my wonderful foreword but spent extra time with me to speak about his vision for the future. I consider myself incredibly lucky to have known his father, Wellington Mara, and I can say with all honesty that Mr. Mara's legacy of class and dignity lives on in his son.

A big vote of thanks goes to the people at Triumph Books; to Tom Bast, who brought me into the project, and Jeff Fedotin for spearheading the editing process.

Finally, thanks to my family: Diane, Andrew, Liz, and Kathleen. The past 2½ months have encompassed the most intense writing journey I've ever undertaken. This was far from a leisurely stroll down memory lane, and I could not have accomplished any of it without your patience. Thanks for giving me the space and time to get it done and the understanding to put up with the swings between elation and despair that such a project engenders.

SOURCES

Books

Burress, Plaxico; Cole, Jason—*Giant: The Road to the Super Bowl*; Harper Entertainment, New York, 2008.

Callahan, Tom—*The GM: The Inside Story of a Dream Job and the Nightmares That Go With It*; Crown, New York, 2007.

Coughlin, Tom; Curtis, Brian—*A Team to Believe In: Our Journey to the Super Bowl Championship*; Ballantine Books, New York, 2008.

Coughlin, Tom; Fisher, David—*Earn the Right to Win*; Portfolio/Penguin, New York, 2013.

DeVito, Carlo—*Wellington: The Maras, The Giants, And the City Of New York*; Triumph Books, Chicago 2006.

Jones, Dhani; Grotenstein, Jonathan—*The Sportsman*; Rodale Books, New York, 2011.

Kiper, Mel—*The Draft Reference Guide*; Mel Kiper, 1995.

Maxymuk, John—*The 50 Greatest Plays in New York Giants Football History*; Triumph Books, Chicago, 2008.

New York Giants—*New York Giants Information Guide*, 2012.

NFL—*NFL Record and Fact Book*, 2012.

Palladino, Ernie—*Lombardi and Landry: How Two of Pro Football's Greatest Coaches Launched Their Legends and Changed the Game Forever*; Skyhorse, New York, 2011.

Schwartz, Paul—*Tales from the New York Giants Sideline*; Skyhorse, New York, 2004, 2007, 2011.

Strahan, Michael; Glazer, Jay—*Inside the Helmet: Life as a Sunday Afternoon Warrior*; Gotham, New York, 2007.

Vacchiano, Ralph—*Eli Manning: The Making of a Quarterback*; Skyhorse, New York, 2008.

Periodicals

Associated Press

The Baltimore Sun

New York Daily News

The Journal News

Las Vegas Review-Journal
New York Post
The New York Times
The Philadelphia Inquirer
Raleigh News & Observer
The Giants Insider
Sports Illustrated
St. Petersburg Times
USA Today
Wine Spectator

Websites
Army.mil
AVweb.com
CBSSports.com
ESPN.com
Essence.com
Giants.com
Pro-Football-Reference.com
Yahoo.com
NFL.com
60minutes.com

Personal Interviews
Ernie Accorsi
Tommy Bamundo
Jim Fassel
Kent Graham
Rodney Hampton
Pat Hanlon
John Mara
Jerry Reese
Rich Seubert